ANDREI BELY

THE

CHRISTENED

CHINAMAN

TRANSLATED, ANNOTATED AND INTRODUCED BY

THOMAS R. BEYER, JR.

Hermitage Publishers

1991

Andrei Bely

The Christened Chinaman
A novel

Translated from Russian by Thomas R. Beyer, Jr.

Copyright ⓒ 1991 by Thomas R. Beyer, Jr.

Library of Congress Cataloging-in-Publication Data

Bely, Andrey, 1880-1934.
    [Kreshchenyi kitaets. English]
    The christened Chinaman / Andrei Bely; translated, annotated, and
introduced by Thomas R. Beyer, Jr.
        p.   cm.
    Translation of: Kreshchenyi kitaets.
    ISBN 1-55779-042-6 : $12.00
    I. Title.
PG3453.B84K713   1991   91-32723
891.73'3--dc20   CIP

A sketch by Sergei Chekhonin "Woman with flower" (1914) is
used for front cover

Published by HERMITAGE PUBLISHERS
P.O. Box 410
Tenafly, N.J. 07670, U.S.A.

CONTENTS

THE CHRISTENED CHINAMAN

TRANSLATOR'S INTRODUCTION

The Christened Chinaman (Крещёный китаец), originally entitled *The Transgression of Nikolai Letaev: (I: Epopee)*, appeared in 1921 to mixed reviews. A. Veksler called it "one of the most artistically vibrant and complete works of Russian literature, if not the most vibrant work of A. Bely."[1] Viktor Shklovsky, the well known Formalist critic, wrote: "I don't think that he himself [Bely] knows what in the world an 'Epopee' is."[2] Critics have also varied widely in their evaluations of the stylistic innovations of the work. Gleb Struve complained of the "artificial, obsessive verse rhythm" of the work, noting "I confess to not having been able to read it through."[3] This same rhythm seemed to Marietta Shaginyan just exactly right for the epic form chosen by Bely for his work.[4] Andrei Bely and his works often called forth extreme responses, positive and negative, from his contemporaries. Now most of his works are met with silence in the Soviet Union, read by few and understood by even fewer in the West.

The Christened Chinaman is an autobiographical novel relating the world as seen through the eyes of a five year old in the prose-poetry of a forty-one year old Symbolist writer. Like all of Bely's works the novel has multiple levels and meanings. Bely is a lover of synthesis and triangularity. His world is broken down into tripartite structures in which the third element is the embodiment and resolution of the first two. This type of structure can be found at every level of the novel. On the stylistic level there are elements of sense, sound and meaning. The structural level consists of content, form and symbol. The thematic level is composed of autobiography, literature and mysticism or myth.

The autobiographical, contextual level is the easiest to decipher: it is simple and direct, a bare skeleton for the work. The novel is set in the mid-1880's in the Moscow apartment of a Professor of Mathematics, Mikhail Vasilevich Letaev. With him are his much younger and beautiful wife, Elizaveta, and their son, Nikolai, nicknamed Kotik or "Kitten." The action of the novel flows through the seasons of fall, winter and spring with an imagined and anticipated summer. Kotik, the narrator, is largely confined to the apartment save for a few strolls in the environs of the Arbat district. There is little or no plot in the narrative; rather, a series of incidents and episodes helps to define the family members and the relationships between them in the familial triangle. The conflict of the work is the struggle of the father and mother over the fate and future of the son. Should he be allowed to develop into an eggheaded eccentric mathematician like his father or into a muliebral musician like his mother? While the conflict is clear, the proper course of action for the child is not. He retreats into a pose of ignorance and slow-wittedness in order to avoid his mother's wrath. He withdraws into his own inner self, into a world of imagination inhabited by frightening creatures who arrive with the darkness of night, but who fortunately disperse with the coming of morning's light into the bedroom. Despite his attempts to conceal his intellectual development, Kotik is eventually discovered and beaten by his mother for listening to the father. Kotik is then bundled up and rushed away from the house by his father to spend the day at his Uncle's. The next morning he returns home for a reconciliation with the repentant mother.

The struggle between science and art, the mathematician-musician conflict of Professor Nikolai Vasilevich Bugaev and Aleksandra Dmitrievna, nee Yegorova, over their only son, Boris, is well documented both by Bely himself (the pseudonym of Boris Bugaev) in his memoirs and by other biographers. Similarly many of the persons and events found in the novel can also be traced to references in Bely's non-fictional works. In a preface to the first edition which was subsequently omitted, Bely warned against too close a comparison between his fictional and actual father. To some extent all fiction is a mixture of fact and fantasy, of memory enhanced by imagination. Ideally the line between the two should disappear for both writers and readers in the texture of the final work. In Bely's case the enhancement and imagination occur more on the levels of style and symbol; memory preserves in large part the real events which become the content. As it is, most accounts of his father including those by Bely himself provide considerable evidence that the fictional Mikhail Letaev has much in common with the real Nikolai Bugaev.

If the content is only the skeleton, then the format, the literariness of the work, is the body. In Bely the style is the substance. Sound prevails over sense. The word predominates over the sentence. The part is often more important than the whole. Shifting the burden of meaning from the forest to the trees, Bely disassembles the linear and temporal components of logic. In place of traditional exposition, in which one word following another is logically connected with it, there is a verbal and spatial logic based on the repetition of sounds, roots, words, phrases and sentences. Connections are made by associating like elements wherever they are found. The chaos of external reality is ordered only by the the imposition of an internal patterning upon the words. Here the narrator is not only a five year old but a middle-aged Symbolist poet sensitive to rhythm and rhyme and asserting the poet's right to order his world verbally. This combination of child and adult in a single narrator is the unifying device of the novel.

In curious ways what the boy and what the poet see and say are often identical, even though the former arrives there through ignorance or accident, the latter through knowledge or design. For example, the father often buys antonovka apples and brings them home to the boy. Anton, the yardman, is a swindler who sells the father's books. Antonovich is a professor like the father, but he is a gangster and kidnapper. Gangrene in Russian is called "Anton's fire." The only connection which exists among all of these is the Russian root "anton" (антон). Later the boy commits an "original sin" and is kidnapped by his father. When presented with an anise apple the boy imagines being thrown into the biblical fire of the book of Daniel. These seemingly random thought-trains of the boy are at the same time elaborate systems devised by the poet.

The poet is likewise responsible for the other systems such as the color scheme. The world is constructed primarily of reds and greens, blacks and whites, blues and yellows. All of these help to order and establish limits in the mind of the child. Another device is the cyclical alternation of day and night in which darkness, fear and incomprehensibility are replaced with light, security and clarification. Finally there is the important motif contained in the growth of sexual awareness. The boy is confused but curious about bodily functions, sexual organs, menstruation and love-making. The middle-aged poet mirrors this ignorance (although he presumably knows what the boy doesn't) with euphemisms, hints, double entendres. In effect both aspects of the narrator (young and old) while seeming to disguise things only reveal them all the more clearly to the reader.

The story is as simple as the style is complex. The prose undergoes that dislocation of language into its meaning referred to by T. S. Eliot. It is a poet's prose in which the denotation or signification of a word often is less important than the connotations, sounds or symbols evoked by the word. Bely's aim throughout his artistic career was to revitalize language, to create the "living word."[5] Words take on new additional meanings, or recapture older forgotten ones. Sounds abound, and gradually the reader comes to see and hear that the sound precedes the sense, the unit comes before unity. Where old words are insufficient for the task, new words are invented. Here again we confront the narrator-double. Is it baby-talk or poetic license? The false analogy of the child or the poetic inspiration of the adult? Names take on meanings: the family name Letaev comes from the root "лет"—"to fly." Metaphors have literal meanings and homonyms confound the youth. The boy's consciousness still before the stage of "figurative" perception combines with the poet's rediscovery of coincidences which have been forgotten or lost.

All of this sound and sense is intended to culminate in meaning, in a synthesis of symbolic metaphysical themes that inserts a spirit into the body and skeleton of the work. There are actually two major themes in the novel. The first is revealed in the title and in the last words of the work: "The Christened Chinaman." In the father are united two disparate cultures, religions, traditions and regions. West (which for Russians is Europe) meets East in a series of unions which alone are capable of bringing fulfillment and release from the search for Truth. The Elohim of Abraham, Moses and the prophets come together with Ahura Mazda and Brahma in Christ and Christianity, the New Covenant. Latin and Sanskrit return once again to the one language understood by all before the tragedy of the Tower of Babel. Professor Letaev, the cultured intellectual with roots in Pythagorus, Leibniz and Kant, respected in European mathematical circles, is also the bearer of the wildman Scythian-Tatar heritage. He is a wiseman and a fool, this genius is an eccentric, the dean is a buffoon. The rationalism and reserve of Europe are complemented by the intuitivism and impetuosity of the East. Professor Bugaev becomes the embodiment of Russia's age old identity crisis: are we Europeans or Asians? The truth embodied in the person of Professor Bugaev is the message that Russia is unique. Russia is descendant of both East and West, but belongs to neither. It is as if the Mongol father had committed the rape of the gentile Byzantine mother and both had decided to disown the bastard called Russia. Yet the son of the father cannot deny or ignore his heritage. Just as Russia is troubled and divided by the circumstances of its birth, so too is the narrator. He loves and fears the father whom he loses as a young man, but as the middle aged poet he will use the literary process to find him and recreate him. This theme of the son is the second major theme of the novel.

The theme of son versus father, the underlying Oedipal complex in many of Bely's prose works, was first explored by Khodasevich.[6] Others have parroted his interpretation, but left it essentially undeveloped. Freud's *Totem and Taboo* does provide several clues for unlocking the mysteries of the novel. His theories on the covenant between father and son, the identification of filial guilt with the inception of religion and his recognition of art and religion as two outgrowths of the Oedipal complex are all pertinent to *The Christened Chinaman*. The issues of sexual awakening, love-hate relationships, and taboos in the work remain to be unraveled, but the Freudian approach is limited because it focuses attention solely on the "gender" aspect of "род."

The key element of the novel is, indeed, the concept of "род," but in its far broader implications of "**genus**," "**generic**," "**generation**," "**genteel**," "**congenital**" and "**original**." Bely, the writer and myth-maker, sets out to resolve the problem of "birth" by combining the Old and New Testaments, Genesis and the Gospels. The "original" sin is birth itself. Generated by the act of procreation between progenitor (father) and the genetrix (mother), it is the son who must be sacrificed. The mock sacrifice of Isaac by Abraham at the Lord's command prefigures the crucifixion. God the Father sacrifices Christ, his only begotten Son, on the Cross. Christ, the innocent one, sheds his blood for all men in the only sacrifice acceptable to the Father, a sacrifice of both man and God. The Christian myth, the mystery of Christ, is perpetuated in the sacrament of Baptism. Water, the sign of the New Covenant, replaces the blood of circumcision of the Old Covenant. In Baptism, man is christened, he becomes Christlike and is reconciled with the Father.

Kotik seeks the same reconciliation. In his own mystical dream world he is crucified, dies and is buried, only to resurrect and live in glory thereafter. The resurrected Kotik can return home to his mother who herself has been reconciled with her son by his sacrifice. In his dreams Kotik, created in the image and likeness of the Father, comes to recognize and accept the cup of sorrows presented to him. The poet comes to a similar realization that he is his father's son, and Andrei Bely effects a reconciliation with Professor Bugaev in his literary creation. In accepting their fate, in resigning themselves to their heritage, both child and poet fulfill their covenant and find peace.

This search for peace and reconciliation was the driving force in the life and works of Andrei Bely. Born in 1880, the lone and lonely child of a mismatched marriage, Boris Bugaev grew up in the Arbat district of Moscow. Intelligent and quickwitted, he was constantly drawn between the two poles represented by his father and mother. The duality of their relationship was to be reproduced in his personality and make itself felt throughout his artistic career and adult life. Surrounded mostly by relatives and adult friends of the family in his early years (his father was already over forty at his birth), he kept himself the center of attention only by acting the part of a child. Consequently, he grew old and yet never grew up. Already in school he displayed his independence and individuality by skipping classes for several weeks and going instead to the library, where he simply devoured books. This particular incident in his life, this "transgression," was to have constituted the central event in the *Transgression of Nikolai Letaev*. In subsequent editions the heading for the first chapter, "The Christened Chinaman," became the title of the entire novel, when the work never progressed to this autobiographical moment.

Boris enrolled at Moscow University in 1899 in a course of studies in the natural sciences. After graduating in 1903, he enrolled for a second degree in philosophy which he never completed. Failure to pursue things to their conclusion is another characteristic trait of Bely, but his inability to finish his second degree is at least understandable. In 1902 he had already published his first major work, *Symphony (The Second, Dramatic One)*, in which he tried to capture in prose the magic of music. In this first decade of the century Andrei Bely (the pseudonym he had chosen to avoid embarrassment for and confusion with his father's name) became a widely published poet, prosaist, critic and essayist. For a while he became the most prolific and polemical theorist of the Symbolist movement in Russia. At the same time he was acquiring an encyclopedic, albeit at times superficial, knowledge of almost everything under the sun, but especially of philosophy and aesthetics. He read so many works, was influenced by so many figures and traditions, that it is difficult to believe any attempts to separate neatly and divide precisely these influences into periods, as Bely and his biographers often do. Vladimir Solovyov, Nietzsche, Schopenhauer, Kant, Blavatsky, Besant, Steiner, all fascinated this impressionable young man at least temporarily. If there is any progression, it can be seen only in the broadest terms as one passing through Orthodoxy to Rationalism and finding its synthesis in mysticism. In the end Bely apparently found the answers to his questions in the rational religion of Rudolf Steiner, Anthroposophy.

By 1910 at the age of thirty Bely had insured for himself a place in the history of Russian letters. Four prose symphonies, a major novel (*The Silver Dove*, 1909), three major collections of poetry, over two hundred articles, essays and reviews and his monumental work *Symbolism* were all being read and discussed. Eventually *Symbolism* would lay the groundwork for the Russian Formalist movement, initiate a school of statistical critical analysis still carried on in the Soviet Union and the United States, and indirectly by its influence on Formalism, have an effect on the later New Critics and Structuralists. Yet Bely went abroad at the peak of his career, and by the time he returned the Symbolist concerns, persons and movement had been replaced in the public's mind. The brash challenges of the younger Symbolists seemed mild and conventional compared to a new generation of screamers and shouters, such as Mayakovsky.

If Bely's popularity declined in the second decade of the century, at least his talent did not suffer. In the teens he wrote and published the novel upon which much of his reputation rests: *Petersburg* (1914). This most important event of his literary life was matched by the single most important influence for the rest of his life: his meeting with and acceptance of Rudolf Steiner. Ten years after the death of his father, Bely finally found a new father figure, a spiritual advisor, one who could show the way and lead him through this earthly existence. The story of Rudolf Steiner and Andrei Bely, if and when it ever becomes fully known, will certainly clarify much about Bely and his art. Bely settled with Asya Turgeneva, his companion and later his wife, in Dornach to work on the construction of the Goetheanum. In 1916 he returned to motherland Russia ravaged by war and soon to be racked by revolution. Bely like Blok eagerly accepted the Revolution as the long anticipated and awaited Apocalypse. In the next few years he participated fully in trying to build the new society. Bely lent his hand to the training of cadres of writers for the Proletkult. There had always been something of the frustrated teacher in Bely, reflected in the various introductions, prefaces, forewords to his works, or the several hundreds of pages of footnotes and commentary to *Symbolism*. Meanwhile he continued work on various manuscripts which would eventually see the light. It was primarily a period of prose: *Petersburg*, *Kotik Letaev*, *Notes of an Eccentric* and a series of critical works.

Bely continued to write prolifically in the 1920's in spite of his complaints that publishers were ignoring him. In the first years of the decade he turned his attention to his father in the poem "The First Encounter" and the novel *The Christened Chinaman*. Having apparently resolved for himself the image of his father, Bely was hit by a severe loss with the death of Aleksandr Blok, symbolist poet, friend, spiritual brother. In November of 1921 Bely, unable to cope with the physical hardships of life in Russia, departed for Berlin. Here he was disappointed by Asya, who had disowned him for a new lover, and he felt betrayed by Rudolf Steiner's restrained and reserved attitude toward him. In spite of these disappointments or perhaps because of them, Bely provided an almost non-stop stream of works for Berlin publishers. In a two year period he published nine original works and several reprints of older works, including a rewritten version of *Petersburg*. Bely left Berlin and returned to Russia in October of 1923. In the next ten years he would produce two major novels, three volumes of memoirs and two major critical studies. He died of a cerebral hemorrhage in January, 1934.

In the end Bely had come to grips with his life, although in a highly individualistic way. Having purged himself and his guilt in his fiction, he could turn to fact. In one sense, however, there wasn't really any dividing line between the two. Khodasevich remarks that "Bely's autobiography is a series of 'non-existent events,' just like those of his autobiographical novels."[7] It might be more correct to say that they are filled with events which often exist for Bely alone. For Bely, appearance is not to be mistaken for reality. Reality is a synthesis of both an event and the individual's perception or experience of that event. In his world it is the word which comes first and then becomes flesh. Art is not merely a reflection of life, but an expression and the image of reality itself. This results, of course, in a vision of the world that is highly individualistic and unique to Bely. The very personal quality of the reality makes empirical verification of it irrelevant.

The key to the *The Christened Chinaman* is not to be found in the events depicted, which may or may not have occurred, but in the writer's perception and portrayal of those events. To read Bely does not require that we have faith in his vision. But to confront, appreciate, truly understand Bely's art we must enter for a time into his world, into his mind. At times frustrating, at other times refreshing, the journey is always nothing less than a "magical mystery tour."

THE TEXT AND THE TRANSLATION

The story of Bely's writings is the history of grandiose plans most often unrealized. Bely was forever drawing up, discarding, modifying and revising not only his works, but also the grand designs which they were intended to fit. He began his publishing career in prose with the appearance of *A Symphony (The Second, Dramatic One)* in 1902. This was followed by the *Northern Symphony (The First, Heroic One)* in 1904, *The Return: The Third Symphony* in 1905 and finally *A Goblet of Blizzards: The Fourth Symphony* in 1908. His next major effort in prose was *The Silver Dove* (1909), intended as the first part of a trilogy to be entitled *East or West*. This was followed by Bely's most famous novel, *Petersburg* (1914), also conceived as part of the trilogy. While one can indeed find the theme of east and west in *Petersburg*, the work itself has almost no connection to the first novel. The third element of this trilogy was to have been a work entitled *My Life*. In fact, a new autobiographical novel, *Kotik Letaev* (1917-1918) did appear, but it had absolutely no relation to the first two novels. By this time Bely considered *Kotik Letaev* to be not the end of his first trilogy, but only the first part of the promised *My Life*.

In 1918 Bely began what would eventually become *Notes of an Eccentric*, announced in 1919 as the first part of Volume I of the new *I: Epopee*, conceived as a ten volume opus. The project was somewhat altered when from October to December 1920 Bely wrote four chapters, only one of which was eventually edited in the spring of 1921 and survived as: *The Transgression of Nikolai Letaev: (Epopee —Volume I)*, "The Christened Chinaman," "Chapter 1." Printed in *Zapiski mechtatelej*, IV (Petrograd: 1921, pp. 21-165), this text will change titles but little else throughout its subsequent reprintings. In the "Instead of a Foreword" to the work Bely alerted his readers that *Notes of an Eccentric*, the former Volume I of *Epopee*, should now be considered merely a "Foreword" to the overall work.

In 1922 "The Transgression of Nikolai Letaev" appeared in the Paris journal, *Sovremennye zapiski*. This version contains only five of the fifteen sub-chapters of the 1921 version: "Instead of a Foreword," "The Study" and "Papochka" (XI, 65-89); "This and That's Own" (XII,

53-68); "Ahura Mazda" and "Papa Hit the Nail on the Head" (XIII, 99-115).

In 1925 while planning his *Complete Works*, which also never appeared, Bely expressed a desire to unite *Kotik Letaev* and *The Transgression of Nikolai Letaev* as "pieces of the unwritten 'Epopee,' which at one time I wanted to call 'My Life.' They should be united under the general title 'Kotik Letaev,' as parts I and II."[8] This idea was obviously abandoned by 1927, when the identical work appeared as a separate volume *The Christened Chinaman* (Moscow: Nikitinskie subbotniki). In 1928 the remainder of the five thousand copies printed received a new cover and title page, this time as *The Christened Chinaman: A Novel*. The work has not been reprinted in the Soviet Union. A photographic reproduction slightly reduced in size of the 1927 Moscow edition appeared as Volume XXIII of the "Slavische Propyläen" series of the Wilhelm Fink Verlag, Munich, 1969. This edition has a brief introductory note plus some useful identification of the major characters by Dmitrij Tschizewskij and Anton Hönig.

Bely's abandonment of his fictional autobiography after *The Transgression* may be connected with the death in 1921 of his friend and sometimes foe, fellow Symbolist, Aleksandr Blok. Bely dates his "Instead of a Foreword" July 1921. Blok died on August 7, 1921, an event which spurred Bely to write his "remembrances" of the poet. Bely spent much of the latter part of 1921, then 1922 working on "Remembrances of Blok," first printed in *Zapiski mechtatelej* (1922) and then later expanded and revised into a book-length project for the Berlin journal *Epopeja* (1922-1923). This in turn led to work on his own memoirs in late 1922 and early 1923 which eventually became *The Beginning of the Century* (1933). Two other volumes of memoirs have appeared in Russian: *On the Border of Two Centuries* (1930, 1931) and *Between Two Revolutions* (dated 1934, actually appeared in 1935). In many ways the memoirs constitute not a break with, but a continuation of, the autobiography. These memoirs record events and personalities, the accuracy of which has been questioned by reviewers, largely because they are seen through the prism of Bely's own unique vision. In one sense Bely merely switched from writing factual fiction to writing fictional facts.

The text of *The Christened Chinaman*, unlike those of *Petersburg*, underwent almost no revision and no major rewriting by the author. Some differences do exist and they are by no means minor. The 1922 version differs considerably from the other variants. As has been noted it contains only one third of the full text, a fact left unmentioned in the text itself and often ignored by bibliographers. It is written in the old orthography, which had been retained by Russian emigrees after the Soviet reforms of the language. Most notably, the 1922 edition omits almost all of the typographical peculiarities of Bely's text, thereby reducing it in the reader's vision to a conventional prose work. Irregular spacing and indentation, the off-setting of passages by dashes and dots, the liberal use of accent marks and italics and the separation by lines of dialogue are mostly absent so that the text conforms to a more standardized prose model. The 1922 version also omits the final paragraph of the "Instead of a Foreword" in which Bely explains the relationship between this work, *Notes of an Eccentric* and *Epopee*. Many of the alterations in typography may be attributed to the never-ending efforts of editors to conserve space, a concern to which Bely was not altogether insensitive. But this version as a whole conceals a major structural element of Bely's prose.

The versions of 1921 and 1927 (including the subsequent reprint) are almost identical except for a few minor distinctions. It is significant that not a single word has been added or deleted in the 1927 text. For the most part the distinctions are purely mechanical ones. We have already mentioned the change in title, which was required when the action of the novel failed to contain the envisioned "transgression."[9]

The subsequent omission of the "Instead of a Foreword" in the 1927 edition has also been noted. Another element which distinguishes the two versions is the number of characters per line. The 1921 version has approximately 65 characters per line compared with 50 characters for the 1927 version. This explains, of course, the increase in pages of text from 142 to 230 in the later edition. More significantly, fewer characters per line result in far more frequent and more graphically distinct configurations in the text. The visual aspect enhanced by the typography is an important element of Bely's overall design and I have tried to preserve it basically unchanged in this translation. Other distinctions between the two texts are minor. There are several instances of spelling having been changed to conform presumably with newer Soviet standards. One does find fewer instances of capitalization in the later edition, especially when used referring to religious persons and places. The lower case is used for the initial letters of the personal pronoun "he" for Christ and for "богородица" (Mother of God). Where these changes are the result of conformity with Soviet attempts to de-emphasize religion, the upper case has been restored in the translation. There are misprints, typographical errors or simply mistakes in both versions, although the 1927 version seems to have cleared up several questionable uses of punctuation from the earlier text. I have chosen the 1927 text as the authoritative one, as the last one to have been printed during the lifetime of the author, but I have consulted the other texts when difficulties arose. This explains, for example, why "безбойные" of the 1927 edition is translated as "wallpaperless" (безобойные) of the 1921 version.

Bely's works have not always fared well in English translation. Some excerpts from *Kotik Letaev* were done by George Reavey (*Soviet Literature* ed. George Reavey and Marc Slonim, 1933; and his *Modern Soviet Short Stories* 1961). Reavey has also translated *The Silver Dove* (New York: Grove Press, 1974). In 1959 John Cournos translated *St. Petersburg* (New York: Grove Press).

While these translations represent various degrees of literary and artistic merit, they are far removed from Bely and his prose, and they fail to explain why Nabokov would consider *Petersburg* one of the great masterpieces of twentieth century prose, ranking just after Joyce's *Ulysses* and Kafka's *Transformation*, but before Proust's *In Search of Lost Time*.

More recently a new generation of American scholar-translators has turned its attention to Bely with considerable success. Gerald Janecek broke important ground with his 1971 translation of *Kotik Letaev* (Ann Arbor: Ardis). Robert Maguire and John Malmstad contributed years of work to a masterful edition of *Petersburg* (Indiana Univ. Press, 1978). This is not just a translation: a solid introduction and extensive notes make this an excellent primer on how to read a Symbolist or modernist novel. Gerald Janecek has also published a translation of Bely's long poem "The First Encounter," annotated by Nina Berberova (Princeton Univeristy Press, 1979). This scholarly notation seems to be the only way to make Bely comprehensible to a wider audience. Also in the last decade a few of Bely's critical articles have appeared, as well as a volume of short stories.[10] Even so, all of these translations represent only a small part of Bely's literary legacy.

Why have Bely's works been less fortunate than those of other writers? Why has this Russian "James Joyce" been denied to an extent the attention and appreciation which he seems to deserve? Some of the reasons are purely extra-literary. This genius was also a very, very strange fellow, чудак, in his looks, in his manner, in his intellectual temperament. Nina Berberova recalls him in the 1920's as a frightening physical specimen, with overdeveloped arms and legs, and the high brow inherited from his father. Others recall him as absent-minded, distant, alone in his own world. Surely he was listening to a different drummer when he eurythmically danced out his poems. Perhaps he would have been happier if he had remained silent. Unfortunately he refused to restrain himself and was no less of a wrangler than his father. Indeed, throughout his entire life he was constantly alienating friend and foe alike in both word and deed. When he returned to Russia after two years in Berlin in 1923, he found himself rejected by the emigrees as a traitor, and never fully accepted by the Soviets. In many ways he was a man without a country and without an audience.

Finally, there was Bely's search for some way out the chaos which he perceived around him and in his own life. Much has been made of the domestic quarrels between father and mother over the son's development and their eventual deleterious effect on the child. Most scholars and critics are willing to follow Bely's lead in assigning the blame elsewhere. Ultimately, the blame should rest where it belongs, on the shoulders of Bely himself. Even as he grew physically he failed to mature intellectually. He was forever searching for that special secret, a synthesis, which would provide a simple answer to a complex world. A variety of solutions were briefly embraced then discarded along the way. From Orthodoxy, through Rationalism and then mysticism, Bely arrived at Anthroposophy and Rudolf Steiner, who would serve as the father figure which Bely had lost. In the midst of the Anthroposophists, in the teachings of Steiner, in the building of the Goetheanum Bely seemed to find the long awaited synthesis. It is in the teachings of Steiner that East meets West (*The Bhagavad Gita and the Epistles of Paul*); sound meets sense (*Eurythmy as Visible Speech*); the rational and the irrational, the physical and the spiritual all unite. Most of Bely's contemporaries dismissed Steiner and his theories, considering them only a harmful influence in Bely's literary output. Modern scholars have been more willing to be objective, but they have been hampered by the nature of Anthroposophy and its mysteries. Only one who has been initiated into the secrets of the movement can fully appreciate and understand them; likewise, attempts to explain them in a coherent fashion to the uninitiated are doomed from the beginning to failure.

Western scholars of more recent times have been able to return to Bely, perhaps because of the time which separates them from the man. With a healthy disinterest in Bely's political leanings, or lack of them, and a tolerance for the man not put to the test by personal acquaintance, they can turn their attention to the works themselves. Here the literary impediments to translation become starkly clear. Evgeny Zamyatin once wrote of Bely's books: "I am not certain, however, whether one can properly say that they are written in Russian, so unusual is Bely's syntax, so full of neologisms his diction. The language of his books is Bely's language, just as the language of *Ulysses* is not English, but Joyce's English."[11]

Zamyatin's comparison of Bely with Joyce is one frequently echoed. Certainly a translator can look to Joyce to find a new and expanded English language. Yet one should caution that Bely and Joyce are allied more in spirit than in substance; both were innovators, but both were bound by the systems of their respective native languages. Thus while one might look to Joyce for inspiration, one ought to translate Bely as Bely, not as a Russian Joyce.

The difficulty of Bely's prose increases with his development as a writer. In his own prose there seems to be an inverse proportion between form and content. There is a steady decrease in the simple narrative structure at the same time that the stylistic devices increase. Likewise, the meaning of words is slowly replaced by the sound of words as the most important element in a work. There is a gradual progression from the most conventional of his novels, *The Silver Dove*, to a greater and greater departure from novelistic techniques in *Petersburg*, *Kotik Letaev* and then *The Christened Chinaman*.

The basis of Bely's prose is the word, both diachronically and synchronically. The word is like a toy snapper, in which you pop open one end in order to reveal the contents. The explosion of a word pronounced opens a world of delightful surprises. Out jump etymologies; the word "объясниться" with the accent diverted to the second syllable points the way back to the "clear" in "clarification." Sound overwhelms, sometimes supersedes all the other senses as a match "chiffichurs." The poet understands and wants his reader to know that words don't always mean the same thing. When is a "шайка" a "gang" and when is it a "bucket"? When do hares become sunbeams (зайчики) and when do kitchen fumes become offspring (чадо)? The poet can imitate childlike vision if he chooses to see metaphors literally. What does it mean to have "one foot on the grave"? Logic is reduced to sound and not sense: **Persians** eats **persics**, **Anton** doesn't have an **antonovka** apple, "a beadle isn't a beagle," **Пудель не педель**. With childlike naivete new words are formed by analogy with old ones: what for the child is a cute mistake is for the poet a neologism, a "blackroach" (чернокан) instead of a "cockroach" (таракан). The poet recaptures the innocence of the child and assumes for a time a selective ignorance of the constraints imposed by the system of language. Nouns turn into verbs, verbs generate nouns and adjectives, new combinations appear (over four hundred neologisms in *The Christened Chinaman*) as the poet expands and then legitimizes the illegitimate language constructions of a child.

Bely also experiments with larger units. Syntax is modified and altered to fit the mood and thought train of the author. One looks in vain for the period ending the first sentence, which finally appears after some thirty lines. Bely is the master of the run-on sentence, that nemesis of high school English (and probably Russian) teachers. His punctuation and arrangement of text also make Bely's style distinctive and difficult.

Several translators of Bely have simply ignored his uniqueness and proceeded to render his writings in acceptable, often elegant, English with traditional punctuation, pagination etc. Others, namely, Gerald Janecek, Robert Maguire and John Malmstad, have tried to remain true to the spirit of Bely. They have sought to maintain Bely's word repetition by employing one English equivalent for any given Russian word. But they have also attempted to retain most of the peculiarities of Bely's prose within the bounds of commonly accepted English . True as they are to the spirit of Bely, even they have had to bend at the letter, as they attempt to recapture the original. It is essential to keep in mind, however, that as the central element of Bely's prose progresses from content to style new modes of translation are required.

Vladimir Nabokov, both theorist and practitioner of the art and craft of translation, once declared: "The only object and justification of translation is the conveyance of the most exact information possible and this can be only achieved by a literal translation, with notes."[12] This doctrinaire attitude is one which Vladimir Nabokov, the writer, liberally violates in the translations of his own novels. The merit of his English translations is that they represent not the Russian Nabokov but the English novelist Nabokov, one who creates original works in both languages. The theory, however, which he applied with more rigor to Pushkin and Lermontov, is well suited for works of the modern age. A translation of a work of Bely should, I believe, be exactly that: the transfer in the most direct way of the Russian novel into English. **My purpose has been to change languages and yet retain the features of the original.**

This broad statement of intention is easy to make, harder to adhere to. But in most cases I am confident that more has been retained than lost. I have, for example, chosen to duplicate Bely's punctuation and typographical distinctions throughout. This may prove uncomfortable for the English reader, but only slightly more so than it is for the Russian reader. Similarly, I have often preserved awkward syntax and word order. Here I have been influenced by an analogy with Joyce and *Ulysses*. Joyce would certainly be easier to read if one would add punctuation to parts of *Ulysses*, or exercise minor editorial control. I chose not to modify or alter deliberate devices employed by the Bely. I simply found no good reason for simplifying the original in the translation.

I have also tried to center my focus on the word or word-root. Almost exclusively I have chosen and then stuck with one English equivalent for each Russian word. The repetition of roots and words is the primary organizing feature of the text. It is the very essence of Bely's prose. Without this repetition much of the work becomes meaningless. Joseph Frank has defined this concept of "spatial" literature as follows:

> ...language in modern poetry is really reflective. The
> meaning-relationship is completed by the simultaneous
> perception in space of word-groups that have no
> comprehensible relation to each other when read consecutively
> in time. Instead of the instinctive and immediate reference of
> words and word-groups to the objects or events they symbolize
> and the construction of meaning from the sequence of these
> references, modern poetry asks its reader to suspend the process
> of individual reference temporarily until the entire pattern of
> internal references can be apprehended as a unity.[13]

The temptation to stray from the norm of one word for one word is
at times immense. How easy "боюсь" can be either "I fear" or "I am
afraid." "Большой" wants to be "big" or "large" or even "great" and
"огромный" doesn't know whether to be "huge" or "massive" or
"enormous." In one way I have had help in keeping track of all of these
strays. In place of a system of index cards, which seemed to multiply
endlessly and yet still lag behind the need, I originally turned to a
mainframe computer to keep track of the some 9000 lines of text.
While the computer should share some of the credit, it certainly cannot
bear the blame for my human error. But I am reasonably satisfied that
in the few instances when I have used two English words at different
points for one Russian word that I have done so as a matter of choice
and not chance. Ironically, the result of this insistence on precise
repetition of words, preferring them to phrases or sentences, will seem
to some the oft-maligned "word for word" translation.

Much of this will be disconcerting for the reader. English seems to
pride itself on the ability to use a variety of words for one and the same
thing. Russian since at least the time of Pushkin has had no difficulty
with calling a thing by its name. Russians don't seem to need a
Thesaurus. The Russian language also builds new formations and words
by adding suffixes and prefixes to a given root. From the root "шир"
(wide) Russians can make "широкий" (wide or broad) "ширь" (expanse
or full width) "ширить" (expand or broaden) "расширение" (expansion
or dilation) "широкоплечий" (broadshouldered). In most places I have
settled on one root-word, in this case "wide" to recreate in English the
verbal repetitions which constitute the leitmotifs of Bely's work. Often
the word combinations which spring from this such as "wideshouldered"
or a "widening of the corridor" will be perceived as strange by the
English reader. I have also turned to several infrequent and sometimes
obsolete usages of words in order to preserve a single reference in
English. This is the case with the thematically important root "род"
(gen-), for example, why I have used the word "genteel" to translate the
Russian "благородный." Other examples include Abraham who

concludes a "testament" with the Lord instead of the more commonly used "covenant." (In Russian the words have one form "завет.") Granny "complicates" instead of "folding" her work for the Russian "сложить." (The concept of folding is actually the first, though obsolete meaning of complicate.) In the above cases the strangeness for the English reader is not present for the Russian reader. The English reader gets some compensation because of the greater selection of words in English resulting in fewer neologisms than in the original. All of the above retentions result in a text which is complex and difficult to read.

This is certainly in accordance with Bely's own desire to use retardation devices to focus the reader's attention on individual words and to restore the "Magic of Words" to their proper place. For Bely the secret to understanding and criticism is to be found in "the art of slow reading."[14]

If much has been preserved in words and word play, any translator must still be aware of how much has been lost. A major loss is the rhythm of the prose. Although he does not state so, Bely has written a prose-poem. In an introduction to *Masks* (1933), Bely notes that it appears in prose format to save space. *The Christened Chinaman* is a work of two hundred and thirty pages of sustained hexameter, mostly amphibrachic, interspersed with dactylic-trochaic interludes. Bely was a serious student of rhythm in verse (*Symbolism*, 1910; *Rhythm as a Dialectic*, 1928) and also wrote an article on "Rhythm in Prose," 1919. Ivanov-Razumnik was to comment on the rhythm of Bely's novel *Petersburg*, which after the revision of 1922 was declared "amphibrachic." Several Russian readers found the sustained rhythm disturbing. I omitted the rhythm not because it is an insignificant feature, or because I agreed with the critics. Simply stated, to have included the rhythm would have meant to subjugate almost all of the other features to that one consideration.

The other element which cannot find its way into translation is eurythmy. Bely was introduced to eurythmy through the lectures of Rudolf Steiner. Eurythmy is an attempt to establish a direct correspondence between sounds of words and their meanings. Bely offers his own version in *Glossolalia: A Poem about Sound*, written in 1917 and published in 1922. While the practice of eurythmy is a fascinating exercise in word association based on common sounds, it is highly subjective and is essentially determined by the source language. The "vr" sound of "время" (time) and "веретено" (spindle) and "вращать" (to revolve) found in all three Russian words is reproduced only in the English word "revolve" and then in reverse order. This sound coordination is unique to each language. If A. Veksler is correct in identifying Mother as the sound combination **mr** and Father as **br** with the son as a synthesis of **r** and **m**, there may indeed be a sound code.[15] If any such corresponding sound code has occurred in the English it is either accidental or mystical coincidence, and in either case I am unaware of it.

For most Bely will remain a "writer's writer," who like Joyce, is admired from afar, studied and taught mostly by specialists and read by a few non-academic aficionados. Ultimately Bely must be read in the original and so this translation is but a bridge across the barrier of his complicated and complex language. For students of Russian literature I hope it will be a tool through which they will be encouraged to begin uncovering the magic and mystery of Bely on their own. For others I hope it is a taste which whets the appetite for further study and acquaintance with Russian modernist prose.

It has been said that a translation is like a wife—if she is beautiful, she is not faithful; if she is faithful, she is not beautiful. Bely's first wife Asya left him to stay in Dornach. Klavdia Nikolaevna, his second wife, was a faithful companion to him and the preserver of his work and his memory.

I too have opted for faithfulness.

The notes appendixed are presented in such a way as not to interfere with the reading of the text. Dmitrij Tschizewskij and Anton Hönig began the process of identifying persons through Bely's own memoirs in their introduction to the 1969 reprint of the novel. I have expanded upon these and added to them in the growing tradition of annotation. We are still far from the copious companions and commentaries which help to make Joyce and his world accessible to a broad readership, but as teachers-turned-translators we can make a beginning by sharing our own limited findings.

I suggest that one consult the notes for each chapter either before or after the chapter. The omission of page numbers from the notes as well as the lack of stars, numbers, dots etc. are deliberate; a desire not to distract the reader from the text.

Many people have been kind enough to provide guidance, insights and suggestions concerning both the translation and the notes. Their help has certainly added much to my own efforts, the shortcomings of which are mine alone. I would like to thank Alexandra Baker for her clarifications of many of the Russian passages. Nina Berberova, Ivan Elagin and Natalya Minihan, all in their own special ways, provided enlightening comments. Gerald Janecek, Alexander Woronzoff, Richard Sheldon and Sergei Davydov were all kind enough to examine the manuscript. Others include my colleagues at Middlebury College who were very generous with their time, especially Thomas Huber for his key to Bismarck's "three hairs."

Thanks to Dodo, Rinny, Steffi and Sasa for making sure that Papa doesn't follow too closely the path of Kotik.

Thomas R. Beyer, Jr.

1 А. Векслер, "'Эпопее'А. Белого. (Опыт комментария)," *Современная литература: сборник статей*(Ленинград: 1925), 52.

2 В. Шкловский, "Андрей Белый," *Русский современник*, 2 (1924), 233.

3 Gleb Struve, "Andrey Bely Redivivus" in *Andrey Bely: A Critical Review* , ed. Gerald Janecek (Univ. of Kentucky, 1978), p. 41.

4 Мариетта Шагинян, *Литературный дневник* (Петербург: 1922), 72-82.

5 See T. Beyer, "Andrej Belyj's 'The Magic of Words' and *The Silver Dove*," *Slavic and East European Journal*, XXII, 4 (1978), 464-472.

6 В. Ходасевич, "Аблеуховы-Летаевы-Коробкины," *Современные записки*, XXXI (1927), 255-279. See also T. Beyer, *"The Chris'ened Chinaman," Russian Literature*, X (1981), 369-380.

7 В.Ходасевич, *Некрополь* (Париж: : YMCA Press,1976), 99.

8 Н. Бугаева , А. Петровский, "Литературное наследство Андрея Белого," *Литературное наследство*, 27-28 (1937), 605.

9 See the Notes for a further discussion of the title of the work.

10 "Gogol," trans. by Elizabeth Trahan, *Russian Literary Triquarterly*, 4 (1972), 131-144; selections from "Symbolism as a Weltanschauung"and "Forms of Art" in *Readings in Russian Philosophical Thought*, trans. by Louis Shein (Mouton: 1973); "Adam," trans. by Charlotte Douglas, *Russian Literary Triquarterly*, 4 (1972), 81-92; *Complete Short Stories*, trans. by Ronald Peterson (Ardis, 1979); *Selected Essays of Andrey Bely*, trans. Steven Cassedy (Univ. of California, 1985); and *The Dramatic Symphony*, trans. by Roger and Angela Keyes and "The Forms of Art," trans. by John Elsworth (Grove: 1987).

11 Mirra Ginsburg, ed. and trans. *A Soviet Heretic: Essays by Yevgeny Zamyatin* (Univ. of Chicago, 1970), p. 242.

12 Jane Grayson, *Nabokov Translated* (Oxford Univ.Press, 1977), 16.

13 *The Widening Gyre* (Indiana Univ. Press, 1963), p. 13.

14 Андрей Белый, рец. *Енергия, Новый мир*, 4 (1933), 274.

15 А. Векслер, 60.

THE STUDY

By the windows:—

—a wiped worn, professorial desk with a very discolored gray-green cloth, sit upon by bundles of books; here a big inkpot had settled down potbellied; here had fallen: pencils, pencil stubs, compasses, protractors, erasers; a lamp: the green metal had blackened, and the lampshade—had blossomed; scattered about were little leaves of paper and letters with French, Russian, Swedish, American stamps, packets of notices, torn wrappers, unsealed and unslit brochures, booklets and little books from Lang, Gauthier and others; they constituted enormous piles, threatening frequent collapse, which were transferred to the floor, under the desk and onto the window sills, from where they were rising ever higher, extinguishing the light of day and throwing a sullen dusk onto the floor, in order to give themselves up to shelves and little shelves, or jump up onto the bookcase, very tightly stuffed with brown bookcovers and to sow densely with dust the wiped off chocolate colored wallpaper, and—gray Papochka; he would sit in his gray flappy mantle, squeaking his chair and dropping his calculating nose into the cloth,—where with a strain he would blurt out in a whisper:—

—"En, em, es!"—

—starting to sharpen a pencil stub; from where in the dust, in a cobweb and in little leaves of paper he sent out little whispers and his letters to Mittag-Lefler, Poincaré or Klein and others,—

—growing fiercer and entreating Dunyasha and Mama to leave the papers in peace:

"Don't mess me up, you know..."

"But the dust, sir,—you see..."

"No, leave it be: don't you know, each little paper is—a document: put it somewhere else,—you'll never find anything..."

From here he would stand up; and scatterbrainedly walk through the corridor, the dining room; and he ended up in the drawing room; stopping before the mirror, as if not seeing himself, he would stand and trace with a finger signs in the air; by chance having glimpsed the self before himself, he would imbibe himself rather bestially, placing two fingers under his spectacles; and he could not tear himself away, he could not tear himself away from the ridiculously constructed head, fullweighted, crushing and flattening Papa (seemed to be square, did he) and which contemplated from under the glasses of the spectacles with deeply squatting, small, very slanted little eyes, an obtusely arranged nose; he would then smooth this fullcheeked face with a fullbodied hand; having turned, he would try to glimpse his own personal profile (and the profile was Scythian), stern, curlybearded, seeming bestial; he is so laughable:—

    —yes—

        —his house jacket had been shortened; it ends above the waistcoat; the jacket is puffed out ever so widely; the pantaloons are pulled out of shape; he moves his shoulders, correcting and pulling up the suspenders; he pulls them up—they fall down; in this jacket of his, like in a sack, he can easily turn around and around —to the right, to the left; and it seems that the jacket has been put on aslant; and because of this—there is something of a slant to Papochka; he was slanted by the jacket; very often he would slant his arms; and he would put his foot on the floor more heavily than he should have.

    I remember, it used to be,—

        —he stands such a bigheaded one, thrust into the hard beard—the fingers of one hand, and his tin spectacles raised to his brow, the brow bent to one side with savagery, a brow slit through with a crease, as if resolving on some terrible act; he would drum with his hand on the door;

    and—

        —the torso had been turned over by the stomach
        somehow slanting down from the shoulders; the legs are
        also placed aslant; he is so heavy and bulky from this
        displacement of the axles;—

        —he stands:—

        —banging his fingers against the door, he grows savage; and—he whispers to himself, whispers, whispers; I am terrified, terrified: there is something here of "one's own."

    "Ah, now what have you done"—Mama cries out to him as she passes by with the keys; she is going to the wardrobe—for a corsage, the raspberry, plush one, and—for the matching skirt.

Papochka here undergoes a change; he thrusts out his head and winks at Mamochka with timid little eyes, as if he had been uncovered in the act:

"It's just me!"

"Nothing much..."

"So!"

He drums his feet to the study, such a slanteyed one:

"Yes, go to your room!"

"Do some calculating!"

He stumbles over the words, scatterbrainedly having turned his goodspirited-scatterbrained somehow doggy countenance, and he looks over the eyes of the raised glasses (of the spectacles).

"Yes I'm already doing so, my Lizok... calculating"...

And Mama indicates with a smile:

"Eccentric."

And bustlingly jangling the keys, she goes for the raspberry, plush, ball corsage, for the plush skirt; the lace is— black; no sleeves; on the breast—a big slit; she is bare-armed and barebreasted, having densely powdered her little head and placed in her hair an egret,— somehow grayhaired—she is going out to dance and whirl about in the enormous *grande-ronde*.

And Papa again falls over the long discolored gray-green cloth to calculate, drinking up the ink of the inkpot—in little leaves of paper, pencils, pencil stubs, protractors and booklets: he calculates all about, waves his arms about, leaps up, begins to run about in the little cobwebs, shaking all over; he jumps up blurting out a whisper—

—"En, em, es: ah!"—

—knocking into a pile of books:

"I've smashed it: ugh, what a diabolical mess!"

Deep in concentration he suddenly starts to sharpen a pencil stub, trying to turn its tip into a mere point: then silence sets in; afterwards the ohs and ahs rise again on the properties of some sort of world, of another one, not of ours; I observed, how he would pace boomingly back and forth, his shaggy head hung somehow bitterly and tartly, hanging down to the right and staring at the even shelves of brown bookspines from under his brow, as though he were doing an inspection of them; he always pressed to his breast his right hand with a pencil stub, throwing into the air his waving left hand and he stuck out two fingers against the background of chocolate-colored wallpaper; and suddenly he began to shine so gently with goodness, when the contours of a new calculation "ef, ex" arose before him; they had reported on it at the Sorbonne; the French mathematician Darboux had exchanged impressions about it with Papochka, and Chebyshev—had trembled.

I know that scorpions bred here—not malicious ones, but bookish ones; Papa once showed me a scorpion, having grabbed me as I was passing by; he pressed me up against the bookcase; and opening an enormous and smelly folio: a volume of Lagrange, he placed it up under my nose; he showed me a little scorpion, rather satisfied with this event.

"Hee-hee... Hee-hee-hee!..." he passed sentence upon it, catching it on a page of Lagrange with his big index finger.

"Hee-hee"—and his face began to wrinkle up with wrinkles—humoristically, almost sarcastically, but goodspirited and joyfully:

"Ah you, look here: you know it's crawling, the rascal is crawling!"

And having winked at me with his little Tatar eyes, he pronounced in a respectful whisper.

"Do you know, Kotenka, he eats microbes: a useful beast."

"Yes!"

I make out the little scorpion on the page of Lagrange; it is—tiny, it crawls, it destroys microbes; a useful rascal! And Papa, having slammed shut the useful rascal, takes it away to the bookcase; and—there came the smell of antonovka (he used to buy these antonovka apples, and bestow on us gifts of antonovka at dinner).

Once a year, donning a dressing gown, he raised pillars of dust with a filthy rag, sneezing and coughing; here he bore out what was unnecessary to coffee-colored bookcases, filling even the width of the corridor (between the nursery), attempting with the bookcases to burst into the nursery upon us and block up the exit all together: to cork us up with books; and now and then he would set out with Dunyasha and the yardman for the pantry, bearing all of the excess of this accumulated mass; but Anton, our yardman, having taken the keys to the pantry, and having entered into an agreement with a swindler, would drag the books out; Papa's books were still being traded after his death by second-hand booksellers in Moscow.

Yes, yes.—

—On the bookcases rose multihumped book piles, draped with green material,—dusty, like everything else; amid them was situated a little bed, which squeaked, with a hard little mattress and little blanket of the same chocolate color as everything else; two slippers stuck out as did a multitude of boots gray from the dust, which struck me by the rustyish-uncleaned look of their tops—amid the barbells,——raised by Papa with a strain:

"One!"

"Two!.."

. . . . . .

"Sixteen!"—

—(he suffered from constipation)—

—the bookcases multiplied; and—new ones were set up, in the sad years overgrowing the bed (at the head, and at the sides, and at the foot!), imaging a room within a room with a narrow passage, to which our Papa would retire: to lie down with a book:—

—it used to be:—

—you go,—and you glimpse: in a gradation of soft tones of chocolate, gray-coffee, gray, gray-green color he lies on the bed with his spectacles on his brow, closing his eyes, his weary hand (with a turned open little volume) dropped to his breast; the other hand hangs somehow forcelessly from the bed; he lies grown gray and pale, in wrinkles; and here he seems older than he should (in general he looks younger than he should: he will be fifty!)

And you think:

"Papochka..."—

—Or:—

—you glimpse: he lies undressed on his side, tucked up, his knees pressed in and his bent body drawn in detail; the head has withdrawn under the blanket; only the nose sticks out and a piece of beard (this was he resting, having dined); and—you say:

"Tea is served, Papa!"—

—He leaps up; sits on the bed, forcefully he wipes his eyes with his fist, fussing, trembling under his spectacles:

"Ah, ah!"

. . . .

Yes, the brazen book threatened the drawing room; as if it were all together an afterthought; oppressed by the collapses of books, Papa came up with the thought to erect a bookshelf: straight into the drawing room. Ai, what happened then!

Having glimpsed the shelf, Mama clasped her hands; and her little face grew thin all over from the tedium; and—it tossed itself straight into one's eyes; and her face stood up in one sheer stare, nagging:

"Out!"

"This junk?"

"In here?"

"Out-out-out!"

Papa whispered something of "one's own" relative to the shelf, methodically slicing his own phrases in the air with a paperknife, which he bore everywhere with him, just like a book, so that his opinion relative to the shelf would lay down before us as obviously as an open book:

"Well then..."

But at this how Mama would begin to stamp her foot:

"Out!"

"Disorder!"

"You're spreading the dust. If you want to spread dust, then hold onto it in your own room!"—

—Yes I knew, that "well then," like all of Papa's revelations, would be quickly sent off by Mama: to the pantry— to gather dust, from where they withdrew... to... the second-hand booksellers!—

—The unfortunate bookshelf flew impetuously back into the study: we feared a movement of little volumes from the north-west corner, where the study cooled off,—to the south-east, where the receiving rooms were resplendent in arrogant booklessness; a stretched out book row, multivolumed, elbowshaped, long, like a tentacle, was trying, having opened the door, to spill over everywhere with volumes, to curl around everything else; often it seemed, that Papa, like an octopus, had thrown out from himself his multilegs from the book rows and he catches us, clutching for an arm, for a leg with a voluminous little volume, trying to force everything to become bookish:—

—it used to be, he is always walking after Mama and always collecting himself to give **rational counsel**, to convince her of the **means**, flowing out of Papa's **point of view**; but the **rational counsel** of his seems to Mamochka, Granny, Dotya, Dunyasha and me merely a verbal kite, let into the heavens like a page of a little volume:—

—I saw paper kites jerking in the heavens a tail of bast;—

—We jerk back our necks: we don't understand anything; where does all this of Papa's live and fly—in the heavens? But all this is called: **giving rational counsel.**—

—Or the means: means were always being proposed by him for everything; and it seemed to Mamochka, Granny, Dotya, Dunyasha and me: if we would start to apply these **"means"** to life, **"The Society for the Propagation of Technical Accomplishments"** would have immediately opened at our place, with Papa being made the founder of the society; and the secretary would sit in the dining room and write down the minutes, and we would have died of tedium.—

—Points of view: how he could develop points of view, so that his little eyes would become imperceptible **points of view**; what would come of them? He would begin to speak at the table about his own **points of view**; he begins to speak and he doesn't eat: he slices his cutlets with thoughts, chews words; thus he spends the main course dinner after dinner; and all this is called **"intellectuality"**; and this **"intellectuality"** towers on high, like a brow (an enormous brow: Mamochka when things were tedious called him **bigbrow**); this—**abstract opinion,** no,—she could not endure it: "Mikhail Vasilich, you should go to your room: you should set off to the club." And the **abstract** opinion, having stood up from the table, banging his chair, trying to be quiet, exits and asks Dunyasha to brush off his frock coat (the floor boards have already screeched with cruel squeaks; Papa, trying to be quiet, collects himself to go to the club).—

—He puts on the frock coat which isn't a frock coat—it's a lapserdak (he dresses not as one should, but according to his own personal means); the "lapserdak" trails almost to the floor, it doesn't fit right on the breast; he fastened it—**"bang,"** it burst open: threads dangle, a handkerchief hangs out like a coattail, and the collar is rolled up and twisted in the impatience of quickly putting it on his shoulders; on the other hand: the little jacket had been shortened, ending above the waistcoat and puffed out horribly.—

—And nonetheless Papochka walks after Mamochka with a little volume, and—he preaches the means, thought of by him,—there, in the study from where he exits anew and anew—to give us counsel, on how to live and what to do: his word strikes like a ton of bricks; Mama's eyes widened from the horror of the tedium, and she grabs with her hand for the guttapercha sphere; and "pss"—she wants to spray the pine stream of the atomizer; but—the atomizer does not work; and mathematics hangs densely in the air;— —our Papa is—a Scythian; he does not like perfumy spirits, saying of perfume: "I don't need it: I don't reek of anything," but all the same he smells: of antonovka, halfdamped stearin candle and dust; now and then of all of them at once; nor does he hear music; it is with music that Mamochka struggles with Papochka;—

—he is always attempting to facet the means of life; and to limit us, to cut us down to size into facets, but not like those clear bright facets on Mama's luminous earrings: but with abstract facets or limits (we do not understand them: Mama, Granny, Dotya, Dunyasha and I); Mama immediately sits down to play the piano; and Papa, having brought out for us a little volume of French thinkers, immediately bears off the voluminous little volume in which is laid out for us the rational clarity, which he once attempted to thrust into the drawing room: there is no bookshelf; and—there won't be one!

. . . .

We struggled with the elbowshaped row of volumes, spread by enormous rapidly rusting masses. There is nothing to be done; having pulled on his dressing gown, sneezing, coughing, Papa grunting and groaning would stand up on the squeaking, longtime rocky chair: to conduct the sorting of the volumes destined to enter the storeroom; it seemed: the pressure of the little volumes would burst the study apart; Papa in a white shirt, with a candle in hand and with a turned open volume of Sophus Lie would fall from the brokenthrough wall onto the bed toward... Henrietta Martynovna, in order to continue his reading.

But the study still held out; and—strange to say: Mama placed a washstand there; she would exit splashing and spraying soap and water on the books: but nothing disturbed Papa from blurting out in a whisper **exes** and **wyes** thunderously passing by the nursery with a lighted candle and a little volume of Sophus Lie through the corridor— into that dark little room, where quite often the sounds of water flushing burst forth stormily, where I had not been, from where they brought me... a bedpan, where quite often Papa used to sit with a lighted candle and a little volume of Sophus Lie; quite often the pipes were clogged up; and Papa went to pour a dark-red liquid and halt the undignified smells:—

—such a **means** succeeded; and black little sticks, it seems, of potassium permanganate stood on the bookshelf amid volumes of mathematics:—

—yes, he spread words, just like black little sticks of potassium permanganate, instantaneously eliminating the foul smell of words with a **genteel** tendency—

—Our Papa was an altruist in the highest sense:—

—now and then: there were so many egoistic smells in the dark little room, that the besmeared plumber, rattling his boots, would pass by on the way there; and he would drag out strange parts: both pipes and little basins; Papa with his candle used to inquire of him then, what, strictly speaking, did the damage consist of; it seemed then: Papa is nearing his aim; and "**The Society for the Propagation of Technical Accomplishments**" would rise up right here in front of the dark room; the plumber would be the president of the society: Papa would take his minutes:—

—Papa was not allowed to take minutes in the drawing room!

. . . .

He was dear to me also at those times, when he would make himself resemble a bigheaded gnome: he used to turn to us with his head withdrawn into his sloping shoulders; and—stare very intently, almost sucking in his lip, emitting a special sound through his lips of sifted air "vvvsss," as though he wanted to say something; instead he would wink and, turning his head, stomp off to his study, like to a remote deaf cave.

. . . . .

Now and then I fasten my gaze on Papa's, very big, ruddy, somewhat full face, framed by a not so large, curly, chestnut beard; the years had made their mark on it with distinct streaks of gray; this face seems especially tender to me (how often I fear it), fullweighted, crushing and flattening Papa; it was ridiculously constructed; yes, the whole head was ridiculously constructed with a very-very big protruding brow and with deeply squatted, small, very slanted little eyes, like those of a Tatar; the little eyes, like arrows: they are sent out to the interlocuter, they prick like safety pins: they seem to be dark brown; or they run about, spin like little wheels: they seem to be gray: but, all out of breath, they stumble upon a new thought, smile, bluening and overflowing with superlative goodness, like the heavens enlightening behind the clouds.

There is thunder—in the beard, under the mustache, in the mouth: the beard and mustache:—

—he has them trimmed, he returns with a not so large beard which has become doubly prickly, with a neck which has become fuller, with a face grown smaller,—he seems so bestial, so fanatical...—

—the mouth:—

—wide, thrust forward by the upper lips, eating on the lower lip, concealed by the stubble of the sternly hanging mustache, which is hard and prickly kissing me; so it seems, the mouth bursts apart into a simplistic, natural bark: "All this, my Kotenka,—yes-yes-yes-yes: is idle babble, babble—the babble of liberals" (it is—a Scythian, not a Westerner: the mouth); and it goes, baring its fists, this mouth, to press down upon the babbler; Papa collapses his breast, withdraws his neck into his crumpled collar running up to meet his head, he lets the whole head down below his shoulders, just like a bull (the nose hangs on his clavicle; the spectacles seat themselves apart); and above the brow—a tuft of hair; the little eyes filled with blood begin to run about unpleasantly, a red vein traces itself on the neck and—how it beats:—

—"Pardon me, old chap, you are talking nonsense! You should read Kant, Spinoza and Leibniz!" and the liberal babbler lets out a *bon mot*: "A most horrible debater!" —

—Once some students asked me at a lecture:

"Who is that savage eccentric?"—

I answered:

"Professor Letaev."

"A most horrible debater!"—

—the mouth is—a debater!

But the mouth bursts into a laugh: and—this dear face is covered with a distinct prominent wrinkle, arranged to the right and to the left of the nose and puffing out the cheeks with bumps; the white, strong teeth, on which Papa prides himself, show themselves; a big, curved, but wide gooselike nose separates, like an old scoffer, spreading his arms apart at his wide sides—the nostrils; and—here-here-here it begins to jump about, like a lively frog:—

—And Papa becomes a ruddy prankster, like a satyr; he should put ivy on his head (it may be he has little hooves); a handkerchief hangs down behind: a satyrical tail exactly! He stuck out his head and looks at a little fly, flying downward from the ceiling: "A little fly is, you know—after all, like a little bird: a magnificent little machine; Professor Zhukovsky could not complicate such a little machine." And—with a "**hee-hee-hee-hee**"—he steals up with his full, bent palm, to the "little machine" cleaning its paws. And—"tsap-tsarap": the little fly sits—in his fist...—

—The nose—is an entertainer:—

—the spectacles:—

—they gleam quite sternly; he speaks, he raises the spectacles on words, precisely propping them up from below with his trembling fingers; his hands tremble from excitement; savage well-defined creases slice through all of the brow, collecting in a little wisp above the nose.

Afterwards he is smoothed out, he reclines: having grown in goodness all over, he shines; and he sits quietly, in great tenderness—thus: neither this way nor that: bigbrowed, bespectacled, with a fallen lock on his brow, a let-down little shoulder falling somehow slantingly to the right to the side; and—pulling the other shoulder straight up to the ear, drawing in the hands of his completely calmed arms toward himself under the cuffs; he had shouted to his heart's content; and—he sits quietly, in great tenderness,—thus, neither this way nor that; he smiles clearly, ever so quietly to himself and to everything there is, re-calling a Chinese wiseman who has mastered the wisdom of the I ching, spreading subtle smells of tea and ripe antonovka apples:—

—strange: for here in the study it smells sooner of an old book, papers, dust, now and then of sealing wax; then where does the smell of antonovka apples come from?—

—after the scandals and the arguments this smell fell away; and it smelled naturally: of dust.

. . . . .

Sunset!

In the distance the horizons were pillared by a strengthening smoke; everywhere pillars hang motionlessly; hardly overhanging, barely moving, not falling a drop; and the heavens are no longer the heavens; what can be yellower? Simply some sort of canarium?—

—and
Papochka is—illumined by the heavens, enlightened by the spirit!—
—In
the completely turquoise heavens singing luminaries come clearly to
life out of the cloud—with a cry: in a cherry one; they go out: and it
became stern, and became lilac: exactly like a symphony, where humor
taking to its wings, flowing together with tears into a crystal little
lake, raises up resounding songs of seethrough icebergs and crystals:
you know not what it is: crystallography, music?

PAPOCHKA

You know: **sanctitude!**

It resides in Papa; and to an understanding soul he seems stonelike, or—divorced from life, which is only a **"disorder of sensitive nerves"** ; and Papa strides through the days as a humorist, preferring the little leaves of lectures to all mysticism: but worshipping... the buds and little leaves of a May poplar; Confucian wisdom filled him; his favorite phrases are:

"Everything is—a measure of harmony!"

"Where there is harmony, you know, there is measure!"

"In the middle ground and, yes, in constancy—the real man appears" ...

"We go to the world, in order, having become the world, to stand above the world,—in the world, in relationship to which the world is—only an atom, moving from world to world; the world of worlds, this is—we; the root of us is a numeral, and a numeral is a harmony of measure."

"Thus everything is a harmony of measure."

I know that Papa lives like a conservator of weights and measures; he reveals the sounds of harmonies with the help of numerals; the incomprehensible, the incalculable he pushes away from himself, delighting both in a small little fly, and in the fact that one can discern a picture by Rizzoni gazing through a magnifying glass; he could spend hours delving deeply into trifles, discerning trifles; and constructing from trifles something which is not a trifle at all.

There sticks in my memory:

"Yes, well, water!"

"H two o: beauty!"

"Simplicity!"

He tried to prove to everyone that champagne is—good for nothing: the structural formulas of complicated compositions are inelegant.

"Water is a great drink, given to us"—and in his tiny little eyes—luminosity; with this luminary of thought he flattens out the tablecloth with a finger—he walks about the room, grabbing a little pitcher with water, from which a run of emanating sunbeams lights up on the walls; pushing his spectacles up on his brow and screwing up his slant-eyes, he admires them; and he enlightens the ritual of water-drinking with runs of a wise word (thus: I have respect for water); the refinement of the senses is not elegance; the compilation of the numerator and the denominator of relations between the irritation of external objects and yes, the sensation of them.

"Complication, the confusion of thought and senses is"—he secretively proposes with his mouth an opinion for us on the tapestried tablecloth—"not depth; these thoughts are not thoughts: the process of calculation is—not a result; results are—good."

"Yes, yes" he fusses with his mustached mouth and tosses about glances—

—"hm, in the result usually"—his paperknife flies up —"the numerator and, hm, the denominator of an unknown relation, hm, are reduced—hm" (the paperknife makes a quick zig-zag in the air, reducing a misty thought—to a result of simple thought) "and we move over: to simple relations!!"—

—here he views the opponent (Mama) victoriously (but Mamochka frowns).

"This is some sort of—yes-yes-yes!—only a third, or only a half, but certainly not a fifth, nor a twenty-fifth"—quite cunningly he snickers

striking a glass
with his index finger—
—"jang!"—
—"Again?"
—"Don't make that ringing sound on the glass!"—Mamochka bursts out in an exclamation...

"The world is—a relation short and simple; it is—the result of multicomplicated processes, but it is not a process: a result!"—

—Sult-
sesult!—

—He snaps his fingers: on an oilcloth circle; and he throws it up: that circle; and catching it, he lays this circle under a circle (he plays with circles).

"This nonsense has started again!"

"How tedious this is: you've caused creases in the tablecloth again!"

"Hm"—he cries back, rather satisfied with his creation of the world and he expresses his satisfaction in unexpected mischief: leaping up, he runs thunderously around the not so large space of the anteroom—to the kitchen.

Flinging the door wide open he screams out his impromptu impetuously—to Afrosinya:

> I beg Afrosinya
> To make us botvinya.
> No butter and no meat
> Kvas and onion we'll eat;
> We'll finish all our peas,
> You'll bake some pies to please,
> Sour dough makes them tastier,
> O, you,—Clytemnestra!

· ·

Yes, he used to put forth his rule: very measured, all would have said: a philistine China, from customs of high society, of laws and rules, filling the rules with an all together different content, taken—

—from Leibniz,—

—from Pythagoras,—

—from Lao-tzu,—

—he stubbornly tried in everything to carry out all of this, cramping us with counsel and bursting like a deaf rhinoceros into unfaceted music:—

—to facet, to facet,
to find results, to weigh
and to fall in love!—

—To which Mamochka replies:
"You, are— a bighead!"

And only special cases come out of this: only laughable consequences of loud theories; Papa himself began to live like a saint, a life limited by himself; he seemed to others to be limited; appearing amid us as a simpleton, he was quite often in a laughable condition—

—meeting him on the street, you
would not say:
"Professor!"
You would say:
"Swindler!"—

—he exchanged bowler hats and umbrellas in just a

massive quantity, always leaving his own and
dragging off someone else's goods: rather old ones,
by the way.

Others caught every chance to lower him; he fell
into the trap immediately:

"You see?"

Once it was said:

"You know, surely Professor Letaev is suffering from a softening
of the brain?"

Yes, yes: the rational means to live did not always succeed; and the
clarity of the French thinkers truly secreted the mists; I used to stare at
him for a long time; and the forces comprising his world would become
enigmatic for me; he used to change sides on himself; everywhere he
transgressed the measure: measurelessly he thought up measures and
means: and he used to forget them; like the means of brewing acids
(manganese and boric).

"Ah, Lizanka"—once he said—"there are magnificent means to
preserve our teeth from damage with a brew of acids!"

"Ah, you: means, means!"

"No, don't you know..."

And he secreted his solution until its time; once he burst in with
an enormous funnel of tin, with a green bottle, with a sack of acid
crystals (for some reason he had purchased a blank bottle).

"What are you doing?"

"But this, Lizochek.. here you see, I... to brew... boric... hm,
acid..."

"But?.. Who is going to allow you?"

" Lizochka, I'll brew it up quickly for myself."

"I won't permit it: it's an outrage, a unimaginable disgrace!"

But truly, with bullish stubbornness, setting aside a tray, he stood
up the bottle; fiddling over the funnel.

At this point Mama, unable to hold herself back, broke into a peal
of laughter; and Aunt Dotya after her—laughed pea, pea, pea; poking
about with his nose in the blank bottle and burning his trembling
fingers on the stream of boiling water, he muttered:

"The solution is concentrated."

And "hee-hee-hee"— the solution of acid, which had begun to
gurgle, set off into the funnel; twice he made a brew in this image,
having forgotten about the means; the means (the funnel) were sent off
at this point: into the rubbish; thus the **means to live** were

demolished: **means after means**: he did not stand in the way; yes, he loved: results, sums, capabilities, which became means; he himself lost these means; he lived by means of the capability: to think up means!

I remember!

Once a grayhaired musk-ox appeared in the dining room; such a highfalutin, important—professor from Kiev; Papochka, having leaped up and wiping his hands in welcome, thundered off to the study, leaving the honored guest in dumb amazement.

"Wait: just a minute!"

I know: it is always like this; they arrive—and he takes cover; to perform in the study some sort of action (he won't say which); which—I know:—

—are two actions being consummated here quite often one after the other; the first action: a run through the little corridor to the dark little room with a burntdown candle; and—with a little volume; after standing there a while, he runs back out; and on the go he buttons up... he does not come out: he stands before the door in the drawing room; from behind the door he is already speaking with the guest; and continues... to button up, putting his nose out from behind the door, the very thing which is not buttoned up; we knew this; and we very much feared that he would come out before he succeeded in finishing all of this; but he did come out, buttoned up; and immediately—with his head into the conversation;—

—and the second, secreted action—consisted of:

—"Right away... Wait just a minute!"—

—He takes cover: leaping up, thundering joyfully:

—"Vasily Ivanych, I'm overjoyed... Vasily Ivanych, are you here from Kiev for long?.. You should have, Vasily Ivanych... I would have, Vasily Ivanych"— "**Vasily Ivanych**," "**Vasily Ivanych**": Vasily Ivanych, for sure must think that this is a mocking of "**Vasily Ivanych**"; suddenly "**Vasily Ivanych**" turns into "**Vasily Ilych**"; this "**Vasily Ivanych**" is pronounced so joyfully, as if in the very combination of sounds "**Vasily Ivanych**" there is a secret which Papa alone knows, but which "**Vasily Ivanych**" does not know; and luminous sunbeams run: here-here-here:—

—it ran along the tablecloth, fluttered under the ceiling, quickened in a zig-zag on the white wallpaper, on faces; it got lost in the windows; Moscow cleared up: it is—the little sun (that's how "**Vasily Ivanych**" is, I can say!)—

—our faces burn with a rosy strong ruddiness!—

—Vasily Ivanych Bykaenko is touched by the amiability, the joyfulness of Papa—

—but what is the joyfulness about?—

—I—know:—

—"Wait just a minute: I'll, be back right away"— he runs off to the study, frightened,—straight to the desk; and he grabs there, over the desk, behind the pockets; behind the thin wall I hear:

"O Lord! God dammit! Ah!"

"I've lost it..."

"Where is the little key?"

"?"

"It's not here."

"Shoo-shoo"— a sheet of paper spread shuffles, a little leaf of paper soars up, and something thunders...

"I'm done for!"

Silence sets in, full of horror: if he doesn't find the key, he won't come out, he'll begin to fool about; the guest is— waiting.

"I've found it!"

The thunderous crack of a drawer: I know, from there a thick, bound book is grabbed; tossing his spectacles up on his brow, he sticks his nose to the pages, covered in writing with a galloping hand-writing; he runs with his fingers, very satisfied with himself and the "**means**":

"Well now, let's have a look?"

And he whisks through like a whisper:

"So-so-so: here's 'a' ; here's 'b' : Badabaev, Badeev... No— further: ah—no: dammit: Bercheev, Berendeev, Berneev, Berseev; no further, my old chap; here: Budaev, Bugaev... Bykaenko!! Here it is."

"Hee-hee-hee!"

"Here it is!"

"I've found it!"

"Here he is"—the surprised and joyful whisper carries—"Vasily Ivanych Bykaenko..."

"Public figure..."

The whisper becomes louder:

"Professor!"

And the whisper becomes an exclamation:

"Eh... heh-heh-heh: hee-hee: hee-hee... Babbler!"

"And?"

"Tell me, if you please, old chap!"

"Now that is something!"

"A babbler!"

"A liberal, an Austriophile!"

"Hee-hee-hee..."

And leaping up, he passes back and forth on the run from excitement behind the thin wall, lights a candle, and quickly runs past the nursery into the dark little room; there to discuss that which had just been learned; there— he locks himself up:—

—I know: already:—

—in a skipping handwriting, striving to get into the book, our acquaintances begin to drop in,—all of them, all (Berendeevs, Berenyovs, Burnyovs, Bernilins, Berniches, Berpovs, Bershes, Berseevs—many hundreds of them!), arranged by surname in alphabetical order; given are short character sketches, first names, patronymics, kinds of activities and inclinations;—

—here having gleaned the raw material for a conversation, my Papa, returning with the candle, runs with a thunderous roar into the drawing room, to the guest; just before running in, still stumbling behind the door, strangely bogged down there, he tosses out one after another one of the handwritten words, which had just been underlined:

"Yes: I am overjoyed to see you" gives out from behind the door.

"You, surely, Vasily Ivanych"—the door squeaked, from where a nose stuck out with a quite cunning, all together goodspirited walrus-like face.

"You, Vasily Ivanych"—Papa behind the door is trying to cope with an unyielding toilette part:

"You've, surely, just arrived here?"

"Well, what's new in Kiev?"

"What about Antonovich?"—the floorboards squeak in the drawing room... "What is Grushevsky writing?"—the armchair already squeaks... "Is Bukreev well? Is Mrs. Zakharchenko-Vashchenko still so stout?"—his hands are thrown about right and left.

"And what about the Kostyakovskys?"

The old professor (babbler, liberal, Austriophile),—all puffed up, shaggy, a grayhaired musk-ox, does not try to breathe his smelly opinion out clearly; he gargles some sluggish words in his throat and phaaeys into a white handkerchief, — he is overblown, swollen up, like a bottle—not a sound; but Papochka knows that this "**bottle**" secretes much fizz and foam; and he walks around in a circle, collecting himself to drink up the conversation, and raises his spectacles, licking his lips like a cat; he sits down with an "**allow me to ask**," in order to penetrate: with his tongue, like a corkscrew:—

—he turns and turns, and turns it, and—tugs at the cork; the "**bottle**" pops; and after phooing forth words, it pours out like fizzling champagne; and all are intoxicated; the "**liberal babbler**" fizzes and produces fir shoots of words; Mama sits quietly in her cornflower-blue jacket; her little breast breathing, like a fan fluttering quietly; I see: her little mouth listens spellbound.

"Ah, ah!"

"Good!"

"So beautiful; so sonorous."

And Papa sits as the little humorist: bitingly, slanteyed he laughs and looks attentively as they placed the idle gossip on a cart: they lash the little horse; and pomposity—was on its way; a prattle a rattlin on! Papa suddenly burst out at him, popping a word like a cork: Mamochka jerks (her little lips pulled together like a little ring); the piercing scream raised by Papa, the opponent of an independent life for those at the extreme edges of the country, depresses her; but Papa goes to extremes with his words:

"Allow, allow me!"

And having driven up quietly in a bass voice, he tosses out howls;—well and he began to shout indivisibly at the top of his voice:

"You are—inveterate, old chap: you are—inveterate... You are—with the Polacks... You, I tell you, are for Austria..."—he leaps up and cries out in stride; he passes like a heavy cleaver through alien opinions, and grabbing hold of an opinion like a frockcoat button with a strong hand, pressing his nose and his own two spectacles to the chin of Bykaenko (he is taller than him), he stands on tiptoes; Bykaenko draws back into the corner; there they trample him with a heavy crushing blow; already Mamochka's little face grows thin from the tedium; and—it tosses itself straight into one's eyes; and they glow white hot, and run, blue, like the little flames of coal gas; the heavy coal fumes make one's head ache; the little coal eyes naggingly burn everything in front of them; me, if it is me; more likely—it is Papa.

The debate strengthens over tea:

"You are for Austria, for Austria; and whose money is holding Ukrainian literature together, old chap?.. We know about that!.. You, I am going to inform you..."

"I am—for Shevchenko... Shevchenko was completely blocked out by you Muscovites."

"Like Gogol?" —Papa giggles bitingly.

"What about Gogol? A Russian peasant... Now—Shevchenko... Shevchenko..."

"Shevchenko Shevchenko" Papa pokes his nose in the air... "And Antonovich? And his gang?"—and he points his eyes at the corner (and I look over—isn't Antonovich sitting in the corner with some sort of gang); our Papa is a Roosky; and I know from Mama, that to be a Roosky,—that means: wrapping red sashes about oneself, stomping and shouting; Mama does not like this at all, but I see, that, these actions have brought us to the Rooskies; I see Papa sitting, straining his sly, "Scythian" little eyes on everything, like beads, sparkling "Scythian" points of view at everything:—

—Papa is—

—a Scythian, a cleaver of questions, a great curser!—

—and Papa seems like a tyrant, ready to slice up with a table knife whomever you like,—with a table knife, grabbed by him scatterbrainedly and in the debate striking it all over the tablecloth,—in truth it had a blunt tip (Mama feared for the tablecloth, for the new one with the cocks, but not for the one with the peacocks); I remember: Papa was always forcing himself to make a cutlet from the tablecloth with this little knife:

"Yes, yes—Antonovich, I tell you openly, is a Jesuit!"

But Bykaenko is going all out (here comes the scandal across the table!):

"What do you mean, you know, after all Antonovich is a magnificent scholar, a public figure: our Ukrainian Erasmus... You, probably, haven't even read the works of Antonovich."

Papa's word crashes down: as he points his extended finger:

" I have so read them!"

And—he tries to put forth an army of arguments,—he quickly leaps up on the chair; his eyes drink in their own reflection on the copper (we have a samovar of red copper). He chops cutlets in the air with his hands: and we can just whistle and snap our fingers: his word jumps around the rooms like a little ball!

" But I'll tell you firstly!.."

" Tenthly!!"

" Twentiethly!!!" —

" Hm, hm!"

I know that his "hm" is pregnant with significance; from the "hm" there follows:

"How?!?"

"What in the world?!?"

"Yes for all of this I could get you..."

But here, suddenly grabbed by a thought, he lets drop:

"Yech!"

Hopelessly he throws off his napkin onto the tablecloth; and he hunches over again, snapping the starch of his shirt, sits down on the chair, placing down his outstretched palm (he tosses his little penknife in the air not taking into account objections); the other hand he hooks behind the chair, pressing it under his armpit, and prepares to jump on all of this—together with the chair; thus they debate for hours:—

—I

saw a playtoy: **"The Smith and the Bear"**; you jiggle the board: **the Smith and the Bear** bang away with their little hammers—in the middle ground between them; I see now, that all of this was playing, here are **"The Smith and the Bear"**: and they sit and bang away first with fists, then with words: in the middle ground between them:—

—all opinions were taken apart; they were laid out by Papa like cards: like this and that,—like in patience: Papa loved to play patience; and he deftly complicated his patiences from debates; he would grab up all of Bykaenko's opinions; he throws his cards on the table, throws them about like this and that, and Bykaenko watches, what will become of Papa's opinions (the devil knows what); and he puffs up—like some kind of sour dough; in his brain— a batter of gray matter; he digs his finger and drips white dandruff from a bald spot onto his shoulders; offended he begins to take his leave, having left all of his opinions; Papa, satisfied now, that he has debated, is suddenly grabbed by a thought—he becomes confused, wipes his hands; and leading the guest into the anteroom, cannot in his soul praise him sufficiently (he did not like likeminded persons: he loved only opponents).

A red and perspiring Bykaenko, as if just from the bathhouse, having wrapped around his shawl, his musk-ox face sticks out of his hat like from behind the hay, he bows to Papa, and Papochka, shining all over, screwing up his eyes, draws his head into the shoulders flying up to meet it:

"I, so to say... Don't take my words to heart!" And with a full palm he slices the air; and—clicks his heavy heels, crawling with his other hand into the pocket of the pantaloons with the rhinoceros creases hanging below the knees;

yes,—

—the pantaloons are longer than they should be; a gray, wide jacket,—it is shorter than it should be; below the knees, hanging cloth, the pantaloons formed a second set of feet inside of which Papa walked like stockings—

—and rocking his stooping back, bent slightly to the right, he goes from the anteroom, sucking on his lips and snapping his tongue in his mouth resoundingly, as though he had eaten his fill; with his left hand set aside which would catch on everything, he would swing about—

—and in the right he always holds: a little paperknife, a pencil stub, or a little volume,—

—and Mama pesters him:

"Did you shout enough?"

"Well, no"—he winks at Mamochka with his running, like little wheels, quick, guilty eyes,—

"No, what for: we spoke like this, debated a little; like... we discussed—

—How they discussed! Thus many people like that, who appeared at our house for the first time, did not appear a second time.—

And in Mamochka, I know, a most malicious anthill of words, very biting ones is already swarming:

"You didn't give me a chance to say a word... No, not a word! I— sit there, like some kitchen maid, to wash your cups... An unimaginable disgrace: an outrage!"

Afterwards the apartment bites for a long time (and here a little ant, and there a little ant); and Papochka—a click of the heels to the study; behind him, following,—Mamochka; Papa moves about the rooms;

Mamochka moves about the rooms following; much is pronounced here; but about "I" or "you"—there is no mention; Mamochka's mouth tinkles, a little bell, about how "others" of us speak in words about a numeral and about a measure, but in action...; yes, there are **"those, who..."**; I do not like these **"those"**; it would be better if she would just say straight out "you"; for these **"those"** are—boors, ruffians, dumb Rooskies—they force my little heart to beat forcefully; and to think, that these "those" are—Papa. **"Those"**—rush quickly along the corridor like rhinoceroses: to the club...

    . . . . .

THIS AND THAT'S OWN

And it is already morning!

You glance out the window; and—the snow has been scratched by crows' little claws; and one crow has pressed itself against another crow at the gutter: it is cold—they ruffle their feathers; the morning is—unsightly, incurious; it is tedious!

The spindle of days turns around and around—the shadow of shadows!

My nursery is—singlewindowed, blue; a wardrobe; Mama's wardrobe; a very small little table, two chairs, the bed of Henrietta Martynovna; and—a little bed: mine; a little trunk and little commode; on the chair a little pitcher and little basin; behind the door on a rack—dresses hung, and skirts, and blouses, turned inside out and staring sillily because of the dress-shield; all of this belonged not to me: to Henrietta Martynovna; in a dark corner an etagere with playthings; the icon image above it is ancient; a secretive emerald gleams greenly on the bloody ruby from the crown of the Deogenetrix, in the pit of her arm grabbing hold of the pearl body of the infant.

I know that Your Silvergentleness, the snow, will come falling out: it will pile up silversheets in the blotched thaw; but—pewter puddles will step through and toward evening they will make a blue patch of ice (there will be a ruddy glow): it will run away in a bustling little stream; it will appear anew: in a greater quantity; everything will turn white into a flaky mass; and the puddles will cool off into icon frames of cold: framed treasures of ice:

"**Es ist kalt.**"

A blowing windchase whistled, ran on—into the lifeless horizon: of savage times; already the shouts of teary piano keys: Mamochka had sat down in the dining room to play; already it gushes into little ears: their peals of laughter are already above everything. The events of life began to flutter away in the eventlessness of sounds; and Mama, bending over the black and slit box, has withdrawn her look into the whitetoothiness of the keys; I see: a bracelet jumps glitteringly from her small little hand; an earring diamondizes in a lilaceous spark; Mama's little head fell to the sounds, marveling with upflown eyebrows (under the little curlicue of hair)—at the sounds; she is—carried away by her playing: she does not see, she does not hear; and with a shake of her little head she says:

"No!"

"No!"

"No!"

"Never, not for anything!"—

"How dare you, sounds?"

But the sounds do dare: will Mamochka dare? Only a lone spark dares "this"; and it began to run from lilac shades into green: it became—orange...

Henrietta Martynovna and I—listen.

. . . . .

Yes, Henrietta Martynovna, a German, is not at all malicious—but dumb, dumb: Papa used to say of her:

"An amazingly, you know, limited nature!"

She understood—everything, everything:

"Do you understand?"

"Ja!"

"Do you understand?"

"Ja, o gewiss—selbstverständig!"

Papa used to debate with scholars; Uncle would roll his little ball of bread, ohing:

"The devil knows what it is: you can not understand it!"

Henrietta Martynovna would blurt out and say:

"I—undershtood!"

And Papa would fix his snubnosed gaze, throwing the little knife up:

"You understood—everything?"

He catches the little knife:

"O, ja!"

"And Spinoza, and Kant?"—and the fingers dance along the tablecloth like peas.

"Ja, selbstverständig!"

"Well, that's good!"

He leaps up, runs into the study with his right, sloping shoulder, rocking his left arm in the air; and he runs out from there with an enormous mathematical book: chuckling at us with his gibberish:

"Cee over eych two, ef-bee-que, the enth root of 'ay', minus, plus: delta 'ey', delta 'bee', delta 'cee', delta 'dee'.. You understand?"

"Ja, o gewiss!"

"Repeat it!"

"Ploos, minoos... **Ja, ja: und so weiter!**"

And Papochka stormily gallops about (and even clicks his heels) —

—he loved, when he was joking, to jump up, clicking about: little busts would fall down because of this (Pushkin had chopped off one sideburn in this way acquiring a new image); and—

—and he spreads his hands like a humorist, leaning over Uncle with a little whisper:

"You see, you see!.."

"I—said it!"

"She won't get far at all: poor thing!"

She—developed in me palespiritedness.

. . . .

And it simply came about thus (much in life comes about thus: tiddly winks, little crumbs, specks of dust); you breathe out of your little mouth; and—something fogs up from the little mouth; you draw an angular mug with a shaking little finger on the perspiring spot, and from it little drops of moisture from your breathing flow onto the window sill; the spot flows away, and that rosy house of Starikov on the opposite side appears anew; under it ran a peoplechase along the road of time; I know: murky whirlpools are the precipitation of the moisture of breathing; and here they have breathed on the mirror for me Henrietta Martynovna; someone breathed on the mirror; and losing its reflection, the mirror became—a whitish mist; they breathed again: and—Henrietta Martynovna sits with a very pretty little face, white like chalk, with a white-yellow braid,—she is somehow this way all over; palelipped, pale-eyelidless, dumbly fastening her gaze at the self before Mama's mirror, which reflected her better; she looks expressionlessly, grinning, at the bloodless, pale gums; and...—

. . . . .

The slamming, loudly banging iron leaves of the rumbling roof rolled under the wind—above us; and with a hoarse doggy howl the weather rose up the chimney flue; and already Almochka howls back a doggerel to it from the dark anteroom:

"What do you want?"

Yes, the snowscript leaves a starlike silversheet, when the windchase runs off into the horizon—along the road of times, when the banging, loudly slamming iron leaves of the rumbling roof roll above us:—

—that is—the wind!

. . . . .

As soon as Mama withdraws,—Henrietta Martynovna quietly goes behind the alcove: to look at herself; she stares, stares at herself—this way and that; she turns up her irresponsible little nose; and—forces herself, squinting her little eyes, to glimpse her own personal profile; I already know; she is—a murky creature of the mirror; you touch it with a little finger—you feel only glass; behind the glass you glimpse: Herr Zett, or Herman; I know: she is—not she; this is—Zett, about whom she speaks with her girlfriend on the boulevard when we take a walk; they call Herr Herman—Zett; and this "Zett" has firmly seated himself in her head.

I tug at her sleeve,—she turns, fixes her pale greensickness gaze on me; and, winking, she shows me her bloodless gums over a gloss of even, little porcelain teeth; I barely hear:

"O du: dummes Kind!"

And—she buries her head again: and—do not await anything; keeping myself occupied, I wander through the blank, quieted apartment; I sit on my haunches under the hand washstand; I open the little doors—and look; and there stands a bucket; I—touch it: a slimy "louse-louse." The faceted, copper handle of the door occupies me; it is—turning green; they wipe it off with a brick; it is ground up; stealthily I licked it: the brick is not tasty; I want to spin off the handle; well—come-on, come-on! A spreadpawed armchair slants like a walnut tree; the lacquer smiles at me; I go up to it and nibble at it with my little teeth; no—it is not tasty!—

—Well, come-on: I go to pick out clay from the stove: I pick out a piece, yes—into the little mouth; I—like it; there is something in the aftertaste! Glinka-modeling clay!

. . . .

From everyone there matures one's own which I can not understand: "ten"—this: is raising the little fingers of the hands; and I—did not answer; "one's own" is —not "mine"; and this "one's own" is a covered object, another person's, each person's: ununderstandable to me; once Mama said:

"Yes, yes: he has 'chic'..." And yes: he has **that here: this— one's own!**

"What? What is it?"

"Like that!"—she waved her little hand under her little brow; her little eyes—toward the tablecloth; that way, somehow all over—agitated.

And she smiled.

It dawned on me: everyone has somewhere concealed "one's own", about which it is forbidden to say what it is: you are only permitted to whisper, as... Henrietta whispers loudly with her girl friend; her "one's own" is—**Zett**, or Herman; Herr Herman is secreted—under "**Zett**"; they call it an "**object**"; everyone has this "**object**"; Mama has one; Papa has—a different one: the very same kind that other men have; they cover up their own object; but if you undress them—the "**object**" exposes itself.

. . . . .

I know, everyone's "this that" grows, swarming with the precise rustle of a whisper, but the clarification is—concealed in the creases of a clenched mouth under the eyelashes; I distinctly heard: Dunyasha — takes walks in the street with a shop-assistant; it is impossible to hold onto this Dunyasha; even I take walks with Henrietta Martynovna; I remember: catching a glimpse of me Mama made eyes:

"Ah!"

"Be silent!"

"Leave me!"

"The child..."

"It is forbidden..."

I understand: I—acted the "child": a somersault! Mama, her braid tossed onto her breast, bit it and cast a slanting glance at Auntie:

"Look at **Kotik**."

"He's somersaulting..."

"I hadn't the slightest hint!.."

She grabbed me up in her arms, and "bash"—onto the little bed; peals of laughter, she plays, rolls; she spanked me; I started to squeal; we squealed; and after...—

—The hint became more than a hint; the gates of understanding distinctly widened—into the distances beyond the gates;—

—I interpret it:—

—Dunyasha walks the streets with a shop-assistant: this is—not important; Dunyasha goes from streetwalking to the shop-assistant: they do something, and this is—more important.—

—The kitchen maid has "one's own": the appearance of Petrovich in the kitchen is permitted; and—they do, something; they have done something;—

—afterwards "Kotiks" appear; how this occurs there,—I don't know; but,—I do know—

—there appeared from somewhere quite a screamer Yegorka,—the previous year; and he set off for the "Foundling Hospital"; and Dunyasha said that she was very ashamed when Afrosinya spent the night with her own "muzhik";—

—yes: that is the way it is:—

—it is indecent to lie with a muzhik; and it is impossible to hold onto Dunyasha for the reason that, after walking the streets with the shop-assistant, she goes to the shop-assistant: to sleep.

Isn't the shop-assistant a muzhik?

"Yes, how should I say, Kotik, perhaps, what,—yes..."

And having measured me with an unseeing glance from under his brow, as if a scholarly question had been proposed to him, Papa knocked against the door to the room, in order to whisper something into the pages: after all everything he has there is his "one's own".

All the more of this "one's own" ("**here this here,**" awful)—is in Papochka; I had shaken with terror more than once because of it:—

—thus: once I glimpsed a nephew of Papa's; and I liked him; and meanwhile—he was a state criminal, a transgressor, sent off to hot Tashkent with Kistyakovsky:—

—I brought him my constructo cubes, and dumped them onto his lap:

"Construct a little house!"

But he waved me off:

"No, no!"

"We do not know how..."

"We demolish everything..."

But I said to him:

"Construct one!"

He—constructed one: such a lovely one!—

—afterwards Papa wiped his chin with a shaking finger and set forth an army of arguments against the nephew, falling heavily with his foot against the floor and slicing his phrases in the air with the paperknife, like a book:

"The singular unity of Russia..."

"Yes, yes, Vyacheslavenka,—do you know—was created over the course of years!.."

"And you—want to demolish everything!"

And Papa's opinion opened up before us like a slit-open book:

"Well, here, Vyacheslavenka, you have recognized in part your delusions..."

And he walked about for a long time, ohing about:

"It's all Antonovich's fault!"

"Yes, yes!"—

—"Antonovich"—he used to stamp his foot at this word, he would stand on this point with eye and nose—"is inciting you, do you know, Vyacheslavenka, the young people, and he himself is—off to the side, to the side!"—

—He ohs: and I know; in his eyes a crushing defeat is being consummated at this, as though they had borne out everything: in place of the full life of thought of the apartment— there remained a blank place; blank—from the horror, that Antonovich and his gang would undoubtedly destroy the unity of Russia.

Antonovich has long been in my imagination, he has long stunk up all of the surrounding Kievan district with his resolution to steal the convictions: of Volodechko, Gorenko, Silichko, Dimko, Vadimko, Oleshko,—exactly like, he stole Vyacheslavenka:—

—yes, undoubtedly, here is **this and that's own,**—

—because the elder, Antonovich is—a professor, like Papa: from Kiev; this is—a deception, this is—"zett," or—a mask: under it Antonovich is, as it seems,—a soultormenting prankster, a bathhouse splasher, even a gangster, and this is filthier than a robber; a robber simply sets down on the road, tosses a sharp knife, previously whipped against the whetstone by the sharpener, and thrusts it straight into the stomach, and—he withdraws, wheezing, with a very stout sack on his back,—to lie low in a burdock grove; this inveterate prankster, modestly donning his professor's uniform tail coat, crawls out of the bathhouse—as the sheer **"Antonovich"** that is, as one who comes into the steam-puffing bathhouse, hangs up his uniform tail coat, exposing the horrors of bare men; and, all soapy and smelling of mould, he throws into his gang's bucket over there Papa's nephew, whom he had just stolen,—he lets into the gang's bucket boiling water from the bathhouse faucet; the nephew—still an unstable young man— dissolves, like soap: yes, yes: understanding—a little girl in a white dress—dances; and dark nannies come in a muttering swarm: so horribly indistinct, yet so terribly occupying!—

—already the windchase has run off, along the road of times; time itself, a frightened hare, ran, pressing back its ears.

.   .   .   .

Torn off from the rest a thundering sign slams with great effort its bent leaf of iron under the little window: everything there is aws, ohs, ahs; and—then everything there is squats to keep silent under the little window until a new runout: I hear sounds from the kitchen:

—"Jang, jang!"—

—This, I know, in the kitchen they are pounding almonds with a blunt pestle.

And I am deep in thought about all of this world—both vicious and pernicious! I listen, how headlessly, armlessly, dumb shadows pass into blackening niches; there is—an assembly of shadows; there is a multitudinous-multitude of them; the corner compresses them gloomily; in the corner rustling little spheres begin to roll: mice; and— quicklegged thoughts from my head run about the rooms; and seethrough handlegs of shadows hung headlessly; a handleg began to run along the parquets—onto the walls; from the walls—to the ceiling;—

—from the shadows a blackhorned-legless suddenly rises, it falls with its multimanus, encircles with its arms, grabs around and will suck everything there is out of me, pouring it into itself; and I will be swept about as an all-together weightless shadow inside of its existence; and—it will dance away with me to the enormous distances, beyond the windows, where—

—the banging, loudly slamming iron leaves of the rumbling roof rolled thundering with a whistle:

"Ai, ai!"

I run—backwards: to Henrietta Martynovna; and tug at her little sleeve; she turns from the mirror, quietly fixes her pale greensickness gaze on me, quietly shows her bloodless gums and—says:

"**Was willst du?**"

"**O du, dummes Kind.**"

And—do not await anything: she will not think up anything.

.   .   .   .

I remember—she would whiten all over; around it would become pale; and the paleness turned gray, and the grayness darkened—in the corners; thus for hours she would sit before Mama's mirror: suddenly she—leaps up, takes me by the hand: we quickly run away from the mirror—through the drawing room—into the nursery; this was the sound of the bell, quite loud: the floorboards squeak; the autowalker starts out; this is Papa going through the corridor from the dark anteroom, coughing, in his uniform tailcoat, hanging his big head to the right and staring at everything from under his brow; in his right hand he pressed a very stout portfolio, throwing his left hand in the air and drumming on the walls with trembling fingers; everything silences; only the wind like thunder passes along the roofs; in the little window a sheer silversheet has been sprinkled with snow; the stove in Papa's room began howling like a hoarse doggy; from the chimney flues tossed tufts of smoke whip along roofs and windows; I look out the little window: whitest roofs have settled down into darkest niches; nibblers mice—play quieter and quieter...

Do not await anything!

Can this really be—Mrs. Malinovsky...

· ·

In gloomy October they reupholstered our armchair in an olive color; yes: and in gloomy October at our place appeared—

—Mrs. Malinovsky!—

—greennosed, greenbrowed: a gray old hack in a black-gray kerchief!—

—she entered bitingly like overflattened ivy: she spoiled the air for Mama with her little question:

"And why, my dear, has a separate bedroom appeared at your place? That's a fact—isn't it: that's—all there is to it!"

"**That's all there is to it**" she added to each word; I noticed in her her own particular attribute: to appear wherever a process of denunciation was being accomplished no matter what it might be; all her announcements always led up to a denouncement; she announces something—a gay society dissolves into malicious little fountains of quarrels:—

—and such a little fountain began beating away between Papa and Mama; yes, yes, they say, a cannibal eats people by gnawing at them; they say of her that she gnaws people to death: such a cannibaless!

I remember the events of the year and the construct of measured months exactly from that time: yes, from October (I was born in October); that October was very snowy!

Winter! All the houses, just like coffins: stern snowdrifts; maliciousness whistles in the chimney flue; a crow runs under the windows with a gnawed bone. Look out: Mrs. Malinovsky will do it to you:

"That's all there is to it!"—

—And she used to appear: she was horribly respected in the professorial circle; whatever Varvara Semyonovna says, that is the law; and she would say such pleasant things; they used to melt in your mouth like the taste of sweet-pears, if you taste these things; but you will surely scream later: from a stomach ache and a pain in the guts;—

—she would say such pleasant things to husbands about husbands; and—such tasteless things: to husbands about their wives; the husbands would say:

"Varvara Semyonovna,—yes! A respected person: she has read Solovyov, the historian, twenty-five times from cover to cover."

Their wives would answer:

"A horrible pedant!"

And once at our place Uncle Yorsh added:

"She is—simply a green old hack!"

She appeared in the green drawing room (I do not remember her when we had the red drawing room!)

She held her own apartment in lacquered sparkle; she had only two dresses: one—palegray; and the other—green; in the first she would go visiting; and in the second—she received visitors; she used to say at our place, embracing Mamochka about the waist:

"Yes, that's all there is to it,—my dear... Everywhere at everyone's place—there is dust... That's all there is to it... As soon as I arrive home... That's all there is to it... I tear my dress off... That's all there is to it... And then, you know, you bring home with you so much dust on the hem from your guests, that afterwards Annushka must sweep up the floor... And Nikolai Irasovich also..."—

—Yes, yes: all of her conversations were broken short by Nikolai Irasovich:—

—Nikolai Irasovich had been her husband who had preferred some twenty years ago to let himself down into the grave, rather than to live by such means...—

—At Malinovsky's it is so clean, so clean, that the servants no longer sweep the waxed parquets, but... lick them; or, squatting, with a finger nail on which they have spit, they playfully scrape up a speck of dust off the floor; it seems to me: they wipe the floors there with their tongues, like everything, that happens in the professorial circle; and by the walls stand boards, upholstered with a gray, cloth material, so that a professor leaning against the wallpaper by chance would not leave a greasy spot there with his head; even the soles of the shagreen slippers of Malinovsky herself are clean, so clean, that they make soup from them, to serve to the guests; and a professor tastes with joy the dish made from this sole; she is full of sweetness; sweets are—everywhere;—

— only in the bed sheets do foul things go on:—

—in the morning she is nauseous from... her own personal rumpled bed; and at the gala nameday dinner at our place she speaks only about this, not fearing, that during such conversations the dish will be left untouched.

"You know,—yes, my dear; as soon as I arise, then right—out of the room, out; that's all there is to it; I can not, my dear, I can not bear the sight of an unmade bed; so—yes, yes, yes: that's all there is to it; or else,—I burst out vomiting."

And the dish is—not touched: they bring it around to all; and no one touches a piece.

"And why aren't you eating, my dear: that's all there is to it?"

"Ah... Varvara Semyonova!.."

"Yes? Do you suffer from indigestion?.. So: yes..."

And she starts, having told everything she could about herself, to speak aloud "**Nikolai Irasych.**"

"Nikolai Irasych had, yes,—my dear..."

We hoped, that with his bed matters stood better...

. . . . .

The arrival of Malinovsky was connected with the green upholstering of the drawing room, with the recognition, that the fairy tale of objects is made up of hairs, felt and dust, with an increasing frequency of quarrels in our place, with interference in our family life of outside ears which distress Mamochka; yes, Malinovsky knew about everyone (and she was—ubiquitous); I heard the fact that even the walls have some kind of ears:

What kind of?

I think: Malinovsky's!

She hangs her ears about our place (at one time I took dried mushrooms for her ears); and she recognizes that a new lamp has appeared at our place:

"That's all, my dear!"

"And I always say: constancy and faithfulness are—the natural decoration of a woman..."

"By the way..."

"Tell me: what did you buy such a luxurious lamp for, when your old lamp wasn't even spoiled."

"And why did you—that's all—move the drawing room about?"

"You are inconstant, my dear!"

"That's all there is to it!"

"I always say: constancy and faithfulness are—the natural, that's all there is to it..."

"My Nikolai Irasovich!"

"Yes!"

"That's all there is to it!"

"He said the same thing..."

"Yes!"

Mama afterwards—sobs; and the hanging sag of the shades becomes green at our place, dispersing the light of day; and we are becoming inconsolably green.

. . . .

Henrietta Martynovna had already quietly placed the smooth little hat with the blue veil on her head; she has on her artificial beauty spots; we are going to the Arbat to take a walk: into the peoplechases. Flights of wide flying spans were opened by a survey of the Arbat: a silverplumed light snow is flying; and it lies down fluffily; a crow ruffles itself up from the cornice: like a little sphere; sleighs slice the snow with their runners down to the stones; a shinynosed, malicious gloom in hoods quickened into a run; and gymnasiasts run in blue peakcaps, decorated with a butterfly; a silvery hanging drop sprinkles in the face; I am—whitish; we—shake ourselves off; we splash the wet snowyslush against the ground; there at the confectioner's Felsh, in the little window are thrown about candies in orange, smooth paper wrappers; and then—"Pectoral": little cough caramels—I wish I would cough! Another little window; I do not like it: a guttapercha little boy stands there, stood up against a little ball; a little ball with such a little end...—no, I do not like it! Once we came here: Henrietta Martynovna purchased dress-shields here; further, in a little window, coffee pots, copper jars,—uninteresting; Monsieur Retteré is more interesting: he sits behind the counter, so blackbrowed, so blackbearded:—

—later I used to see him grayhaired: in the end, I recently stood before a cross on a grave where he had taken rest from his labors!—

—so blackbrowed, so blackbearded, not like the men running here in the frost: they are— whitemen; they are—bluelips; and there even passed a blackpuss—a Negro!

Here is the cobbler Greenblatt, where they recognize me, where they indulge me; here is Blank and Arbat Square (at Blank's I admired a stuffed wolf and the cages with the motley birds; ah, I do not like the corner coffee house and the sign: "Karl Morà...").

Ai, ai, ai!

A flaky mass poured down: downy snow flakes fly down; a passing gelding has turned all gray; an overpowdered poodle ran by, knocked into a silly curbstone; and suddenly he howled as if he had met an acquaintance: he sniffs greedily the calling card of a doggy—valiantly he lifts a hairy leg against the silly curbstone:—

—Papa used to tell me: doggies write postcards to doggies on the curbstone; and a doggy, having read with his nose the letters of the doggy,—valiantly lifts a hairy leg against the silly curbstone!—

—Here children are running: little whiteheads! The little faces are red, like cranberries; one downy whitehead ran up importantly to me: to play a bit; him—I know:

A capricious child!

We turn onto Maly Kislovsky alley; I fear indistinctions; and here is an indistinction— "this and that's own": two griffons, winged: and— I fear the two winged griffons, raising two paws over the busy entrance; I fear the two yellow, grinning lions on the gates of some house: here they will jump off:—

—just like now—

—two griffins, raising two paws over the busy entrance—sit: still. And two grinning stone lions sit on the gates of the same house: the same house! Recently I was walking along Nikitsky street (the Soviet "Nikitsky!"): a female motorcyclist was gunning the gas; a member of the All Russian Central Executive

Committee in a bigeared, snowy hat, was borne by in a black auto:—he
glanced with a firm face at me; I turned onto Maly Kislovsky; and I
glimpsed that which I had feared back then—thirty-five years ago: I
glimpsed—

—griffons, winged, two paws raised over the busy entrance,
two yellow, grinning lions on the gates—of that very same house. I
was struck by the **"one's own"** expression of the griffons, a bloody
sort of grin of the yellow lions; this again was **"one's own"**; and
along with this **"one's own"**, so horrible...; I know: the **"one's
own"** of Afrosinya, Petrovich, Mamochka is not as horrible, as the
"one's own" expression of the lions: ununderstandable, monstrous!—
—This **"one's own"** is so monstrous only in ...Papochka:—

—Yes,
Chebyshev, the mathematician: his **"one's own"** is the same: i.e.
indistinction, delirium; it is impossible to utter— **"Chebyshev"**: it
is still possible to talk about Antonovich: **"Chebyshev"** is—
forbidden; say "Antonovich"—I immediately glimpse the veins filling
on Papa's reddening brow; just say:

"Chebyshev!" and—a deathly paleness appears on the brow.

If you knock Papa into Chebyshev,—a nasty scene will occur:
instantly they'll become all shaggy; and without a scream both will
come down on one another, consummating with heavy breathing
something base; and—having previously snapped the door loudly shut;
they glimpse only one another, they grab at each other—by the arms,
and—run into the study; and Mama pours out tears:

"Let me in!"

In answer there is only—a deaf row: of Chebyshev on top of Papa,
or Papa on top of him; and—they send for the firemen: to break down
the doors; they break down the doors; they enter: amid the blood a
bloody Chebyshev trembles—senseless; Papa is —no longer; or there
is—no Chebyshev, but Papa, tufted, worn out, covered in blood, is
digging—

—in the red beef!—

—just like some sort of a dog!

They once spoke of Chebyshev, having forgotten about Papa, who
hanging his head down to the right side and waving his hand with the
paperknife (the left one)—went out on tiptoe: and everyone forgot about
him; soon I ran off to the study; and there two windows of the study,
just like two enormous crimson eyes (it was evening), widened, quietly

crimsoning the door jambs, the hand washstands, the glasspanes; in all of this red—

—Papa was pacing back and forth,—

—oh, no, he was not pacing back and forth: he was running on tiptoes, quietly shouting to himself; and with a hand pressed into a firm fist in sharp turns—"bam-bam-bam-bam-bam"—he kept pounding very quickly in the air!

He fell with his very big head onto his arms: as if the head had been seated on the shoulders by two men with great force who had first strained themselves: it sat—somehow to the side.

. . . .

. . . .

We turned from the Arbat onto Maly Kislovsky—look; peoplelessness; I know: griffins await with raised paw; and— they are stretched out for me; but I fear and I cry; I ask to turn around; we turned around—the peoplelessness ended; peoplechases again went by; the golden boot above Greenblatt's rocks in the air; everything darkened; and it seems to me to be lonely and severe; beyond the snowy mists everything has tensed up extraordinarily: it horrifies; and here a spark occupies a spot—so prophetic; it malices from a nearby house; and everything Chebyshevizes, griffonizes, grimaces and lionizes; everything howls; all the windows—blacken; they take a seat under the window; and the night fixed its blackhorned gaze: in the windows: and in the windows—eyelessness!

. . . . . .

GRANNY, AUNTIE, UNCLE

I know Granny's herstory!

In a delicate, cretonne armchair, in wiped worn spots of the worn out seat, Granny droops in her bay roan, bigeared cap and chews the fat of her daily fare: carrots had become more expensive, they were selling frozen slop; she coughs up the word:

"Carrots!"

"Frozen slop!"

"I touch a bunch..."

"I brought it home, and what a—stench!"

And in vexation she tugs with her hand at the tatters of her yellow-flannelette Chinese-jacket; and calmly chomping her lips, she again tries to make a marriage with the satin suit of the cards: the marriages do not work out:

"She's an old maid!"

"And she'll be left that way."

Here she fixes her punynosed gaze on some junk. They lead me in,—and she puts a hank on my hands:

"You ought to, little one, hold your hands like this!"

And the rough hank winds; granny's herstory quickly swells up; I am—simply a hank; I'm bitten from behind; the couch is—a fleabag; downyplumed Granny twists a gray hair out of her nostrils; and fluffy cotton tufts from her right ear; she casts a slanty bloodshot glance, speaking in a bass voice, just like a billygoat; a blackroach smacks against the floor; and the clock is in full swing with a weighty hiss; and everything smells of death, under me a spring pokes about.

Everything will cool off in the frozen slop: it is freezing!

Granny sits here all week; resurrected on Sunday she goes to Mass in such an old fashioned "manteau" and in a wrinkled hat, with "marmots" (people no longer wear such hats); she turns about: she cools off in the frozen slop, gets aches in her bones and meets monthly with Marya Herodovna, with a fever.

On the window sill stands a punypalmated little flower, long ago molded; beyond the little window—wetslush; freedances of snowflakes—flash, flicker; there comes—a yawn: I yawn apart my little mouth.

Here is—Auntie—from her job: ribless, punybrowed Auntie—with
a troubling thought:

"The marriages—didn't work out!"

"And you'll be left that way!"

Auntie sits by the window, tinyshouldered, a little stick; on her
blankface a fluttering of eyelashes stands blankly; she is—in selfspiritedness; silently she secretes her unenlightenedness; you ask her
something—she marvels; and—her cheeks puffs up; she fixes her gaze
on blankflights of dust specks, on the soot of the ceiling, she is
chained to a spot out of the dusk by the paleness of her eyeless little
face; her tiny little nose sniffs very thoughtlessly, it draws into itself
the smell of kasha, she moves her big chin and—is attracted to under
the ceiling by the blackness of the thinning lines; she is—blankeyed;
her dark brown little eyes are only for looks; they are like two outside
stick-ons; a moth flying by with a flutter sits on her little brow,
marked by little curls; it makes its point here—with a shake of her
little head:

"Liza has a new Canton crepe for a dress."

"So what!"

"You don't say: for the tarlatan tablecloth there at the Letaevs'…"

"I should go to the Letaevs'!"

And Granny in a temper tears off a tatterdemalion from her jacket;
but Auntie out of malice to her—begins to walk back and forth under
her nose and glimpses her goodlooking self in the mirror, she tries to
look younger and begins to sing:

"La-la… Little wind…"

"La-la!"

"Can barely breathe!"

"La-la.. Little wind…La-la!.."

"It doesn't heave!"

Granny to her wet-lipped:

"Hey, you, spinner: you'll probably callosify even the mirror with
your dear personal persona!"

Auntie answers her to this:

"I—want to live!"

She reproaches Auntie:

"You are—a proud girl!"

She chases suitors away from herself; but—she wants to live; here
is Pyotr Savvich: a suitor's suitor; both a widower, and a simple

fellow; after all he tried: he forced, forced, forced himself; and received only "chuckles":

"You pay attention,"—chirps a laughing Mamochka, a slim and shapely convolvula,—"pay attention: Dotya!"

"Everyone has on their desk someone's portrait... some—a suitor, some—an admirer, and some, some"—and having caught herself in the mirror, she chains herself to the spot and looks at her own personal curve of her figure, so all over, whitenecked, satiny, in a kaolin necklace, and she tries the golden galloon of her hair comb (won't it fall out?)...

"Some have... Some have... Yes, what was I saying: she has, Dotya has, her own personal portrait of Dotya on the desk: ha-ha-ha!"

At this Papa opines:

"Yes, you know: no matter who comes close—he gets a 'chuckle!'.."

Mama is—a slim and shapely convolvula, of medium height, pulled in by a strong corset and puffed up from below by a bustle, in her heliotropic skirt, in a Basque shirt of shiny satins (I loved that "massicot" color), on which little berries of pale blue kaolin gambol and jump,—she curls like an eel, when she is gay; Auntie Dotya, like a browless, very tall little stick walks behind her: breastless, flat; Mama touches her—everything is like a little board there:

"You're—not wearing a corset?"

Her little eyes look quickly, and the two dimples of her cheek look cunningly:

"Well, what about Pyotr Savvich?"

And Auntie Dotya fastidiously covers her covered breast with her arm:

"Ah, leave me alone!"

Mamochka pushes the "tear" pendants into her earlobes: and faceted sparkling begins to drip like rain from the blue luminary with greenish senses turning into red passions; but Auntie—does not drip; Mamochka fades like a sparkling little star and rocks like a dewy branch; Auntie is stretched out in a sorrowful resolution:—

—to try to overcome her job at the telegraph office!

. . . . .

She comes like a sour apple; and she beats on you with a bitter taste; and she begins to affirm over and over for Henrietta Martynovna facts about our apartment known to all the house:

"Yesterday you had suckling pig..."

"Liza has a new **"cream"** dress, a **"prune"** dress."

"Liza is going to the ball."

Henrietta Martynovna, the German, with a very pretty little face, white, like chalk, with a white-yellow braid, eyelidless, pale-lipless, inexpressively she puts out her miniblooded gums:

"Prune," "cream"...

"Yes, yes..."

"Gewiss!"

"Selbstverständig..."

"And you forgot the 'massicot'..."

Here Auntie looks at the German from the blankflights of her winks:

"No—I did not forget:—but **'massicot'**—is barely *comme-il-faut...*"

And both turn their little noses irresponsibly to the mirror, in order... to glance at their profiles.

Auntie speaks exclusively about Mama,—in words belonging to Mama and addressed to Mama, informing Mama, tiring from the tedium, about things which Mama had already lived through.

"You have a cream dress!"

"I didn't forget the **massicot**..."

"You had suckling pig at the table..."

Mama to her:

"Well what of it?"

And she begins to sing:

"La-la-la... Little wind... La-la... Can barely breathe... La-la... It doesn't heave..."

And Auntie seconds her:

"La-lya... It doesn't heave..."

. . . .

I remember:—

—it whitens, it pales; and grays palely; and darkens grayly; it ashens:—

—pewter grays deceive you with a wink, and Mamochka, pushing her bust out of the satin, raising the splendor of her breasts, bustles her wraparound skirt with the Canton crepe lining—

—a twi-
ster, a turner!—

—she sits down in front of Auntie, and her splendid bustle bends immediately to the side; I see—she is not in good spirits: Auntie Dotya is going to catch it:

"Yes, our Mikhail Vasilevich is—a rare one, yes-yes amazing; he is—a benefactor!"

And Auntie is—speechless, sensing an ambush:

"What do you mean?"

Auntie Dotya begins to draw on the outside of her palewhitish face, like with charcoal on white paper, a lightly wiped thin coating of flying dust,—her expressions:

"Yes, yes, our Mikhail Vasilevich, is—a rare one, yes-yes: amazing."

Mama replies to this—with ridicule, with a flutter, with a persistent spinningabout:

"A luminous personality!"

And Auntie winks, blankfaced into the glasspanes: and Auntie yes-yesses:

"A luminous personality!"

In the little window start up windwaves: and Mama—used to say:

"You—say the very same thing... I say: our Mikhail Vasilevich is—such a phenomenon, that..." Mama tenses her lips, she twitches maliciously her nostrils in vexation at Auntie; here she became before the mirror—a spin...

And Auntie crawls with her eyes into the windows:

"Yes, I say the very same thing: there is such a phenomenon, that"—and beyond the glasspanes—there, where the mist, a pewter overhang, fell with a flutter of snowflakes, welded into little drops,—a sprinkle-rain began to fall: a blinking! Already from the gutter-drainpipes the melted snow tumbles down:

"This is—a force!"

And Auntie tries to grain out an opinion:

"I say the very same thing: a force!"

"And you are obligated to it!"

Auntie jerks her little brow in tiny curls:

"Obligated!"

"Thanks to him—you exist!"

"We exist!"

At this point Mama can no longer hold herself in: and correcting the very slim fringe of her bodice, she flashes:

"You really are a jerker: you jerk out—other peoples' words!"

And Auntie tries:

"And you have a prune dress, a cream dress..."

"I always say something: then you always say something..."

Mama presses her chin bitingly:

"But it is I—who says it: but what do you say? You mince, you mince my words, the very same ones, like a mincer!.."

But Auntie minces with dignity (a proud girl!)

"These are my words: I always say the very same thing... And I cannot say anything else—but that which I have in my head..."

"You say only, what you hear!.."

Auntie's eyes are —"wet-ones":

"No, I say what I hear: and I always affirm that your husband is an amazing, moral person; and you are obligated to him for everything!"

—"What do you mean by that?"

—"Yes, yes: obligated for everything; without him you couldn't sew yourself anything!"

Mama passes her little eyes over Auntie and shouts at the atomizer; and she grabs it by the little sphere and throws it away:

—"Ai, ai! What rubbish you speak, you piece of rubbish! You come here, wag about, just like a fox, and then you talk this crap! First put your own life in order, and then go... You've been sitting tight until you've become an old maid!.. Pyotr Savvich—yes, yes: is no fool!"

And—hipless Auntie—goes home: to sniff the smells of kasha!

And it pales whitely;

and grays palely; and dar-

kens grayly; and the darkness ashens;

beyond the windows—the cornices of the houses

grow weaker into barely visible traces of fleeting weakening

lines wiped from a blackboard, like lightly drawn chalk; here faded Granny in the worn-out seat of the old armchair again picks at her kerchief with two boney hooks in the graying pattern of the wallpaper; and a violent vein completely swells her ailing hand; already the glass lamp hangs sternly in murkiness; Granny complicates her work; the fire of her cigarette, like the eye of a jaguar—admonishes:

"Well, why did you return so early: what's up at the Letaevs'?"

And—into the cigarette with her teeth; and the bright-red eye describes for us in a fiery reflection of light a malicious face of "nothing" and then it—takes covers: Auntie boohoos:

"And I'm, here: so unfortunate."

The eye of the jaguar opens.

"Well, you've tooted your own horn; you raise dust and stir things up over an unfortunate life "—the dark corner under Granny resounds in a bass voice; from Granny; and from the other corner from under Auntie gives out:

"Yes, you have it good: you've lived out your life, one can say, on what constituted our fortunes... I—want to live!.."

And objects fly into the lifelessness, into the fathomless: they become the deception of the night—

—at nights the holeless walls stand;
at nights the eyeless people come;

I look:—

—Auntie Dotya is without eyes: only two eye sockets blacken strangely in the dusk: I fear, that in the nightly gloom eyes will exchange people: how is one to know who grows kinder in the light from his eyes: with inconsolable malice it looks out from the gloom; here is—Granny:—

—one can say, she lived out what constituted the fortune of Mama and Auntie; just so: Auntie Dotya—used to go to her little bed when she was small; today she wants to "live"—without a man: and she puts on her little desk her own personal portrait of Dotya!

The crooked lamp with its kerosine flame barely glimmers...

. . . .

I remember we are with Granny, and with Auntie at Granny's; Granny is looking at herself maliciously with the red-lead of her little eyes; and Auntie, having put on a durable dress, gazes inimically; and then skinny Uncle Vasya comes home from his job.

He is—a bumbler-mumbler, light chestnut colored, bisideburned cougher, he uncovers in a buttercup of freckles his yellowtoothed mouth; he shows his Adam's apple, tufts up his sideburns; one eye— on Auntie; one eye—on Granny.

"Heh-heh: Mamasha!"

And Auntie—at Granny: they both already know that they know.

"Mamasha!"

"Mamasha" it is (something "their own" is imaged by the word "Mamasha"), cockplumed Granny struts all about: she evileyes— Auntie, Uncle.

And Uncle—passes through!

. . . .

Uncle Vasya has: a cockade, a hearty job, a medal; he—had been recommended for a medal; but—he cackles; and—coughs a cock-a-doo-dle-doo; for five years he has been beating on the doorstep of the Revenue Department.

And—with what? It's simple—if done with a piece of felt, but not so simple—if done with a stone; he hunches down over a soiled little desk with one foot in the grave—with a very legible handwriting:—
—How can this be? One foot in the grave?—

> — I think about this one
> foot in the grave:—
> —I

pity Uncle Vasya; he—bellows: he bends over,—surely his head
will fall on the

parquet, and he will sweep with his sideburns; and
maybe this bending
with one foot
in the grave
is worse—
—bending
down he sticks
his head between his
legs: with his teeth he drags
his own handkerchiefs—out of his coattail!—

And—
—ah—
—his little room: is cold! Granny beats felt around the door in the winters, in order to protect her feet from the frost.

"And—I simply can't stand it!"

"In Vasily's room"—

> —Granny pronounces this **"in Vasily's room"** with such deep malice, as though in **"Vasily's room"** someone is guilty: the guilty one is —
> **"Vasily!"**

"In Vasily's room—there is a fierce frost!"

"Yes it is impossible to say, that—Vasily…"

I know—what is impossible to say: it is impossible to say—what? **"Vasily should"**? And what—"should Vasily?" But—I know: "Vasily." A comrade, Letkov, calls him a poor soul.

Vasily is blamed by Granny for **"everything"** there is: that there is a draft under her feet, that there is a tart scent from the kasha and the glue, that a rotted leaf of appliqué has been granulated by the flies, that there is a lot of crooked cardboard covered with a press; that a belch rises in Uncle's catarrhal composition.

Here, returning from **"one foot in the grave,"** Uncle sits down: to exercise himself in the bookbinder's art: and he bellows, bellows to himself under the nose.

"Yes, yes!"

"A trade!"

"A thing—that's useful!"

This is all—Papochka: their provider! Both tailor, and—gardener of impulses; the family is grateful to him for the fact that it is given his counsel, kindness, money and produce.

"Here is—some woolen material: for Dotya for a dress; it can't be—worn out; it is better than last year's."

And—I know: this year's material is always—unwearoutable and better than last year's material; I think: if such gifts continue year in and year out,—then, surely, in about twenty years they will have to bestow on Auntie Dotya a gift of brocade, because the other materials, (those, which are worse) will for sure have all been given to her.

"Don't thank me: this is—Mikhail Vasilevich!"

Papa is giver, keeper, healer; and—eternal counsellor; he recommends that Uncle turn his tedious leisure time into a trade.

"Yes, yes, a trade is—a useful thing..."

"You see: it distracts from obtrusive thoughts!"

"If you happen to want to,—you, Vasily Yegorych, take it up... You can bind the **"Mathematical Bulletin"** for my library...

"You'll—get paid, and I'll—get some use from it: I can give you about eighteen years for binding."

Uncle forces himself to become a bookbinder, but—he is so devil-may-care.

So: after occupying himself with a little bowl of kasha he sits with a loud **"hic"**; he tries to insert something into the printed skin,—it will not go.

"It's freezing!"

"Brr-brr!"

And he goes to warm himself about the rooms.

Then he thinks, that—he is being caressed; and he caresses himself in the mirror; he puts aside his foot and straightens his sideburns.

"And why ain't I a brain?"

He stands like a winker; and his Adam's apple is —like a race horse; it spins about like a dandy; and he clicks one black boot against the other boot.

"Look at you: just look at you!"

And—he slaps his heels in front of Granny: Granny—like a billygoat at him.

"Well, what do you want?"

"Carrots, I dare say, are very dear!"

"What are you fumbling with?"

"I bought some cabbage, cooked it, cooked it: frozen slop!"

"The stench!"

Uncle Vasya, remembering himself, quacks:

"It's freezing!"

"Brr-brr!"

And off to his room: to visit the "**Snorers**"...

And soon he sends a penetrating snore from the frozen little wall, from the threelegged bed, a bellyless, birdbrained mosquito, broken in two with one sideburn pressed to the pillow, the mouth opened wide and yellowing in freckles; such a malcunning worker! The little cloth blanket is gray; and on a gray field sing cocks, wiped worn by much lying; on a nail—a hat with a cockade; and—a violin; a meower sits under a geranium; the wallpaper is of the same color; darkened—spots of dampness; where the corner is swept by the frost,—snowflakes come off coldly with fingers.

There he lives: what a Mister Lay-me-down!

From here he goes to dine—at our place, on the holiday; he stagnates; during debates in his head—there is a brainbreaker; he sits— like a brainshaker; he rolls up all his slices; he eats, he laughs pillared to the ground; and—he bats his eyelashes; infrequently he tries to boom out his thoughts; and—sweatbrowed from the force of these efforts, he cannot use his brain at all.

"Yes, yes!"

"A trade!"

"A useful thing!"

"Thing!"

"Trade."

And—again he falls wordless.

Auntie comes with him.

"Well, how are things at your place..."

"Ah, 'Mamasha'!"

She sits propping up with a propped-up arm (the other one)—her little head; she winks in such a condition: like a little stick, her breast is like a little stick; so riblessly she stands, riblessly she passes over to the window.

"The telegraph!"

"I'm fed up with it!"

. . . .

Uncle Vasya's ragged life is—in halves; I recognize one half:—

—Uncle Vasya is wifeless, wenchless, and as they say—is not a **"brain,"** but he has twenty-twenty hindsight, his brains are in his behind, but all the same with dignity, he sits modestly, curling a sideburn with his hand, wrapped in a white napkin, and widening his eyes in conversation,—

—and with the other hand he rolls teeny-weeny bread balls of dough; and Papa leans over to him with an opinion, with his agitation:

"I'm telling you: you, Vasily Yegorovich"—he sticks his beard into the starch:

"You, I'll tell you straight out..."

"You ought to leave this!"

And with this opens another, **"one's own"** half of the burst-apart life of Uncle:—

—where Uncle, such a Mister Quiet, faded, chomping teeny-weeny bread balls into dough and trusting any words—

—appears before us—as another person: eating Granny out of house and home, quite a screaming cockler, who raises his voice at everyone:

"You are all good: waterhogs!"

He barks loudly, having sloshed down his rowanberry vodka; a silly womanizer, hobbling along the floor, he grunts to himself under the nose, carries on like in a tavern:

"Hey, you, waterhogs!"

And he starts to dance to slap his heels like a spinning top—propped up:

> My name is Vaska Pazukhov—
> I'll quaff my rum and be right off!

Yes and he womanizes indecently and grins all over and shows his "lalaks" (these, I know, are his eyelids: that is what Granny calls them), he cackles-gackles, begins coughing, lets out a word on the fly; and—disappears for about three days; and Granny says:

"I'm telling you, he will wench himself to no good!"

Once she appeared; and began to blare, to bray, and—there rose such a blast over the matter.

"What do you mean?"

"Again?"

Granny bristled.

"No matter what you say—he is a scandal monger, this Vasily Yegorovich of yours!"

And shielding herself with her hands from the nose which our Papa was trying to drive into her face between the palms, she announced: "Intoxication"; I thought: this is for sure an upset stomach, with a big scandal: he needs chicken soup; from Granny's words was revealed to me:

"He is—a bouser!"

And what is a "bouser"? You'll find it in Dahl's dictionary, but in your head—take a look!—Again:—

—understanding, a little girl in a white little dress, dances; and dark nannies come in a muttering swarm: so horribly indistinct, yet—so terribly occupying!

. . . .

And Mama plays:—

—taken off, borne off; the events of life fluttered in the beinglessness of sounds; again there came during the years someone tall; that's—Uncle; he stood up on the skinny stilts: on his legs; he is withdrawing from us—forever along the whitening roofs: he is withdrawing to the heavens; and he starts to bang out to us from the heavens:—"Yes I am tired of bending 'one foot in the grave:' it's enough!"

"I am tired of beating the doorstep of the Revenue Department!"

"Here is—the felt, here are—the stones: let others beat it."

"I am tired of trades: a trade is not a useful thing!.."

"I am withdrawing from you!"

. . . .

"Uncle, Uncle—dear: and I..."

Mama strums her little hand along the keys; and agitation arises in the sounds; she became so tiny, so dear; she sticks out her neck; and—

as if growing timid, she passes among the sounds—on tiptoes: like a little girl; and—she bows with her congenital birthmark; she translates the sounds so expressively with her eyes which jump up from the bottom of the page: to the little hook, to the note:—

—and I withdraw into this life; and

—as it is not bad, this life; his

—little room! Cold: Granny
beats felt around the door, in order to
protect her feet and—

. . . .

Ah!

Temporary is the time,—but burdensome is time; it mumbles by in days given up; and it—gives out—into our ears,—into our souls!

ROULADE

And Mamochka sounds the same as a roulade; the piano starts speaking her sounds to me.

Mama sits down to play; her hands pour out sounds; the roulade flows, foaming against a key with a handpouring trill, splashing my soul with a discant: the concentrated bass falls into the precipice, gravitating to there by its weight: the surfaces of the keys have parted loudly into combs, winking sharps; the sea deceives.

That is—Mama: again she started speaking out; she shines with gracefulness, with a shiny gradation, with a gesticulation of the scale: from a bird's singing to... a howl, to... a tiger; it smells tenderly of a little lemon flower; she marvels with upflown little eyebrows: her little eyes are—pansies.

Tenderly she pronounces her steps with a silky whisper, shiningly enlivened by perfumy spirits, having donned her shiny rose kazakin, hanging creamy lace, exclaiming resoundingly with a bunch of keys— she pronounces her steps on the carpet: to the chiffonier, where dresses are flattened out in a clear mass of satin, where this bustle swells up — —found under skirts—

—even, I know, the German girl has such a little pillow; I know, they deftly tie up such a little pillow where necessary, in order to be fullsided.—

—Sides turning around and around and with her birthmark jumping, Mama passes by with a bustle in her hands, throwing her eyes in passing at the little window.

The sunset, like a little lemon flower, smells tenderly: of an infusion of flowers; the rooms are filled like a perfumery.

. . . .

From the past a transfluent image gushes into her soul.

"Goodness," or "maliciousness"—is only the foam of a gulf of that, one's own, which is in everyone; "one's own" shouted out in Mama like a phantasy of palms and like a bunch of gabbing wenches of baobob, in which was revealed a fountain of varicolored humming birds, elephants stamped and hyenas stank: a zoological garden, but not

Mamochka; India, but not the professorial circle of the nineties, not Arbat; only an old Chinaman, my Papa, could convert this circle to the philosophy of **"Tao"** of Lao-tzu, counselling one to see big breasted professors' wives not as old wenches,—but as parks, and to remake the flies you are fed up with into **"very occupying, you know, little machines."**

Professors' wives,—are not even **flies**; Bobynin the professor is not silly, but... if you sit yourself between them a tropical forest will turn into a gabbing tedium of scholarly uncombed old women, who at one time married their husbands on **"one's own"** convictions;—

—these professors' wives do not like Mama: they accompany her with crookedmouth malice; for them she is—a little girl: and—they lay in a circle wolf traps of customs: they catch Mama in the custom of the professorial life: in the kitchen dry mushrooms hung like ears; Malinovsky—is listening; the walls have—ears...

"So, yes, my dear!.."

"Why is it,—yes?"

"Why is it that you do not attend the Temperance Society, yes..."

"All of us, that is, attend!"

"Sofya Dragonovna, and Anna Gorgonovna with Anna Grinovna."

Dragons, gorgons and grins haunt me: very terrifying is the "grin"—the crookedmouth malice of professors' wives:—

—I saw a little picture; a little red fox which they were hunting with dogs; somewhere all of this was barked out: Mamochka, the little fox, grinned strongly at this:—

— I feared the professors' wives:—

—especially that one, Doktorovsky; yes, yes, she has a very stout one of those thing on which they all put a bustle; all the time she would twaddle with whomever was giving a paper, burdened with a dissertation; and to the one who still had not declaimed his paper, she would present up that very stout thing represented by her bustle; she even presented it to Mamochka, covering her eyes with patches of ice;—

—and the old rats the Sleptsovs stick their little noses out from their lair: to sniff her beauty and to peep aloud, that—no, no: she is not beautiful, that she needs to have her braids trimmed; she is distressed by the squeals: her little eyes are—icy whirlpools, they freeze;—

—and then they let go along the cheeks
a little bead: into a little handkerchief; they melted: they flutter anew
like a butterfly among the palm trees: it smelled of spring, and—of a
white lapdog, Almochka, with a part on the little brow combed with a
little comb; having sat gayly in a rocking chair with a silky whisper,
she tossed one little leg on the other little leg: a red slipper hangs rather
playfully from her tiptoe—

—Almochka began scratching with her little
paws on the floor,—with her little tail in the air: hum-hum; and the
little tiptoe turns around and around like a little finger, just like a goose
puss: the red slipper smacked against the floor; the lapdog—starts
running in circles like a hare, gripping with its teeth, like a delicacy,
the slipper; I, getting down on all fours, crawl in a lump under the little
foot, like Almochka; Mamochka, flowering shiningly in her
selfspiritedness, tosses back her braid, laughs:

"Look!"

"Catch him!"

"Hold him!"

"Kotik is putting on a show!"

Snapping her palms, she flies down from the rocking chair.

And—she chases me; she grabs about, rolling with me on the
carpet, letting her hair fall down with combs of hanging braids over me;
I see—in the pit of her neck, under the skin, a little mouse began to
move; I stick my little head right into Mama's skirt, into the sheer
rustling of her crepe de Chine, and she—lifts the hem of my darkblue
dress: she loudly smacks there, where one should smack: let her smack,
this is—such playing between us!

. . . .

She breathed a sigh, that I would become, like the fly, "**a n
occupying little machine,**" complicated by Papochka.

She daydreamed—of a **young man**, a mathematician, heeding
conversations about "**modules,**" preferring them to the shiny force
beating in her, not hearing music and bespectacled—

—it is impossible to
hang Tintoretto side by side with Flemish hares or with a Flemish,
even if virtuous, corpulent and red kitchen maid in an overstarched cap;
Papa—hung: an Italian landscape, next to a landscape... of a scholarly
kitchen maid:—

—next to the professor's wife Kislenko—Mama!—

—And
Mama trembled, fearing, that they would cripple me, clothing me in a
going-out frock coat of science.

If you had asked Papa:

"And what should we order for Kot?"

He would have answered:

"What?"

"Buy him a bowler hat!"

"Yes, yes!"

"Order him a little frock coat!"

He could have, for sure, brought me a spectacle case for my nameday celebration.

He was always forcing himself to clarify for me the phenomena of
life as a complication of impetuous centripetal forces with centrifugal
(ones); this gift was similar to the "case." I looked in the forces, as in
reinforced spectacles—very sickly; he piped on his pipe:

"Therein is the force!"

"Here is a force!"

"There is no force in that!"

"But what is 'force'?"

And—"force" responded with the image of Firs, the son of Yorsh
(i.e. Uncle Yorsh). This one—looked "sickly"; and—he died; and—the
thought occured to me:

"Yes there is no force in that!"

"Therein is force, that 'force' is—Firs!" And this Firs grew—sicker
and sicker; if I could understand "forces," then—I would become sickly;
and I would die, without achieving "force."

And everyone said quite reproachfully to Papa:

"Leave him be: he'll develop even more prematurely, and then die,
like your Firs."

"And you!"

.   .   .   .

And—it used to be—

—like a roulade sickly forces rolled out, like a
thread of little crystals on the floor; notes on the scale were threaded
just like little crystals on a thread:—

—from among the stormfelled trees,
a triad, of one chased somewhere, a delicate note starily sparkles out;
another stars from the first, smashed by trills of a descant little lake
into a downpour of clear little flies; by the shore: the sparkle of

Mama's little fingers mature along the blackish bones; and—they begin to beat anew in a precipitous bass, banging out into the abyss and beating resonantly what is lying into howls; and—it washes with a jangling joyfulness, the stones of chords are covered with fizzling foam; and—the precision of the roulade contour is screened by the smoky haze of the pedal; there gives out:—

—between the descant and the bass—

—a suffering, human voice, and—

—it is oppressed by the bass; and—it perishes without a trace; I—cry: some sort of whirlwinds rise as if grabbed away, like a luminouspawed flame, from the little breast:—

—curling into space and into the quickness of events; it grabs onto space: like the space of eventlessness—

—spaces disintegrated into instabilities: like a daily composition; where the lilac night grew dense,—the morning shone through transparently; the matter of night is sliced shiningly by shots of clarity; the unknown has past: all across the land bluens, in order to become the light blue, wave of day,—

—that is Mama, playing, again she is amazed with upflown little eyebrows; a wreath of curls dances on her little brow; her little nose became clarified by a little drop of perspiration; and—

—ah!—

—grown timid, she passes through the sounds,—on tiptoes; like a little girl. And—with her congenital birthmark she looks dumfoundedly into my soul; her little eyes have totally emeraldized; how they jump up to the top from the bottom of the page,—to the little hook, to the note.

I stand, I look: I love!

This is—poison; the sweet poison of the Renaissance, where people perform actions, they look with resolution, they love and destroy without rule: in sounds; not a moral life at all—a musical one:

"My Kotik!"

"Force—is not in this, but in that, where..."

"I can't force you!"

Only the little bees, flying from Mama's lips like honey—sweeten; but now and then they sting: where is—the law of foundation? Papa applies this law to himself: he leads a young, bespectacled youth,—on the foundations of strict, old faithful trials he leads him to the post of docent; but Mamochka says with a sparkling:

"Yes: he is a bureaucrat!"

"He reeks of trash!"

"You'll deceive yourself..."

In about twenty years the former **young man** is—the administrator of a surrounding school district: all of the district moans!

Mamochka is right after all: without foundations!

. . . . . .

I love the little face grown thin with the proud birthmark, with a slim, sharpened little nose, and with—rosy little cheek; and the little mouth, slightly offended, complicated, just like a little flower,—the pearly, even little teeth dew; a playful little chin with a dimple barely visible; and the little brow, not fullgrown, clarifies itself by running arcs of flying, sable eyebrows, raising arcs of wrinkles, and then squatting down to the halfbent black eyelashes of the pansy eyes, faithful, or offended and suspiciously sharpsighted, like leeches—

—how

they drink in!

She is offended:—

—the little mouth becomes like a little worm!

She laughs:—

—and dimples appear!—

—A swollen lip rises; and—the little teeth—can be seen... She screws up her little eyes, waving the veil of her eyelashes and glancingly flinging two sparks; her little head leans to the side; it sprinkles down in a dense thicket of splendid chestnut hair;—

—and—

—Mamochka becomes such a Moscow beauty: from the painting by Makovsky; "The Wedding Feast"!—

—In this pose of the bride she loses herself in admiration in the mirror!

Papa noses about like a thickset gnome (the floorboard squeaks): he slaps her on the little shoulder; Mama submits to him, barely rosening with a smile which has mercy on us, our life and flies to meet some former experience, after which—is it worth living, without which—is it worth believing? The smile, the unfortunate one, lasts a second;—

— apparently

another smile, covering up the first, is borne away with Papa; but the first—takes a seat somewhere: all in the little corner.—

—The second is a little river of domestic cares.

Papa notices this smile, but the first one—he does not see; and—he continues to fumble about with Mama's little shoulder.

"Here: I purchased—two tablecloths!"

"Here: look!"

And Papa, not glancing, slaps her on the little shoulder:

"So!"

"Don't so me, look attentively..."

"This one, here, you see: with the cocks—all over; it cost me..."

"This one, here!"

Papa pounds his opinion:

"So: superlative— magnificent... And—with cocks, and—it did not cost you dearly."

And he continues to snap.

Papa had his hair trimmed today: he is emboldened—with a beard not at all large, which has become doubly prickly; because of it his neck seems thicker; and the face more bestial: ah, what did he get a trim for?

O, no: they surely never will understand one another, but I—understand already: Mama is—exactly like the "bride" of the painting by Makovsky **"The Wedding Feast,"** well, and Papa,—such a bridegroom? Consequently?

I think about this:—

—but these thoughts are—dangerous things:—

—things prophesy how they should be in this case; to understand prophetic things, this—signifies: to set aside the borders between them and me; and I set myself—

—to acknowledge me already as Papa: Mamas and Papas; they do not permit this turnabout in me; I am sliced off from them in the understanding of very dangerous and prophetic things; I withdraw into dumfoundement, I transgress the line;—

—and my transgression—

is the revelation of truth without the realization of the fact, that it is—a revelation; not to realize the rightness of one's own learning—doesn't this signify: to be in transgression;—

—yes!—

—The sin of transgression
is—timidity!

. . . .

I had already heard from Mama: at a dinner given for Turgenev they
seated Mama with Saltanova in such a way, so that Turgenev would see
the beauties: before a splendid bouquet of flowers; and Turgenev, having
put on his pince-nez with a wide black ribbon,—stared at Mama
closely; Papa, warmed by champagne, spoke better than all of them;
and the weak Boborykin, who let out a word like a toy steamship—
forward, but left his idea like a toy rowboat—behind,—

—Boborykin,—
—who was all in yellow, who was called **"Petrusha"** by Sofia
Aleksandrovna ... Boborykin...—

—I saw him in Lugano in sixteen, it
seems (of this century); and he recalled:

"Mikhail Vasilich used to!"

Yes, yes: Boborykin counselled Mama to study diction with him:

"I am telling you!"

"You have very many magnificent, artistic gifts!"

"O, Russian women, Russian women, I do not understand you; no,
how is it possible: housekeeping, and children, and the kitchen, when
the artistic world is—available to you!"

"I am telling you..."

"You listen: **'Pyotr Boborykin'**"—he said (I remember him—
tall, fidgety, all in yellow, all in motley; he puts a lorgnette to his
spectacles; and his skull fills, and beats with crimson veins; he leaps
up, and sits down; and grabs with his finger for the curlicue of the
armchair's back), and Mama used to heed him: and—she was drawn to
the stage.

Everything shiny about the way I live—this is the Mama in me: it
bubbles like a conversation; and out fall: a golden little fish, a
crystalline lense and a shiny rag; I raise the crystalline lense to her
face—she pushes it away with her hand; to narrate more resoundingly;
rather scatterbrainedly she messes up my little hair, she catches her
bracelet on my little nose: it smells of spring—of meadows: the
narrations of Mama's childhood cooled off; she places little bouquets of
flowers before us:—

—yes, they called her Little Star: this little girl,
Little Star, came out of Mama's little eyes; she, is like I; she is—a

little girl, Little Star; we ran to the meadow: cannibalistic time was chasing.—

　　—I remember: she speaks like on a stage; significantly she measures with her gaze and places a finger to her lips:

"Do you know what?"

This "do you know what" sounds all through the room; I throw down my clown, crawl across to the carpet, sit under her little knees, open my little mouth—at how the bent little arm, gleaming—like a yellow-flowing beryl the elbow relaxed on the table; she is—a wordgiver; Henrietta Martynovna, that one is,—a wordtaker, Mama is mimicking:—

　　—she sets her little arms apart: to the right—to the left; and—amuses herself with a song:

　　　　My Pippo, I'm just as always,
　　　　Loving you so many old ways—

　　　　　　　　　　　—and I throw myself down to shout:

"And now—the cockroaches!"

She:

　　　　Yes, where the cockroaches are many,
　　　　O, yes, where there are many,—
　　　　In that house there is a-bun-dance:
　　　　A-bun-dance!

I know that **Mascott** is—Zorina (in the operetta by Lentovsky: Lentovsky walks in a tight fitting coat) **Pippo** was—Ognyov, Roman Yaklich, now appearing in the Mariinsky Theatre, bedeviled by the passions of Mephistopheles instead of Kondratyev and begging Poliksena Borisovna in the aria of the Demon to take his hand and heart; she does not agree; but, but—calling Ognyov "**Romasha**"—she answers him:—

　　—and Mamochka here licks her lips, bends her little head, and from under her brows jump her little eyes, like Poliksena Borisovna:

"You, Romasha, should go to visit Napravnik?"

After:—

　　—the little mouth grins, and—
　　the eyes are bedeviled; I hear—

　　　　　　　　　—how the long "**Romasha**," grinning, booms like a bass at the top of his voice:

"The devil take you!"

"I won't go!"

He fears Napravnik: for that reason he does not go; they tell him:

"Ah, Romasha, Romasha: you should go..."

All these conversations are about the time when Mamochka lived in Petersburg, at the home of Poliksena Borisovna Bleshchensky: near the Moika; a persona from the czarist family came for tea: wild Romasha sat behind the alcove, not daring to blow his nose;—

—she looks at the turquoise ring; and—collects herself with a new thought; from her left hand, from the elbow a cigarette curls a curly stream (yes, Mamochka had begun to light up something); it passes,—the smile— that one, the **first one:**

"Ah!"

"Petersburg!.."

She says all of this for her "own" self: she wants to say it aloud: she's singing well; everything is—impossibly shiny and impossibly understandable to me, like... music; that here,—I do not know; I close my eyes,—with my face to the crepe de Chine blouse; she places her little hand on my head, playing scatterbrainedly with a lock: she looks at the lock; now with a totally extinguished face she herself lives through all of this...—

—with an exclamatory whistle jangling the snows against the glasspanes,—are the gusts, beyond the glasspanes, there: the views are drawn shut... beyond the glasspanes; the Arbat curls itself anew in a whitecoronal veil: beyond the glasspanes; someone has started to mutter in the chimney—the same thing:

"O, God!"

As if to narrate—the same thing:

"O, God!"

In the chimney someone has started to mutter: about something. Suddenly—

—there was a crack: the floor settled down:—

—Papa, with his closely trimmed hair, long attracted by narrations, heavily stomps his foot, placing behind his back two hands with the paperknife and protruding his full stomach, he settles down his big head, smacked into his back; scatterbrainedly he stood up before the mirror, as if not seeing himself; having glimpsed the self before himself, he imbibed bestially the trim of his beard, placing two fingers under his spectacles; and—he could not tear himself away, could not tear himself away: from Mama's loud words ("Petersburg, Petersburg!"), or from the wild Scythian countenance with the bestially trimmed little beard;—

—Mama again dissolves in a word, like a row of her own cartons out of which she takes feathery hats; here Papa cannot hold out: rather hurrying little eyes ran like flies; his fingers—jerk like marionettes; the vein on his neck swelled:

"Leave it be"—he raises his petty little eyes at Mama—two little points, two tips of pencil stubs (these hurrying little eyes disturb me!)—"Leave it be: Petersburg, this is—the Germans."

But Mamochka, clenching her lips, tossing one leg on the other, rustled with silken whispers of her skirt; and—the tiptoe jumps rather significantly; and Papa sharpens his words like pencil stubs, this way and that, into a tip of his own thought: he is disinfecting opinions:

"All of this, Lizanka, is nonsense: trumpery, dumbness; we do not need this, we simply have to face it!"

He was dragged again to the mirror (here is how he is after a trim! He had become—a consummate Scythian): and he smooths his face with a fullbodied hand, having turned around, trying to glimpse his own profile; and—again he clicked his heels from the mirror into a dense thicket of questions:

"What kind of life is that there? Of this Poliksena Borisovna? Singers, highbrows, hussars,.. And isn't it tedious for you, my Lizok,—in such a society?!? I do not understand this!"

He is blind as a bat: and he does not see—Mama's face has thinned from tedium, and—it tossed itself straight into your eyes; it went over suddenly to the eyes, and the two eyes widened apart and were tossed about, and (ai!) they naggingly burned everything which lay in front of them; but Papa is already collecting himself to display an army of arguments; he turns around on the chair; he chops cutlets in the air with his hands:

"Moscow, so to say, is the natural, our Russian center,—of any intellectual, moral, literary, social life..."—

—he passes by in a waddle on his powerful, short legs; he stands flatfooted with a boot on the parquet—"Moscow is the commercial center: it is the junction of the railroads, that which expresses the province..."—

—Papa strikes his words more forcefully...

And Mama, tossed one leg over the other, and her little red tiptoe began to jump bitingly:

"Yes, Petersburg has prospects, the czaritsa rolls along Nevsky in a carriage: bows—to the right, bows—to the left, and Yablochkov's illumination—sparkles!.."

And quickly, quicker—until he is running on tiptoes Papochka is swept about over the floor on his thickset little back; suddenly he clicks his heels totally sarcastically (he even jumps up, clicking and—a wave with the paperknife!)

"Phoo-you. Princess Dagmar,—I beg your pardon—eh, that there 'goes for a ride': ah—dumbness, dumbness!"

And already Mama's little eyes become apparent little adamantine eyes; she cries: they do not care about her; for her to live in the Moscow milieu is—completely impossible: as a professor,—she is a fool, as a professor's wife,—she is a scamp-vamp; and—she passes her eyes over Papa; and—turns to the spoon lying in front of her: and grabs it, and throws it away; and the rosy little mouth is—a sheer bluebell——ehe: yes, he is a piper!—

—and here she goes on and goes on: that she will leave Papa, that Papa is—a degenerate, the likes of which are few, and Mama is a beauty; she looks on us with ailing little eyes:

"It's not a disturbance of sensitive nerves—no, no; I'm—well…"

"I—you!.."

"Get out of here, all of you!"

And—she takes us all in with such a look, that no matter what you say—it is nonsense: and she—will show everyone; how crabby she can be, the old crab apple; and—she displays her birthmark:—

—Papa squeaks a floorboard in his study: a fivefingered hand trembles over a fly, still whole from flight; and—"tsap"; he catches it:—

—and the fly sits in the fist; its head is torn off; that is not a fly, but—Mama; not Mama, but—Mama's nerves…; suddenly—he jerks: he begins to run quickly, strongly pressing his fist to the starch of the shirt and grinning a white sparkle of teeth; and with the other hand at sudden turning points—

—bam,

—bam,

—bam,

—bam,

—bam!—

—very quickly he strikes in the air; once I looked in on him: he was all tufted up: just like two eyes— enormous, crimson—the study windows widened in sheer sunset, crimsoning the doorjambs, the hand washstand and table: all in red— Papa paced back and forth,—oh, no, he did not pace back and forth— —he ran on tiptoes, strongly pressing to the starch of his shirt his whole jaw, separated by a mouth with a white sparkle of teeth, as if he would shout out without a voice—

—one hand presses to his breathing side; the other, clenched in a fist, at sudden turning points—

—bam,—
—bam,—
—bam,—
—bam,—
—bam,—

—he beat in the air, as if performing Mueller's exercises;—

—Papochka's running, this wide open mouth, shouting at the dusk, pressed at the chin to the starch of the snapping shirt; and—

—bam,—
—bam,—
—bam,—
—bam,—

—stuck in my memory: I ran away!..

. . . . .

Having shouted and run a bit with himself—in his own room,—he came out to make peace: completely calmed, even somewhat softened (I used to see him like that coming home from the bathhouse); having settled in the armchair, he took off his spectacles with relief: to wipe them rather gayly: the narrow shoulders slopingly fallen under a very large head brought a confession of guilt: the head had been seated by two men with great force, who had first strained themselves; it sat somehow,—to the side...

. . . . .

Mama also gets over it easily; she cries a bit; and—dresses up: for a soiree; she walks under the mirror like a pliant peacock; her bustle gives her a slightly comical look; and—she evens herself out: the train, shuffling silk lace; the waist—like a liqueur glass; worthy splendors rise up in the charming slit, smelling of opopanax Pinot and blindingly from the diamond, falling in the middle ground, between two bodily creases, with a velvet ribbon; just like Venus, she burns in the dawn—before the sun which is concealed: lower in the corsage; admirers of Mama, surely, are trying to guess:

"Will it rise!"

"It won't rise!"

And—they try with a glance (as if by chance) to penetrate beyond the line of the horizon: and—no, it will not rise! Mama was a bit worried: the pinned-together slit rocks like a dewy, rosy rose, when she walks, pulling on a glove to the elbow and tacking together with an overwound tower of hairdo on the motley carpet her small hairpin; she stumbles in her train; grabbing at it with a deft hand from her tossed little leg, she weaves about us with a rosy whisper of the silk lining—

—what a lining in this dress! I loved the linings in Mama's dresses: she should turn her dresses inside out: the inside facing out; the insides used to shout: with canary, rosy, red,—

—so big: she stands—ceremoniously; don't approach: no, no, no! And she used to return, and then: unfasten herself; the corsage falls to Dunyasha, and the skirts—one after another—fall on the carpet; and from them Mama jumps up to me,—barearmed, a skinny little thing, just in pantalettes, having left behind her splendor, to fawn over me; this was—after; now—no-no-no; ceremoniously she stands, ceremoniously she passes by:—

—in the little window, where there was the bigheadedness of the clouds, where only multibrowed mountains stood in the line of the horizon,—browless planes; and—from behind them, sitting down and illumining us with a brief departing ray, clearly transparent, coming down under it,—a twinkling sphere, a red sphere, squatting down into the earth: to sit out the night;—

—they laid away the twinkling sphere in a special case with a lacquered cover, upholstered with satin on the inside, like an expensive ring,—from Faberge or Deibelle,—

—weighty and burdensome!..

Temporary is the time; but—burdensome is time; it mumbles by—in given up days; and it gives out: into our ears, into our souls!..

. . . . .

The ante—

—room is—

— small:—

—from there the wallpaper stared with yellow-orange malice into the blinking light of the kerosine lamp; a clothes rack, a little table and chair: all is—orangy here; on an orange background in a brick line pass by welldefined: squares, squares; a multihumped clothes rack hangs there; dumbly; three doors: to the dining room, to the kitchen, to the dumb corridor; there hangs, gathering dust, a curtain on the kitchen door of such green color, that it ails one to look, closing the door glass, so as not to see the kitchen; and a greasy little mattress for Alma, who burrows there the bones and fat into the hair scratched by paws;—

—it used to be:—

—in a coonskin coat and sealskin cap Papa crawled in, rumbling in his bootees, bent over Almochka: on the yellow-orange background of the wallpaper, illumined by the spectacles of a blinking flame; Almochka was gnawing a tough yellow bone; and—she looked bloodily askance: and Papa, having put on his spectacles, said:

"This is—a proper doggy occupation: reading newspapers!"

"These bones, Dunyasha, in a dog's life are—the same thing as newspaper reading for humans."

"Almochka nibbles on a bone, and—knows everything."

Behind Papa hurried Mama, in a rotonde and in a tiny plush cap with a toque (an enormous one!); looking askance at her, he indicated with a finger, the big one—the little mattress:

"And Almochka, you know,—is reading the newspapers!"

At this bit of knowledge Mama's birthmark jumped under the little veil (the white one, with the black beauty spots like flies); the little eyes, clouding up, were covered with patches of ice: she squeezed with selfspiritedness her rounding chin to the neck which was filling out, puffing up importantly; it seemed: she would make an:

"Oof!"

These jokes of Papa offend her, grieve her; with one hand leaning on Dunyasha's back, pulling on her fur, soft bootee, she clipped the silence like with scissors:

"It smells again!"

"It smells doggy!"

"What a stench!"

"I have told you, Dunyasha, that you have to air out the mattress: on the snow with it, with snow!"

And—the door was dissolving; and Papa ran away to there, into the darkness, letting his nose down into the fur; and Mama ran out after him lowering her nose in the fur; the cold wafted through the doors: like a heap of howling times; multilegged peoplechases were borne along the Arbat:—

　　　—borne along are the not so loud thunder of events into the enormous darknesses of deadly gloom: tired time limps from the hours; it is— lamelegged!

MAMOCHKA

I know: our Mamochka is ailing!

Papa often said this behind her back. I know that she fell ill crying, when she sat down in the sleeping car from Pieter, in order to cry about the Petersburg life; she fell faint in the professorial circle;—

—her face appeared with ailing eyes at dusk:—

—all the time, remaining dumb, her head hung on her breast, her braids thrown on her breast, and—ailing from reflection; suddenly—

—she raises herself up:—

—she sets out: to wipe off the knick-knacks with a linen rag; here, with aimless wiping she covers space with a murmur, an exclamation, a squeal, an angry nose standing before Papa's door: in a night shirt—before sleep; and she looks naggingly not at the door, but into... the diluvian past,—

—into childhood!—

—From where she had settled down as mistress of the house amid the walls of the Kosyakov house: I remember:—

—the Fourth Zachatyevsky Lane; from where Papa had brought her in a gala carriage, in tails, with a bouquet of flowers—

—and Maksim Kovalevsky, in a tail coat, with a similar bouquet of flowers sat opposite Mamochka; when Mamochka recalls all of this, her eyes always begin to ail: she raises her ailing eyes: she keeps silent with a diamond glance (from tears):

"I—you: all of you!.. Get out! Go, go, all of you..."

"Away from me... Ah, leave me be!"

"Leave..."

"Me!"—

—I do not believe:—

—(ah, little star, white from the sparkle in the indigo sky on whitish middays—

—she is all sparkled out!)—

—Middays are filled with the horror of the old, professorial life and—

—with beardbushes of the old scholarly high priests;—

—from which:—

—her little eyes widened into a—wheel: they began to run, they ran, they run... yes and out of her little eyes rolled; little adamants rolled into the handkerchief:—

—the damp handkerchief is left on an armchair;—

—well so what: she cried a bit?

Everyone cries at our place!

. . . .

The ring with the turquoise settled down on a little finger; she returned from Pieter; and—green spots appeared on the stone of the ring—

—very bad!—

—everyone knows,—

—as soon as the turquoise blue is spoiled by turquoise green, family happiness in the home is lost.

And so:—

—already an archgreen: the happinesses had been grabbed away; pockets were searched, the shelves in the cabinets were rummaged through, but no happiness: where is it?—

—I know: it never was!—

—The best man, Maksim Kovalevsky, lost it in the carriage!..—

—So the little babblers began: Mama is ailing from an illness of sensitive nerves; having sat down, she is silent; she let down her little head onto her breast, tossed her braids onto her breast;—

—Papa walks about and ohs about!—

. . . .

Yes, between Papa and Mamochka—there is: there is something; there can be no argument here, that there are arguments, there are: very prominent ones; only there's noone to ask:—

—but, is there anyone to ask?—

—Only with a howling whistle on the glasspanes do gusts answer beyond the glasspanes—there, having drawn the views shut with muslin: beyond the glasspanes; yes only brutal time answers with a frost; and the crackerjack sun of cruel color hangs; and all the whiteplumed glasspanes have frozen; from all the window sills soon will begin to drip...

. . . . . .

Ah!

I am—alone: I alone; I heed the arrival of tiny sounds; from two to five someone booms at Pompul's; they are chopping cutlets in the kitchen; Dunyasha is cursing; earlier: Mama sounds words like a bunch of keys, all about **ruches, boas, jabots**; up until two she takes cover; three: the loud sound of the bell; Papa booms his galoshes in the anteroom—to wave his signature across leaves of paper; I know,— under each will appear the signature: "**Dean M. Letaev**"; he yawns and screws up his eyes; the light eats the eyes; the iceplumed window diamondizes in winter:—

—it rattles in a lightplumed spring!—

—and with a whistle, with flying snow run-ons of a blizzard whistle against the glasspanes; beyond the glasspanes a white gurgling; the white runs— like thunder, runs with a shudder along the roofs—from our place to Retteré, over Greenblatt's,—

—over Blank's—

—somewhere—

—from where!—

—Papa, bent, cracks his starch, sneezing, and—places his signature: "**Dean M. Letaev.**" Already the winking of lighted lamps; something is happening: trashy, foolish; the corners sat down quietly: in the nontransparent, in the black; in piles, in rustles—

—Mama is crying soundlessly!—

—about what?—

—Papa stands up, rocks from the strain, looks; and wants to say something: he is unable—he bellows, a sad bull; he winks at Mamochka with the red-lead of overfilled little eyes (from blood); he waves his hand, withdraws to the study: to sit in the stu—dy.

. . . .

Dinner time is—heavy:—

—Mama satins her sides up to the table; dissatisfiedly grabbing a napkin, she throws the napkin; with her eyes at the ring with the turquoise—

—it is turning green: it is greener than yesterday!—

— there was nothing left of the turquoise: just an unpleasant green throws itself into Mama's eyes;—

—and—

—dinner crystallizes like the pitcher, like glasses, with the resounding sadness and frosted glass blown—

—of Mama,—

—who, no matter what she sees and no matter what she hears,—at everything she pulls back her little lip, swelled in a quarrel...

And—Papa is lost: how should he sit and what should he look at...—

—He begins simply to mouth words: this way, and that:—

—"Leave it be: your keeping silent... What has gotten into you? Well what did you say? Again—this rubbish... The same old nonsense!.."

"You think so?.. Ah!"

"Rather silly!"—

—and displaying her childhood birthmark, Mamochka regales everyone; no, not with a glance, but with poison: everything she is told, she knows better; and everyone is guilty: all around guilty;—

—and the eyebrows flew up on her tiny little brow; and they construct without a word such hooks of opinions that—

—the soup sticks in the windpipe: I cough; Papa has completely lost his head; from terror he leaped up in a loud question.

It is all the more terrifying for me that they turn to me with their questions: they begin to develop in me at the table a curiosity for exact knowledge; I know that Mama will frown at this; and—she will look from under her brow; and I—hang my head; and I—choked on the answer; to Papa's question—not a goo-goo: I fall silent:—

—because for sure,—

—Papa will withdraw, and when I am left alone with Mama one on one, then—

—very painfully she will grab my arm, jerk me to her; and grabbing for a thick comb, she will jab it.

"Ouch, ouch, ouch!"

"What's this? Ouch, ouch? You present yourself with 'ouch-ouch-ouch': be silent!"

And she combs out my hair with the comb: it would be better to flog them, than to torture a little child so with the comb: I cry; and here I receive: a turquoise on the little nose.

"Well?"

"Get out of here!.."

The blankcolored heavens caress pale-eyed, without warming me; the sunset rosens from a crystalline icicle; and rosy smoke runs like muslin along a rosy roof.

. . . . .

—Or else she would quietly threaten me with a little finger, showing the ring with the turquoise:

"Listen, Kot..."

"Remember this is right under your nose: you will be an alien to me!"

And she presses a chin suddenly grown stout to her neck; she sits—she looks unkindly.

Time darkens; and then: a triplet flows from a violet flute; and a tuft of withdrawn light becomes cherry: it blackens in the sky; a serpent, striped time,—crawls; and old age grins toothlessly in the blackish blanknesses of a ruined world; already blackhanded darkness had extended its enormous digit through the glass; headless, legless like a pillar Blackhand rose to the ceiling, dropping his fivefingered hands on my little neck; and—he compressed my little throat; with dark terrors.

I compress myself: to conceal my development (I am—developing, alas!); unsuspecting Papa, turning to me over dinner with a wise guy question, wishes to expose development all the more quickly, in order to bestow a gift of a little bowler hat, to bestow a little frock coat and a case for spectacles, and a chain for a watch; I answer with intentional silliness; Papa's dark brown little eyes begin to run about, rather sorrowfully they begin to spin, and—they let down straight into the bowl of hot soup (he blows on the spoon); and I look from under my brow at Mamochka:—

—Mamochka's glance changed when she was ailing: it became somehow animal-like—

—and Mama throws her own animal glance, falling upon us: and—it is impossible to understand: you glance at Mama into her little eyes, beyond the little eyes; Mama's little eyes are left; they do not answer my little eyes; not accepted by Mama's glance, my glance begins to run like a baby mouse, away from Mama's little eyes; and I see, that my Papochka is winking from his bowl, attentively glancing at me beginning to wink; his little eyes, baby mice, are swept about toward Mamochka; Mama's little eyes, like a birthmark: they look—but do not see!

. . . .

Papa and I are rarely alone—just the two of us; we were dissolved by silence; I recall unreturnable time, a time not long ago, when Mama was still well; Papa would joke so freely, carefully penetrating into everything that happened with me; and he would cure my upset tummy:—

—I remember;—once I grabbed onto my tummy in pain; I cried; and Papa—stern, bigheaded, stocky, suddenly ran out from behind the door with a bottle of castor oil, shaking his beard with put-on savagery; the buffet plopped; he struck the parquet with a very heavy footstep, dancing around my screams like some jumping jack; and waving a table spoon under the little nose, he stamped out the words of his loud verse, composed for the occasion to entertain me:

> Kotik is a little dummy!
> Does not listen to his nanny:
> Day and night his little tummy
> He fills up with slop and candy.
>
> And the castor oil I'm bringing
> Sure is better than a whipping...
> The punishment sure ain't yummy:
> But it'll clean your little tummy...—

—And everyone broke out laughing; and here having already poured some castor oil on the table spoon, he poured the castor oil down my spreadopened little mouth; jokingly he clicked his heels and loudly jumped up at the occasion;—

—soon they dragged me into a separate room: to clean my little tummy.

. . . .

I remember, yes, unreturnable time, when I did not fear sharing caresses with Papa; now I do not share caresses with him; I am more suspecting; I understood, that scandals are dangerous for Papa: I secreted myself from Papa, loving him strongly; and it was bitter for me, and I cried on the insides of my eyes; but I kept my tears a secret: we lost one another (I had lost another friend!); and this loss was lost in the years, when I lost the capacity: to be sincere with Papochka; nevertheless I always thought: this was my virtue; I bore this cross for years, as an unseen help for Papa and Mama; when they collected at the table then they could burst out at one another: with words and glances.

Strange!

I used to walk amid shadows; and a shagginess of shadows hangs airily; beardbushes appear everywhere; I force my way between them, but through them I stumble against horror, and the horror—peals with laughter: it wants to embrace me...—

—I could break through the floor where the dentist lives, brewing up a foul smell from below by the artificial making of teeth; he would tear my tooth out and triumphantly put in an alien and foul smelling one...—

—I long thought about the brewing of teeth and I long heard the heavy moans (there—teeth were jerked out); and thoughts of the grave, the abyss and the brewing of teeth arose at dinner time, when the soul took to trembling heel from the terror, that Papa, grabbing his bowl, would crash off to his study, locking himself in with the key, and would not exit: there he disappears forever; having collected her suitcases, our Mamochka meanwhile runs away to Petersburg; and "**Zett**" kidnaps Henrietta Martynovna; I—am left alone; in a lonely apartment; and here they sound the bell:—

—and there arrives, opening the door from out of the dusk—a gentleman in a frock coat, in a very black one: with an intention very ignominious; I am left with him one on one; he bellows at me with his bullish puss: he is—

—Blackpuss!

. . . . . .

Once I saw in a tormenting dream, that—it came to pass: that Papa and Mama were lost, that I was borne away to an apartment, just like ours; but I know—it is not ours; some woman (not Mama) comforts me (she does not comfort me in the right way!), she assures me, that she is Mama; suddenly Papa walks about the room; I toss myself at him, catch at his frock coat; he turned: I see—that face is not Papa's!

Something strange is being created at our place; Papa shuts himself off from Mama; and there he produces horrible things, of which no one knows; there he becomes—a fustigator: bright-red; he trembles his fivefingered hand above a fly, whole from flight; and "tsap": he catches it; and the fly sits in his fist;—

—its head is torn off—by jerkers, trembling fingers; Papa sits on top of the fly—bright-red, horrible, I know, that this is not a fly, but—Mama...

And it is strange, and terrible now in the rooms blown out by the storm; all the same it seems to me: something is howling; suddenly: everything is illumined by a candle: Mama can be seen behind the candle; she slams, smacks her slippers, mumbles with her slippers straight into the anteroom: surely, to listen in, on what Afrosinya is saying about her (in the kitchen); suddenly a sound: first began to beat, then began to run a little stick of a tail from the little corner: that is Almochka slamming her little tail on the floor;—

—no—

—she did not listen in: in the kitchen—silence; Almochka gave away Mama...—

—And Mama stamped on Alma: the little stick began to bang anew; everything is illumined anew—only in reverse order; they pass through with a candle: Mama behind the candle... She smacks, clicks, stamps, mumbles...

Something howls:—

—last midnight there was, I know for sure,—

—a procession of malicious blackies from corner to corner: along the carpet, past the chairs; I—saw; I can't really say what it was; they, the blackies, passed everywhere: the years passed (from corner to corner) along the carpet, past the chairs; the moon fell upon them with luminous swords; and crowds of dumb blackies fell, as if dead, on the floor; the moon sailed behind a cloud they—

—the blackies—

—having arisen, lumped together in a band from the black corner lair: along the carpet past the chairs; and—there was no end to them, no name for them!

MIKHAILS

November, a snowgift, chasing out the sleighs, beset the days with woundaround flakes; Papa hangs in the anteroom an enormous torn fur coat (they had already sewn the hem in it several times, it tears; for sure, he rubs it in the gutter while walking)—

          —he hangs in the anteroom a coonskin coat, coughing loudly and shaking off the snow; he stands in his own very high cap of the softest sealskin, with a yellow bastmat bag and a portfolio; in the portfolio—the action files of the department, in the bag—goldheaded wines: twelve bottles—Madeiras, port wines and sherries; these are the eves of Saint Mikhail's day; tomorrow the congratulators will come running: the Mikhails—will be left at home.

The floorpolishers are—at our place: they put aside the furniture, the beds, the tables; and—they complicated the carpets; one crawled about the rooms, standing on his knees; with one hand compressing the wax, he scratched, sullenly perspiring, whitish, wax zig-zags, (he showed a dirty heel), which Almochka, sticking out her puss, tried to bite and squealed out as if the floorpolisher had kicked her with the heel.

Afrosinya arrived with a white wicker basket; she had—a motley-plumed wildfowl: a headless bird; I see—a bloody neck and yellow paw; and I know, that tomorrow for dinner all of this will be served differently at the table.

Mama sternly buries her little nose in the motley-plumed hazelhen: she sniffs:

"No."

"No,—no—no!"

"I won't take it: not for anything."

Oh, I wish tomorrow would come sooner.

. . . .

And here it is "**tomorrow.**"

Oh, how many rosy, ruddy noses glow ruddy in the ruddy frost. How many rosy ruddy dragon flies set down; to sparkle in the cold; and beyond the window they sprinkle sand, so one won't fall; no, it's not November, but—December: and in the Nativity snow, and in the sparkling cold feet will scrape on the street; smokes will sniff out; shovels strikingly scrape their hard iron against the frozen ices.

And the sound of a bell, very resoundingly: they bring in a carton; from impatience my heart is—all agog; and Mama's eyes are—like a wheel; Mama's little mouth opens like a flower: there the little tongue is—a little worm; and she—licks herself, like a kitten, from satisfaction: Tolstopyatov had sent a torte; and they bring the carton straight to Papa; very curiously he fixed his gaze out of his dressing gown on the torte, correcting the tassels on his belly:

"Say it, please..."

Mama bows, extends her lips:

"Well then: congratulations..."

And the little eyes are—two caresses: lookthrough, like lampshades: if you take them off—two little fires; and our nameday boy bows his brow to the thrust out lips; I know: they are now ignited from the eyes; everyone's fiery little eyes flame up; yes, yes,—how many times had Papa celebrated the nameday: and—how many will he still celebrate: but if you already glance there,—and—striking old age stands with its gift: with an ungrateful stroke.

And Papochka is old: already fifty years old.

He sits at the table, resting before his difficult obligation: to treat the visitors, proposing first whitefish, then cheese, then butter, then sherry, —before a piece of chocolate-colored wall, leaning his big head on the jambs of his coffee-colored shelves; he sits without spectacles in a palegray dressing gown; he sits—in great tenderness—thus, neither this way nor that, having placed before himself the cream torte of Tolstopyatov, falling with his let-down little shoulder all falling to the chair, —so bigbrowed, with a fallen lock of hair; his head, barely leaning to the side, amazing us faithfully with totally light blue eyes (not brown):

"Now that's a scandal!"

"The nameday boy."

"Tell us, please."

He smiled very quietly to himself and at everything there was; and he seemed like a Chinese ascetic, seeking the "Middle Use and Constancy" of Confucius; such clarity—no, I had not seen.

But meanwhile first Dunyasha, then Mama would approach him:

"The beadles have come to congratulate you."

"The yardman Anton has come..."

"The night watchman..."

"The plumber..."

Papa winked helplessly at us with guilty little eyes; and he thundered out his little jokes:

"A beadle isn't a beagle."

"Anton? Without an antonovka apple?"

And, obtaining his wallet, he spread around his money.

It was already past eleven o'clock in the morning: a crow eyeballed us in the windows:

"Shoo, shoo."

She flew past.

In the dining room the tables had now been arranged; and the leaves, enormous boards had been covered with a snowwhite tablecloth; mountains of resounding china plates had been wiped to a sparkle; the knives jingled against the forks which are being placed by Dunyasha; displaying a silly puss, a greasy whitefish, golden-brown, had been smoked on a plate; and there appeared cheeses and sausages, and liqueur glasses and a flock of bottles; and bent semicircles of benches surrounded the table; there was cleanliness and order—in everything.

This was managed by Mama, elegant in a checkered skirt, wagging an enormous bustle, rustling a kazakin, magnificent and rosy, with a hairdo, pointed like a tower, pierced with a little golden comb; and with little eyes, painfully biting the horny hand of Dunyasha:

"No, no."

"Not here."

With a lighted rosy little face of a tiny doll: the throat pierced by a brooch which is—round; inside of it—a whiteplumed lady sits with hair totally rusty-red: this is some sort of favorite: a **madam**; I see; Mama's little eyes, misty eyes, now sharpened like leeches' eyes; greenish little fires began running along the earring with the diamond:

"You've let the fumes out of the kitchen again."

And—reddish little fires began running along the earring with the diamond.

The sound of the bell—very resoundingly:

"Mamasha."

That's Granny: in a luminous, brown velveteen dress with gala ribbons of a fresh velveteen headdress, with a lilaceous Mass card in her hands; and she is without a bustle; behind her browless Auntie pales like a thin little stick; following behind her—pillared to the ground unable to resolve whether to enter, all gilded with freckles, correcting, just imagine, his white tie, was Uncle Vasya himself. And Mama says to him:

"This is the height of impropriety! A white tie with a frock coat."

And here from the kitchen came the smell of pies: with cabbage, with rice—with fish, with viziga, with carrots and with meat.

Oh, how many rosy, ruddy noses will glow ruddy, running into the anteroom, clicking their heels, wheeze, blow their noses loudly and push aside their fur coats into Dunyasha's hands, bringing in after them from the frost the tickling smell of something burning; how many will shake off the sparkling snow from icicled mustaches, so that, having played every game to beautify themselves, to fly in kindlylooking, stumbling against the dish of borne-in big kulebyaka; the sound of the bell: the bull-legged professor, a gray warted one, here passes in white-browed with congratulations, sits down, thrusts a piece of kulebyaka into a smacking mouth; and he begins splashing out slobbering words; the sound of the bell: Mrs. Malinovsky becomes a ragged skeleton, with a white, bloodless face—like flattened ivy; it reminds one bitingly; she sniffs at the air with her violet little nose; she spoils the air with a foul-smelling little question; with her swims past a lady, a multigenetrix, with a big belly; Malinovsky asks:

"Which one?"

"The twelfth."

A selfpraising smart aleck, a juicymouthed barrister, cracking his starch, shows himself, he sets his gaze somehow cherrily at the sherry, he squeezes through his teeth his double entendre, and, pecking at his liqueur glass, he burps like a ram; an overstarched chinker—there he is: chink, chink—talks like a tinker. Someone, strangely stained, sullen, like iodine solution, forgets to withdraw; and he stays to dine with us; a crackerjack ne'er-do-well rises from his place and, having made a general bow, to which no one answers him, passes into the halfdusk of the anteroom, leaving without having sampled the bread and salt of our hospitality; in its full complement, as it seems, all of the department roars at the table at our place; the administrator of the surrounding school district himself brings his calling card, but he does not enter; bowing caressively, such a kind and shamefaced Professor Zhukovsky will screw up his eyes: a man's man, but he cries in a voice, like a woman; through the door, bumping into the already withdrawing Zhukovsky, bringing with him his gray streak from the creation of the world, unchangingly comes out the very tiny kindly winking Anuchin; he seemed to me a small little fish; but very bony (if you swallow it—

you'll choke: he sits down at our place to look at the mood of society: hold your ear sharp. Surely the "Russian Gazette" received the knowledge):—

—I recently met him again on the street: having met, I recalled that for thirty-five years I had known him completely the same: he was always very oldish, grayish; surely, he has walked from diapers with a gray little beard, with whirlwinds of whitening hair, jumping above a tiny, wrinkled little brow, with a red, hanging nose, which he grabs with his fingers;—

—in breaks the cloudy, always panting a word, Sergei Alekseevich Usov, cobbling on three-four warts, exactly like on a very tasty berry: yes, a wild strawberry is growing on him; his one-pound, heavy word totally slams the chinker; that one, slammed, phooeys, like an anther; and in a cloud of phooey, green phooey,—settles down on the tablecloth:—

—none other than Veselovsky—

—different, ox-eyed, blown up with such weightless, high flown air: he always blows up the lightest, ornate word, which is borne like a blown-off down of fluff (if it falls in the nose, you'll sneeze so,—you can't believe); and either Aleksei Veselovsky is giving us a speech, or he is so haughtily blowing off the blossoms of a dandelion; here is borne like fluff, not knowing where and why, on the words framed with hairs—

—Sergei Alekseevich Usov, smoking, sprinkles ashes, listening sarcastically; suddenly he hisses, and lets out a joking word like a smoky ring:—

—the joker flies off for a smoke:—

—yes, I know, that they will all be here.

. . . .

Well now, it begins: I hear the sounds of the bell; I sit down—to observe (under the little window; there beyond the little window: a crow knocks blacknosed on the window from a white snow fluff): clouds have begun to move; and a silverplumed snowflake fluffily flies: into the dining room quickly flies a first-year student, bignosed, with a black beard, with a sword; and Papa goes out to meet him; he flies up impetuously, ecstatically jerks Papa's hand; and clicking his heels, from the force of the click he flies through the room to the corner with a torn-off poor hand (oh, how many hands were torn off by him); he passes through from here to the table: to let down his nose above the plate: this is—Batyushkov, the grandson of the poet; theosophy waits ahead for him; and two more students arrive: one is—Aleksei Nikolaevich Severtsov, gaunt, tall, bent in the image of an old man; Pasha Usov, a student with the look of a folk hero, passes, in passing tossing his palm in the air:—

       —and a silverplumed fluffy snowflake flies beyond the window, fluffily lying down; the crow was crestfallen; she has become a little sphere: she has long been chained to the spot; I look both here and there: beyond the little window and at the door; they are serving kulebyaka; snowy elders pass by respectably; stern elders stare inspiredly: in the space of the dining room they boom words; Papa stoops with unnecessary help; widenosed, at times indicating at the table:

"*Pâté de volaille.*"

"I offer for your attention."

And Mamochka looks kindly:

"With meat."

And always the silverplumed snow flies by like weightless fluff tacked together; crows pressed against one another on the roof: they bleat with the laughter of sheep: yes, yes,—Malinovsky to the taste is—a dry sea roach, and by her bones—a prickly smelt; why does she make it look like she is a liberal calf. And she sets aside an arm, and sets a leg, and simply milky rivers flow;—

       —they bleat with the laughter of sheep; she stands: ga-ga-ga,--ba-ba-ba—"Dey rabb... They robbed... They are voting" — the phrases intersect:—"But no,—hurry to serve up a resolution... in the departmental order..." "Dunyasha, what are you doing?" —"Madam, there is no place to hang the fur coats..." "Hang your diploma on the wall, my good sir..." Dey rabb... Ba-ba-ba—ga-ga-ga,—

       —The buffet begins to shake: this is Papa, his eyes shining, passing with a bottle of rowanberry vodka and bowing in quick service:

"Some rowanberry vodka." —

       —"Eh, yes, he is a soaper: blown up with words, he flew like bubbles; he burst. I am telling you, that he—burst," hisses from smoking Sergei Alekseevich Usov—

       —but here appears Aleksei Nikolaevich Veselovsky himself, arrogantly blown up; and everyone—falls silent:—

"Ppss."

"Ppss." —

—The atomizer whistled a piney stream: that is Mamochka wanting to cleanse the smokefilled air:—

"Mimochka, Fimochka, Fifochka, Fofochka, Misik, Tosik and I are going for the holidays to our brother's place in the country…—

—Ga-ga-ba-ba-ba." —

—Papa leapt up quickly, the pocket of his mantle caught again on the arm of the chair, he tore off the pocket:

"Turn your attention over here: caviar!" —

—he bowed down over Grot, who, entering, intersected the crooked mouth malice of the professors' wives, had already settled down blackbrowed in a magnificent (isn't it too magnificent) pose, natural (too natural), his black curls with his beard bowing into his hand; and he makes very beautiful gestures with his other hand:

"Pass the *dos d'esturgeon*."

But stooping and so goodnosedly fixing his gaze with his spectacles, my Papa stands behind his back, finding a minute to indicate with his hand:

"The *pâté de volaille* is very tasty…"

And Grot:

"I give you thanks."—

—He turns to the multisuckeress of sour lemons; and Papa, bespectacled, bigheaded, but tossing and turning, having left Grot, spreads funny points of humor everywhere, he leads parallel lines with his dark brown little eyes; and—tosses off (one after another) parallels: from the cheese to the sausages; today there is no time for him to philosophize; and Grot is philosophizing before the important twolipped fool, Professor Kislenko's wife; yes, they say—in her are bigbreasted passions, but she is held by a pulled-in deerskin; her lips are pulled up like a small pea as if she's collected herself to whistle: if you let them go, they will burst; Mamochka timidly indicates to her a bunch of grapes; she—turns away, as if she hadn't heard; and Mama, insulted, offers again: the twolipped fool answers her with excessive rudeness; she turns her bustle; and with pulled-in deerskin she listens to the very handsome Grot: and with a pencil stub she makes notes very submissively in her little book; listening to Grot is the venerable phrasemonger, all blown up by two jubilees; compressed by his prepared phrase, like by a strong corset, he sits waiting an appropriate occasion,—he tosses up his pince-nez; and—he is drawn like a white bald patch; and—then: the occasion struck; and—he raises his glass, raises himself, and rising on the back of the chair,—he blows his mouth—

      —and a wispy bubble is imaged; the veins fill; and from his forceful efforts sand sprinkles down; and he raises with his right hand the champagne higher and higher; and with his left, hardly waving,—
—near the mouth he starts to develop all of this: he develops it to such length, that there is not enough hand; here—it bursts: and all look with respect at the blank and general place; a finger rocks in the air, and in space hung being weighed the glass,—

      —and everything else has burst: there is no one; only—a chair; and under the chair a sandy handful; they carry out the handful; they clink glasses with Papa: this was said to him: he, he is—a dear nameday boy; he attracted the phrasemonger, who, after all, every day—so (until his jubilee, his third) blows about somewhere: somewhere he had spoken a library full, but written—two brochures; opposite—sits an unimaginable mischief-maker: he had grown his hair to his eyes,—to the small narrow slits of the eyes: to the most malicious, most clever: and—he scratches himself: some kind of monkey. But they say,—he is a clever one—

      —Vindalai Urvantsev:—
—I fear that he will bark; he barks,—everyone's hands shake from horror; his mouth widens apart to... the end of the world; from there comes the smell of the ocean; he is called the **Trumpet of Jericho**; and no matter where he trumpets—it is the first day; and—chaoses; and—twenty-five babblers simply burst; then he closes his mouth; and—scratches himself; and—he looks around: wild and red, confused; after him—five minutes of silence: I see—mouths are moving, but I do not hear: I have gone deaf; Vindalai Urvantsev strikes like the Czar cannon; he strikes—an oceanic width wafts by; he, having struck, grows confused; timid: there is no way at all he can marry; —he is always getting married, getting married, but from the wedding crown—he flees...

It darkens in the dining room, it thins out: beyond the windows, there,—oh, what burning enthusiasm, transfiguration and—shining; transsubstantiated, arising from the noncolored day—selfcolored, enlightened: purplish red, crimson, violet; and—it seems new; and the day is—aerated, illumined; it flies straight into the night;—

—but in the dining room there is sheer disorder; the collection ate and perspired, sat, made a racket; it seemed—everything was in accord; everywhere discords began anew, it seemed that at our table were imaged—**Smiths** and **Bears** were everywhere separating one in front of the other; by turns they tossed fists and words—into the middle ground between them; in the middle—keeping silent is Uncle Vasya, frightened by a shout; they had already torn off the smoked skin; under it the pale white *dos d'esturgeon*, having shown its meat, had been eaten: only the fishy smoked puss stared totally amazed with an unmoving eye, afterwards going into the bone pile; from the *pâté de volaille* remained a yellowing fat and lead paper, and from the caviar—a drying knife; no one is sounding the bell; a hubbub filled the anteroom; and chairs remained everywhere, imaging here doubles, and there triples, frozen in argument; here—a rumpled table cloth, and there—a spill.

And it is—always thus: they always used to look blankly into their own thunder of words; one snitters, everyone—chuckles; and—then fall silent; and suddenly they begin to run like thunder around the rooms; chairs were moved about, they take their leaves; and—press invitations on one another; the hors d'oevres are—all eaten up; a multitude of dirty dishes is being borne off to the kitchen; everything is first washed, it will be concealed again in the buffet; everything begins to flow like old times, as if there had never been a Saint Mikhail's day; but—

—it will be again; this will all—be repeated; it has been repeated since Adam; and it will be at the raising of the dead; yes, the dead, having risen from the snow, will come, thundering with their galoshes on this secretive day to our place at the table:—

—oh, what burning enthusiasm, trans-figuration, beyond the windows; everything there has been trans-substantiated from the noncolored day,—to the selfcolored, enlightened: purplish red, crimson, violet; and—extinguishes. Everything is—blank: and our dear nameday boy has withdrawn to rest; Mama also rests; but from the corner appeared a blackoak-bigbeard; this is—a shadow; it—exits quietly; and wanders—lightly; it scratches quietly the wallpaper... with its... cockroach...;—

—blackthoughts pass, big-beards pass with a noiseless gait; they stand up in crowds, take each other by the hands; one hand flows into another; and—

—there will be single
blackness:—

—night is —a presence—yes: of very many; and—no: not
the absence of them...

. . . .

Already beyond the windows the cold has bluened—there at
everything with a crawling smoke; a gradation of all darkenings has
composed itself into light bluish dims: from blue-gray and—to blue-
blue; and from it to blue-black, even to black-violet; all this darkened—
into the poured ink beyond the little window: dense, sheer.—

—And our
nameday boy:—

—lies on the bed: on the hard bed, crammed in by the
bookcase, totally without spectacles, exposing wrinkles around the
eyes, secreted by the glasses,—pale, tired, having thinned during the day
and growing darker in the darkenings of the day: and passing dusk
throws a row of its gloomy veils on this face; in the blue-gray it is still
white, but in the blue-blue it—began to grayen; in the sheer blue-black
it barely bluens from the bed:

"Yes, Papochka—is growing old..."

He leaps up from the bed; and wipes his eyes:

"Ah—ah—ah."

He stirs about over his spectacles; and—bustles about, searching
for a pencil stub and striking a match: the blackpaths of the nights have
burst apart—in the sparkle of the candles.

"What are you doing—it's harmful to boil about such: the whole
day."

"No matter, no matter."

And he withdrew—into calculations.

"Shouldn't you go to the club."

A flowing tear began to shudder from the eyes: I fear that I will
break out crying: in the time running past we run inescapably; I... with
a yellowish constructo cube, Mama—with a hat carton and Papochka
with a new brochure: **"On the radical e - x"** : I fear: I break out
crying: well, I can still run, Mama still can, but Papa—where can he
run to? He had already knocked off fifty: was a nameday boy; and—he
ceased to be one: he ran from his nameday along the road of time—

—and
I exited quietly into the drawing room: armchairs stood in gloom; and
in the chairs sat: a company of glooms,—and they teased here the

sitting guests; and such glooms gazed at the glass window panes with weighty glances; the glooms stood under the light shades; glooms stood in an espalier:—

—of dumb cavaliers—

—who had donned their tail coats.

AHURA-MAZDA

I stand by the window under the strong walnut baguet: a rolldown shade is hung on copper ringlets; and—the samovar is served, sending into the air a development of steam: under the glass lamp; I stick to the window, where Moscow is firming; and beyond it forests, cities and fields, along which are borne from the border Swiss and German girls to us, to the children, and along which the French girl will go.

Here rhinoceroses walk along the corridor (the buffet stomped its feet: the little busts jumped about); then from the doors—Papa heads in, gazing at me with his tin spectacles; he stands, having consummated behind the door the fastening of his pantaloons; here he had already plopped into the passageway, waving with one hand, pressing with his other a green little book to his side: he hurries behind the table, his mustache growing savage:

"Well, Kotik, my little friend!.."

"Let's do some learning."

He places me in front of himself: he takes it upon himself—to teach me to click my heels; I click my heels, shaking only my head (I'm—in a little dress: my curls, having flown about, tickle under the nose):

"Well now then!"

Well then I!—

—But at the Dadarchenkos' place the boys can not click their heels; one slobbers, his little fist thrust in his little mouth; another is still crawling; Sonechka does curtsies; but she doesn't want to do one for me; we simply kiss:

"One!"

And—ready: quickly now...—

Papochka, loudly clicking his heels, sits me on his knees; he's—in his uniform tail coat (he will break away to a lecture); hurriedly he stumbles with his meaty face in front of the opened book, stooping and slanted off to the side: he bites a rose-drop, he runs with his tongue to far distant countries, where the sun brightly shines; where an olive-bronzed Hindu wrapped in a turban walks, where a Persian in a striped dressing gown champs on a persic.

The little sun, a radiant pheasant, spreads out now its lightplume through the wintry smokes; it's know-it-alls—sunbeams— run to us from the windows; and in it are—blankflights.

"Now then well, my Kotik!"

"Russia, brother,—is!"—he tosses out his palms, reminding me of the gesture of the Sabaoth under the cupola of the Cathedral of the Redeemer (the nose of the Sabaoth was taken by Koshelyov from Professor Usov: a nose—almost three yards long!)...

"Enormous!"

"It comprises"—he throws up his little knife and deftly catches it—"Turkestan, and the Caucasus, and Siberia, Bukhara and Khiva, and Finland"—deftly he throws up the little knife...

"The Urals"—and catches it...—"Repeat..."

I repeat:

"Siberia, Bukhara and Khiva..."

He throws the little knife:

"In Siberia, brother, it is cold, but in Turkestan reeds grow: striped tigers sit there and they eat Sarts; the Sarts have dressing gowns, motley ones, my little brother."

He smells of antonovka, he walks with words:

"We have Kamchatka; and we even ruled Alaska, but... damn it"—and his face is slit through by a sullen wrinkle, and he looks with eyes blank from the horror:

"Damn it! Germans, sharpy bureaucrats, winked it through: we sold Alaska" he snaps his finger under his nose and cocks his fingers into a fig:—"for a million, my little brother!"

His face sours and he shows his tongue:

"They sat those German minsters on us: Lamsdorfs and others; Bismarck with Kalnoky were trying for this: Bismarck has three hairs... We sold—Alaska!"

Here he grows silent, as if he is listening inside of himself, he screws up his little eyes and presses apart his mouth, lifting his spreadnostriled nose; and—savagely sneezing, he hastily gets a handkerchief out from the tail of the coat; then on words,—yes into a hop:

"But nevertheless, hm: something was left for us."

And he is embarrassed, rather pleased with the wealth of Russia:

"Well that's how it is, Kotik."

That's how we are: we are developing ourselves!..

From the dining room—an open door: there—the drawing room door secretly opens Mama's bedroom; behind the screen with the lacquered field of heavenly color, from where goldenwinged storks fly on the cutwork, under a light-blue blanket, her head placed shaggily on her bare elbow,—Mamochka is all ears; secreting her breathing, she is collecting herself to prove to us, that it is forbidden to develop ourselves,—with a threat:

"Kotik!"

"Come here..."

"Don't you dare listen!"

"It's too early—for you!"

"Come here now!"

How to withdraw?

"Kot, stay!"—Papochka gnashes his teeth...

What can you do?

"But?"

"Aren't you listening to your mother?"

"But?"

"Well then from now on you should know: I'm—not your mother!"

How not my mother? I, growing timid, start to go; but hardly do I start to go, when behind me stumbling Papa stamps his words, spreading out his hand with trembling fingers: "**tsap**" at the little skirt, and the smell of antonovka suddenly falls away; and there wafts another smell, also characteristic of him; this smell of extinguished stearin candles and burnt paper was familiar to me, when Papa with an extinguished candle went to the study from the dark little room; here—the vein on the brow fills; the vein on the neck fills; and—the silence lasts, full of horror:—

—in the chimney treeshaking winds howl; and distinctly is heard the sound of prattlins being stitched on the sewing machine (an impromptu is being stitched: a masquerade costume);—

—the sound of falling logs is heard (it is from the kitchen); the surety (what a naughty thought) is borne that the kitchen is all smelled up with sheepskin; Anton, the oakcrusher, woodchopper, blockhead, a chopping block of some sort, drops a bound bundle of logs there; and having sucked on a hang nail, he withdrew reeking of sheepskin:—

—I would like to go: to
sniff sheepskins!

. . . . .

All this is brought to my memory inopportunely,—from the terror
that Mama awoke, like a tiger, laying down behind the screens, in order
to jump out from there, snapping her teeth; and to drag me, a Sart,
behind the screens.

And because of that: when Papa rolls out words (so does a swarm
of wooden figures roll around in a chess box)—my memory runs from
my heel to my toe: from the terror that Mama will awake; from terror
some altogether unnecessary thoughts revolve in my little head :—

—not
long ago I saw to the right and left of the sun—two false suns; two
suns grew dark, but one sun was left; the Persian sun will darken, the
Hindu sun will darken, like Papa disappears to his lectures: Mama—
will be left!

At this point Papa loudly stamps:

"You, Kotenka, you know, don't listen at all?"

"Such a person!"

And jerking up the tablecloth, his fingers start dancing along the
tablecloth—like little peas; he jerks out a word:

"In Russia there is... what?"

I—stumbled: I keep silent; I—sit so bowlegged; I—stagnate so
boneheaded.

"The Urals!"

"The Urals"—he thunders and exhorts.

"What else?"

I do not know: he leans his weight on, jerks:

"How, how, how, how?!?"

I look: Papa has—slanting, malicious, little Tatar eyes: I want to
answer; but... behind the lacquered little screen howl, snapping, the
tigers:

"Kot! Kotik!"

"Don't you dare!"

"It's too early for you..."

"This very minute—to me!"

"No, allow me! The Urals, and—what else?"—Papa puffs out of
breath with his palms in the air.

I'm—not alive and not dead: I hear how Mama smacks: with the
sleepy, with a dreamily swollen face, growing unattractive, having

forgotten her capote, without corset, without jacket, without slippers, she runs out to the dining room with a concentrated look; and here—she swings, stamping her foot in a not so very pretty way.

"Am I—your mother?"

"Your mother?!"

Here having grabbed my little shoulder, she jerks the little shoulder: she twists and turns the little shoulder; dimly she falls with her face under my little nose and leads with a finger, settling by the nose, pressing with a full hand the shirt to the legs and baring her shoulder; she brushes me with a turquoise along the nose:

"Am I your mother?"

I—resolve, that—no: I do not have another choice; I know, I know everything, but—there is no choice, because grabbed by Papa's fivefingered hand by the skirt,—I cannot run from there: ai, ai, ai, ai—so she can twist and turn my shoulder: there will be black and blue marks again—an unimaginable disgrace!

Tach-tararach: a chair falls loudly; a struggle has arisen—for me (they tore off my lace): Papa let go of the skirt; he sat down threateningly, like a billygoat, before the already seated Mamochka; they look one another in the eyes (just like cocks, before they jump in front of one another,—they sit down: and—look at one another); and—Papa cannot hold out: with a biting slice of his slanting, Chinese little eyes, bloodfilled, like red-lead, he suddenly winks, and—he started to go, slamming the door; I am left with Mama.

Snapping the doors shut, spreading her little legs and sticking out a very angry belly, she bites her red lips with angry teeth: and—smack—smack—smack—smack on the cheek; Mama's fingers don't hurt me so much; the malicious little ring hurts: the greenish, hardish little stone really bites; to Mama—under her legs: like a little lump; I kiss her little foot with love: Christ commanded us to pray for sinners.

Mamochka—also begins to cry; and—she exits; I sit—on the floor; along the parquet a crawler-spider runs like a multipawed little ball;—behind it; and with a little foot I smacked it on the parquet: under the little foot was smeared a black **louse-louse**.

Here—it turns evening: and the burned oculus burns,—far away; and shadows cry out from the East; hearts burn; and under the heart is compressed some sort of **something:—**

—and it grows dark beyond the windows: the cold bluened from the darkening house; the long ago whitewashed with gray streaks day showed that it is—a Negro, having turned black from its evening face; and—misting from snows on the roofs; onto the bald head of the earth's sphere they put a cylindrical top hat, very black; with a fateful hand they had pulled over the head the night; lonely and stern.

I sit down under the window; and the night is blackhorned: it gazed in the window; in the corner the multiplication of darknesses had begun; I went into the little corridor: orphaned up to the stove; the stove savagely crackled the logs; the red flame walked along the red, already eaten from the edges firewood,—it hissed, scattering gold and feverish heat: blackened charcoals; everywhere cornflower blue butterflies of coal gas fluttered shinily.

In the drawing room,—there Granny has sat strongly in the worn-out seat of the armchair with hank, with hook: for me to unwind, to mumble at me: from me myself—my life and to look, having gleamed a glance, like fiery steel, from the dusk:—

—black Granny is—life; and Granny became this Granny; we will become her, when we become tired; and we are becoming somewhat tired: we are growing old, like others, who from youth just, like I, lie down, like a caterpillar, in firmly wound diapers, then fly out, like butterflies, eat much, like Mama, become stout wenches, like Mrs. Doktorovsky, walk big-breasted, sit bigbellied, and flabbily hang wrinkles, they dry out, like Granny, a little hunch, or hanging dry ears, like a bunch of mushrooms, made ready for soup—

—and here toothless twotoothed Granny breaks out laughing; and—blankeyed Auntie winks from the shadow: in such a condition; and sprinkling her own blankgeneration of sounds, with me, beaten, smacked, she carries out her own strange ways of playing, she embraces me and leads me through the shadows, like through the days; someone stuck out a paw from the dark darknesses, and I pass through the paw, but there:—

—tou—

—tou—

—tou—

—black-

walkers began walking along the corridor: to knock out! Black tailcoats pass by legless, headless—one after another, bowing one to another with a removal of faces and then rising up an armleg of shadows into the septiped of days: to twirl around the ceilings and burst in a ray of whitepawed flame:—

—this is Dunyasha passing with a candle: a seethrough, blacksmeared grimacer—jumped behind her, casting a shadow, in order to hover weightlessly in the burdened dusk;—

—in the orange flame and in the chocolate wallpaper Papa stoops, having returned from his lectures; Mama, tossing back her head and withdrawing with it into a boa, heaves her bustle, trembles her wide-open raspberry toque, sticking her hand into the muff,—passes, from the snow (all white, in snow) to her room:

"I have no thoughts of grieving"—she jerked her little nose; Papa sits, delving deeply into calculations, and making it look as though he doesn't see Mama; if he raises a little eye to Mama, very clever and not at all malicious, then she will stick out her lips; he very scatterbrainedly, blinking before himself, buries himself in the green spots of the cloth, and—sharpens a pencil stub:

"Well"—I think—"the quarrel continues."

I'm—weak; yes I'm—a slave: I drown again in the mutterings of wenches,—having dug into the little mattress until morning: but an old wench—bowed down; and—she smacks with a black jaw;—

—suddenly!—

—it dawned!—

Not a black wench, but white Mama glitters with a candle, digging into my little brow,—into my eyes; with a merciless hand tossing aside the curls,—as if to look at the little brow; and the little brow is—big:

"Bigbrowed!"

"Takes after his father..."

. . . .

How tousled are Mama's curls: the belly is malevolent; a bent little finger threatens; a second chin blows up under the chin:

"O, no!"

"Not after me!"

"All after his father..."

And she smacks in the dusk; I fear: the blackhorned boogeyman, a seethrough unknown one moos from the armchair at me with a cow puss...

. . . .

Nights I'm—a prisoner; nights the sheer spindle mutters in me with a broadening of sound; and the small tiny hair of a rustle, booms like a loud log; and a black little spot, like a slicing gritting of teeth, quickly rises on the run: to force the moon's beam into submission; it stops, squats heavily like a little crab: a cockroach!

Here the minutes ticked off, they weaken with the hardly noticeable dawn; I see: the black ink—has bluened; and I know:—

—the little day, a whitelegged infant, shouting at the top of its lungs already runs into the ancient arc of the vault of heaven; shaggy Mamas set out after the white infant: with concentrated fury; and—a murder is consummated: the minutes begin to tick like drops of blood and tears; the soulslayers, in a column of mourners stand to the right and stand to the left; and someone bearded, and someone winged stands up with a shaggy miter over the little grave; he will loudly read:—

—beri-beri-beri-beri—

berberi:

—berberi-berberi-beri;

—eri—arii, arii:—

—Papa once told of the great Persian prophet by the name of **"Zoroaster"**;—

—and I see in a dream:—

—they continue to nail the little coffin shut, until it bursts from the rays of the centiarmed sun:—

—Ahura-Mazda!—

—And here I awake...

. . . .

Morning!

Lightest chases of snowflakes smoke under the glassy, sparkling, bluish morning; some sort of an adamant: the universe has just put on an adamantine miter and sprinkles its precious colors like a Persian carpet; Papa is drawn to Mamochka: he tugs at her little shoulder; Mama, her little lips blown up, allows him; I—squeal from joyfulness; I know that toward evening there will be a loud sound of the bell: little cartons will arrive (Papa will send a little gift from Kuznetsky Most); and my heart is—all agog, and Mama's eyes—like a wheel, her hands begin to shake, tearing the twine; she takes from there a big lampshade, hung about with lace, and—licks her lips, like a cat, from pleasure.

. . . .

In our drawing room the fir tree has been saved since the Nativity; this evening they decorate it again; and it is—in clear little spheres; all of the selfcolored little spheres are filled with a lightness; touch it just a bit, and—the broken blown up little sphere cracked its shell; I know: again the dragees in the little cardboard boxes; they bought some more snappers...

. . . . .

Already the golden snappers have swelled with powder; and the yellow, paper cap is dragged out from it; and already on the head—it is torn; another pooped; and—it bestowed on me its gift of little trousers of blue paper; but—they are too short; such a pity; well—I jerk off a nut; all the boughs began to shake, needles fell, and a torn off sphere cluttered onto the parquet; the golden shell now crunches under the feet:—

—how everything is enlightened, how everything is illumined; it diamondized, eyed one clearly; a bigeyed adamant, or a miter; my Papochka, luminous, having put on his cap, just like a miter, hung himself with a golden, paper chain and walks like some Zoroaster:

"For Russia, my friend, in the far away future stands—the light; 'Rousant' this is—luminous; and 'Russian' or 'russet' is—a luminance!"—

—"Yes!"—

—I look at the seethrough translucence; I stuffed my mouth with pastille; from the scent of greenery the red-bright little lantern is so ruby-clear to us; we grabbed each other's hands; and—we whirl: a sparkle—in rotaryflights!

PAPA HIT THE NAIL ON THE HEAD

They sit down in our corners to overhear!

. . . . . .

Mama is—in thrownabout feelings: she sat down under the screen, by the little closet; she opened up the little doors of red wood with her little hand, filling the room with the smell of stuffy spirits; a little drawer rode out blindingly, smelling of lacquered cleanliness and sparkling, from that which filled it:—

—a dried little flower, a scented little handkerchief, a little glass dragon, a cut-glass little flagon: flagon behind flagon, gleaming of orange, faceted glass, of frosted glasses of the wiped ground-in stoppers, gritting at the turns, sparkled paradisiacally; rock crystal, bugles; bangles and beads in cardboard boxes, two agréments:—

—all of this was arranged in a little row on the blinding wood, languid from the smell, spread from a salmon-colored sachet, where a little pile of tiny handkerchiefs was kept, orange, rose; small bundles: of blue, lilaceous ribbons, clearly proclaiming themselves with the sound of little bells (from the cotillion); here are fans—lace ones, cut-out ones: of kidskin, of ivory,—with finely sharpened handles; there are little boxes with powder;—

—truly, there is nothing to rewipe: Mamochka rewipes all this! Risking being chased out, I steal along the little wall into the gleam of cut-glass little flagons, into the world of smells… I see myself from the mercurial surface of the toilette mirror, blown up lacelike, in very light bluish bows: before the bed is tossed out a little screen like a lacquered, bluish field; on it—golden reliefs of spreadwinged storks in the air, hanging eternally in the heavens; beyond the heavens—the bed, where on its quilted, shiny azure blanket—little pillows have been fluffed up under the lace; Mama in an azurish "pouf," complicating one leg over another leg (her legs are— bare) in a whitening blouse, in a slantingly put-on and strawcolored skirt (her underskirt), is wiping a flagon with her little towel, pressing to her knees the wiped ground-in stopper:—

—a powder compact, cut-glass from crystal; there is—a powderpuff: puff-puff-puff-puff; and—I powdered myself: I am powdered! Here there should be another little corner: I would have stuck out my mustache and nibbled: to crunch my teeth and show a black tongue to Henrietta Martynovna:

"**Ach, was wird sagen M a m a?**"—

—But "Mama"—is here; and does not see: she is rewiping the little flagons; it seems: everything has been rewiped and rewound; but—

—here with a hand she raises up under her little nose a little flagon, sniffs it, screwing up her little eyes, she keeps looking at a speck of dust; and, grabbing the little towel, she presses it to her silkrustling, yellow knees; and—

—wipes: she rewipes everything anew: in the same order; words, like babbling flies, fly from her little tongue into... the quietude of the study with a buzzing: up to Papa's ear; for this she had purposely opened the door to the study:—

—thus a fly flock buzzes under the ear into the sun; you wave a hand: it—jerks, sparkling shiningly, like a little emerald of little backs; and—it dances anew under the ear: buzzing awfully: "**buzz-buzz**" and "**buzz-buzz**"—not at anyone personally; just so, in the air!—

—Let, let, let:—

—"**those, who**" can hear, hear about "**those, who...**"—

—"Those, who think, that they've taken over science, but in life they stayed babblers,—yes!.. To have a brow with a bump and to beat the walls with it does not necessarily mean to be a clever person...

"Tfou!"

"Well, tfou to you!"

"A big brow?"—

—a rewiped little flagon is placed back; another, unwiped, is taken; and is—wiped and rewiped; and there gives out a submissive:

"Hm!"—

—behind the little alcove, from the door; it's— "**those,**" who silently sat down in their own study;—

—February is overtaking us already; it's—a windywintry month: outpouring winds are wrapped in slowpoke snows, they walk along roofs; the day is a windbag, a white whistler:—

—a smokeflight burst off from the roofs into a rotaryflight, curling into all the crossroads of Moscow, blowing about hems and fur coats in the white air, splashing snowy slush; yes; and throughwinds were borne into the windchasing days, when the darkening middays were shadowed by misty melancholy; a damp raw, multidropped gutter begins to drip: drips, drips, drips!..

. . . .

Mamochka spreads apart her hands (with the towel—one and with a flagon the other); and—bows her head onto her knees:

"Yes, this is something I understand: an apartment of twelve and more rooms; others have—an apartment of twelve and more rooms, we have"—

—a cut-glass little flagon is put back; there is taken—a cut-glass little dragon!

"Yes, this is something I understand: society balls!.."

"But what do we have?"

"Deadly mould is collecting: bald mould... Whom can we tempt? Not even a moth..."

"Yes!"

"Having complicated their hands on their bellies, they begin running finger against finger, like this Bobynin..."

"Doesn't give a tinker's dam?"

"Bigbrows!"

"Pave the roadway with brows?"

"There are stones for that purpose."

"But the hair has been eaten up by moths: should you sprinkle naphthalene on the mould? Even the flies freeze to death from the tedium,—let alone me, poor one..."

. . . .

In Papa's room—gray-leaden dusk; grayish Papa, blind and deaf, in the gray overhanging the dust of a cloth of unpleasant, gray-green color, begins to honk his nose, quietly raises his eyes and withdraws with his eyes along roofs: into the gloom of firesmokes; and—again he begins to go through the little leaves with a pencil stub; from the roof, under the cloud a very cruel oculus puffed up: of a cyclops; and—it burst with blood; and it poured downward: the blackbrowed heavens in the window:

"Others here, make use of very lucrative official apartments,—yes, academicians!"

"If you really had a brow, and not some stone, we would have long since not been living here: on Vasilievsky!"

"Yes, that's—what I say..."

"Chebyshev is—an academician, and for Yanzhul—they are preparing a place; for Yanzhul someone is going to great lengths. From Pieter..."

Book heaps throw from the windows onto Papochka a shadow, as if they were hands; and here is a curtain with which the shelves are covered, it was let down like a lamina (if you glance in on Papa, he is not an academician, but—"naphthalene mould"); it let itself down, just as if gooselike, or, more exactly a lizard puss,—not a lamina—

—a

green dragon, residing here, on the shelves, letting down its goose puss from the shelf, for sure resolved to glance in on Papochka, what he is doing there over the integral.

The stooped shoulders do not tremble: only a chair squeaked, and a leg twitched imperceptibly:

"I'm—a martyress: the Marshall of the Nobility Ball is at hand, and what am I going to go out in? In the lace one, in the altered one?"

"There are those, who suppose, that it is so: cut up carelessly some rags, and go... Mrs. Lepyokhin—sewed... We are not—Lepyokhin!"

Tearing himself away from the dusty papers, he submissively fixed his ear to the door, displaying his good, his doggy, slightly careworn profile:

"Listen, Lizochek: Lepyokhin is a man of action... Don't disturb, my friend, my calculations,"—and he shows his stooping back, having buried himself in the paper; but Mamochka, in a whitish blouse, leaps up, completely come apart; and she stamps from the screen into the blind study, fluttering with her hand the towel with a highly upheld cut-glass little flagon:

"But?"

"Are you working?"

"What business is it of mine?"

"Lepyokhin works too, but he does it—for the family; the Lepyokhins have chances to go out..."—and she begins to put under the stream of the hand washstand the red facets of a cut glass little bottom: the water splashes a cold, pearly spray; and the pedal of the hand washstand jangles resoundingly; her bustle is placed up against Papa.

Dropping his pencil, he leaps up; and—jerks in an unhurried movement toward the lamp; and—the lamp with its glasses loudly exclaimed "ding-a-ling;" and a match goes chiffuchir; and a rusty-orange light leapt up, unlacing the interlacing of flying mice; mice flittered into the corner (not mice, but shadows); but the match went out:

"Ah, damn it!"

And—from corners flying mice fly out over Papa, who hunchbacked is swept about along the table: one solid back!—

—Just as if trying to cover himself up from loud reproaches; but Mamochka, stamping her foot, turns a fluttering about little blouse, exposing an open breast with an uncombed hat of half-undone braids, sprinkling hairpins;—

—and the lamp flared up (a lampshade is put on); and—the orange color began to run along the cloth, laying down in stripes on the yellow, waxed little squares of the floor; and the former gray-lead and gray-green now turns into a shiny everything: into chocolate-orange and into green-orange (the wallpaper, the shelves are chocolate colored; on the shelves—the curtain is of green color; the cloth of green color is—on the table); and I see the stooping back of shaggy Papa; and I see the back of his head, stubborn with a difficult resolution: to keep silent no matter what, or—to burst; and I hear: from the loud little mouth against the back strikes a buzzing of yellow-orange wasps:

"There are such, **those, who...**"

"Having neither heart, nor feeling, sit, plunged into these foolish calculations..."

The fingers begin to drum along the edge of the table—

—tararach-

tachtachtach!—

—Very impertinently and firmly: a despairing challenge; but—

—stamp-stamp-stamp—

—very firm little legs began running to the back, and, sticking out a proud tummy, purposely stood so bowlegged; the elbows took a walk, the ground-in stopper had been rewiped at the heart; the little mouth foamed from sobs and screams:

"Take that: that's for you!"

And she spit on the floor...

.   .   .   .   .

"Aha: fine!"—

—the face turned with very malicious, slanting eyes, with an all of a sudden very dishevelled head:—

—just like a dog: if you chase him into a dog house, he—obediently turns, putting his puss under his tail; but there, in the dog house, don't tease him: he'll toss himself with a loud bark—

—yes: the face turned with very malicious, slanting little eyes, with a head seething with rage; and—the face with very malicious little Tatar eyes fell apart in wrinkles; it became exactly like a morel, threatening with its prickly bristles; and it became a hole, out of which gushed:—

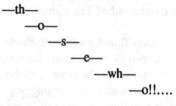

—th—
—o—
—s—
—c—
—wh—
—o!!....

. . . .

"Ah!"

"You—tyrants!"

"You—despots!"

I see: Mama's right strand of hair has become unwound; and—it hangs like a curled ring; and the left strand snaked out on the little shoulder; the mouth—was stretched out from fear and malice; a facial spot—a medusa which smacks; stings; the lips—bitten, the lips bloodily puffed up; she—steps back from Papa, whose red mask of a face, decomposing, greened; whose fivefingered paw is extended:

"If you don't be silent..."

"I..."

"Will make you be silent."

"I—give you five minutes"—

—and the heavyweighted onionshaped hourglass is placed: at the edge of the hand washstand...

. . . . . .

Mamochka concealed herself in the shadow, snapping off to the alcove and howling from there like a dog which has been kicked:

"You're not allowed to wash yourself, you brute forcer: it's mine, my hand washstand—not yours!"

But someone responds with precise malice:

"So!"

"It wasn't I who put the washstand in my room!"

. . . .

Oh, I know, what will happen: it will be horrible!

Those, who... fear nothing, who break ministers and stamp on the administrator of the surrounding district and turn Pafnuty Lvovich simply into a cutlet (raw and red), th—

—o—sss—

—sss—

—sss—

—wh—

—ooo—

—ooo—

—ooo—

—like the terrifying Lawgiver, the Sinai one—

—ooo—

—ooo—

—roar, peace, yelp,...—

—others fear the shade of the monstrous rusty cloud, secreting in itself spherical looking lightning, which sends not thunder, but straight behind the red lightning—"bash," splintering the pines around the house,—

—and I am horrified by the silence of the five quietly crawling past minutes—

—("I give you five minutes!")—

—where a second is eternity; and—I cover, squatting, my ears—until... until... until...—

—until   what?..—

—Meanwhile: until... until... until... until "**that**" (**that very!**): "**those, who**":—

—having flown up into the air, they let fall the jacket weightily to the side, to the left, the face, laid out by a black wrinkle, a gap of Chinese ink, and shading, an old deadman of lifeless face with a mouth spread-open to the ears, and screwed up slanting little eyes, decorated with red lead,—

—reminding one of the mask of the face of a Samurai, waving his saber,—

—Hokusai showed him!—

—This mask of the face of the Samurai, waving his saber is —

     —the countenance of Papa, with nose fallen to the hand, pressing... a rusted-orange nail, in order to strike the nail deafeningly: into the tin plate of the hand washstand!—

     —He had thought up this device; a device for subduing shrewishness, which at the sound of the nail... plunges into a faint: with its head onto the pillows; and—drowns in tears...

· · · · ·

 The minutes flow by until... the terrible "bash," and the darkness bangs into the red-orange color of the study, from open doors, where the precise-yellow lace of a malicious, lantern light lies... like a salamander; Mama curses from there (she doesn't have much time!) everyone: mathematicians, Granny, Grandpa (Papa and Mama are—not Mama's: Papa's...) all four of my aunts and sixteen nephews; I stop up from horror my ears and little nose with my hands, falling on my little knees to the floor; and I bow down:

 "Lord, Lord, Lord, Lord: you—bear us through this, bear us through, bear us through! Save us and have mercy on us, save us and have mercy on us, o, Lord, Lord, Lord, Lord!"—

     —suddenly: I, waved about by clouds of dust from the rusty horror of Chinese typhoons,—I hear through the fingers, with which the ears have been stopped up:

 "There are—fifteen seconds left!.."—

 O!

 O!

 O!

· · · · ·

 I open an eye; I see—

     —bash!—

     —a leg falls, a head and an arm; the leg—onto the floor; the arm—to the hand washstand; and a rusted over until it was yellow nail strikes against the tin plate of the wash hand stand:

 —"Bash!"—

     —From a mouth come-apart a bloody tongue runs out with its bent end; the spectacles fly into the air; and in an arc a handkerchief flies up from a pocket; "he" runs like one solid back, spins around and around, waves his arms, and beats the orange-rusted nail along the iron bed, along the washbasin, along the tin plate;—

—grabbing
the lighted lamp with his fivefingered hand, he stands with this lamp,
trying to smash to smithereens the lamp against the floor and crack the
lampglass, fanning up the black-bloody flame and soot, in order to push
through into the flame, to disappear in the clouds of soot...—

—The lamp
is placed down by the hand again on the desk; and for sure:—

—there is no
study: the wall flew apart in red circles:—

—and Papa;—

—growing savage
with a lance, sharply squeezing in with his legs a hairy horse, on a
collected hide, into the expanse of the far away past he chases off—like
a bent Scythian: after a Persian; more accurately: after the hide of a
Persian! And the sun burst in a flame; and the steppes smoke where
they have been burned; and the Persian makes off away from him;
pressing his head to the mane of the horse, tossing behind the neck his
shaggy hand with a shield covered with hide, on which suddenly
sounded the strike of a weighty lance, smashing the shield and sewing
the Persian to the nape of the stumbling horse: by his pierced neck...—

. . . .

When I came to: then—the study was locked; and there was
silence:—

—only in the chimney was this wind carrying on, again a drone
beginning to buzz: again this pipe-playing was carrying on: amid the
blowing days we are flying: into—

—into the little spindles of days and
shadows: without fires!..

THE SCYTHIAN

—Yes:—

—in the rounds of time:—

—a captive body, making a racket, frenzied; and in a cloud of dust: the countenance of a stooping Scythian, bent in the rusty specks of dust, beaten up by hooves, shaking a red, orange shaft of drowsy antiquity, grinning wildly,—galloped, galloped (after the Persian, a flickering miter):—

—the Scythian—barefoot, stout-heeled, in patched-up old trousers, hanging from the skin like a not skinned hide, shaggy, pock-marked; a green and wenchlike stomach pushing out above the trousers, he smiles with a navel in the shaggy ribs, from which flabby overhangs babble weakly:—

—a stupefying smell was borne spicily: of caraway grasses; howls of the lance through the air,—in an arc; and the pinned by the neck Persian, sticking to the nape, senseless from pain, glittering from the golden metals of the miter,—and he gallops, and cries; but the red sun, sitting down where it has been burned,—a brown circle: denseness, darkness; only the feet of the horses stamp, burdened in time; in the cloud of dust only two bodies pound, stooping:—of the slanteyed, wild Scythian, shouting with a raging grin, and of the dead Persian;—

—and—yes: a big arc was drawn by the times:—

—the galloping was bound up in a consolidation of dust; my body is—solid dust; and it gallops under my little breast, gallops in my little head; and I am torn apart in gallopings of thought, in gallopings of the heart:—

—so it is in the body:—

—in mine!—

—is con-summated the run along the minutes: both of the dead Persian and of the wild Scythian; hooves pound; in the little breast—a growing little lump, a bloody little lump: my Scythian!—

—sending with red lances of dreamy arteries poison; and from it an outpouring motley of Persian ornaments of thought, grow dark with the misty masses in the frosted, in the soft,—

—in my!—

—brain!..

And with leaden pains the deadman gallops along the little head...

. . . .

The picture which I saw,—was Papa with a nail, he raises an enormous fragment of the past:—

—o, it is recalled!—

—Papa once set the curtains on fire with a burning lamp, leaning over masses of books, near the window; the walls flared up shiningly, but he, tearing off the curtains, with his altogether bluntnosed heels stamped the crimson tufts of the dressing gown sticking to the floors in the bleakbrown soot; he stood, besmeared with soot, in the soot; and, very satisfied, he laughed at the exclamations:

"You ought to get a fireman's helmet!.."

Thus he became a fireman!..

Beyond this event of memory, I felt, another event taking a seat— an ancient one, ancient one: in the rage of the flame—

—were recalled—

—greater rages: wild ones, Scythian ones!

. . . . . .

Everything there is hangs: paper, wallpaper, the roll-up shades, a whisper of damask materials; and everything turns into the lace of soot after, a kerosine, red-black phoo-phooeying pillar from the lamp, which they had not turned down, beat into the ceiling:—

—in me decompose to ashes cobwebs, hairs, the felt of our apartment into a bloody fire; and like the curtain, the flaring darkness of the surrounding flies up,—into the past: I see—out of the dust, out of the caraway: the Scythian and the Persian (their struggle is in me)!—

—here the little lump started to stamp under the little breast; and—to the little throat; the vein on the neck pounds; pitter-pattered in the little rib—

—I wait until—

—there will rise up a deaf wall, like a roll-up shade, with very soft red creases in a red ray of the lance penetrating the brow: to expose the horrors of a multitude of decomposing rooms, widening away from me, like a ravine; into the expanses there—I walk, past walls, smashed apart, accurately cut apart in red bricks to the right, and to the left: there—into my past,—

　　　　—I see—

　　　　　　—walled breaks, decorated by a sunny peal of laughter, beating from distances, fallen apart into chiseled, bigheaded brows by the bass of babbling stone wenches, tearing apart their biglipped mouths; to the right some malicious deadhead has gone mad and doublepawed grabbed over the stone belly, like a silly post, with fingerless stones; I see to the left: someone has fixed his chiseled-through navel; and—it seems bright-orange, rusted, grabbed around by a flame of threatening fires; crushed stones clink from the rotten countenance onto the marl:—

　　　　　　—kee—

　　　　　　　　—ka!—

　　　　　　　　　　—some sort of countenances, some sort of keekee!—

　　　　　　—from where, out of the red I see: a Scythian; he whoops wildly, grabbing with his fivefingered hand the sparkling in the air lance and tries to smash the air to smithereens with the suddenly whistling, like a meteor, point, writing in a whirl a malicious arc on my little brow; and the little brow cracks—a broken lampglass; I fall, the Persian, bleeding; on red circles, rapidly beating out from my little eyes, splashes out my life!

PHOOEYNESS

In our apartment long ago settled in an "elder," who comes to the rooms at night: from rooms, closed by him; there—the storeroom, in which I have not been; there, probably, they pass through the dark little room (the plumber exits from there); the "elder" has long been rooted in the storeroom—in cobwebs: Phooey! barefoot, stoutheeled, in patched up old trousers hanging over from the skin like a not skinned hide, shaggy, pockmarked: a green and wenchlike stomach, pushing out above the trousers, the navel smiles in the shaggy ribs, from which two half-woman flabby overhangs babble weakly: he is bearded with chewed up felt, quietly having opened the squeaking doors; and—

—rooms!—

—rooms—

—are constructed in cor-
ridor construct:—

—running wild, cobwebs hang; bare little feet smack loudly—there, to the elder, leaning against his own cobweb, falling to his own personal paw, both gray, and dirtily overgrown—to suck; he picks with it, compressing a rusted-orange nail; he picks at a mushroomy, dried ear; but the paw is shackled by a rusted ring, exclaiming with the bunch of keys from the apartment.

He phooeys,—

—like a hedgehog!—

—evenspiritedly tossing himself on anyone who awakes; and from the tiredness of a quick run he sticks out a slobbering tongue; he begins to run through the rooms (ah, the way is long, the way is long!) to the dining room, where Granny is dolefully telling fortunes, fearing that the king of hearts, or our Church elder, Svetoslavsky, will be covered in spades; and—I rush to her knees.

"What is it, Kotenochek?"

"It's—Petrovich!"

"Come in, Petrovich!"

Petrovich comes in.

If you gasp for breath on the run—one thing is left: to fall, covering your little face—with your brow into the cobwebs: onto the floor; and you the clear bright hot phooeying of a wet nose in the back of the neck: you hear it; no, no, it doesn't bite...

At night the covered-up door is opened; and with a bunch of rusted keys the barefooted one—"stamp-stamp" about the apartment; he appears: sniffs, advances, rustles, suddenly beginning to scratch behind the ear with his foot; and I hear the stamping of the elder's foot, striking the floor, and smackings of a slobbering lip, actively clawing into the fur: to snap a flea by the tail between the teeth; he is being searched for there; and—he begins to pull, to pull:—

—with bare little feet I stamp into the past; ah,—there everything is fiery: two eyes flare up like candles; I, am grabbed,—in the wild jumps (on the back!) from the floorboard—onto the chair, and onto the table, and onto the door: through the years, through the centuries,—to the window sill: the cotton is extracted, little glasses with poison; I hung like a Berendei, I hung above the Arbat; from stone grapevines: here a green gutter,— along the gutter to the roof, there, to fatherlessness: we do not climb up; the twelfth, the twenty-fifth, the one hundred and first floor; there are no walls; only the gutter—like a stalk in unboundlessness... came to an end!

The gutter, shaken loose, here begins rocking under me; time flows from out of it under me into the widening of the gutter; twitching a hung little leg,—above which I—collapse, into knowledgeness—ah, because to sit down **"in such a condition!"** Resoluteness begins to take root: to sit it out here without a grasp of no matter what it is; that which can be grabbed onto, —is in me; in order to grab onto it, I turn myself inside out; so what? Having surpassed the limits, I exited and— sat down: on the stalk of mathematics!

I am—a mathematician, a crazy man—I shout like crazy.—

—And— ah!—

—proclaiming **"nothing,"** I impetuously fall thus,—

—like the lance of the Scythian gone wild on the dead Persian, and like a star which has punctured the earth,—the uncovered crown of an infant's head— inflames: in the brain—

—everything flared up:—

—from the sparkle of a candle!..

. . . .

"Kotik, my Kotenochek, my Kotosyonochek: what's with you, my little one? What do you want, little dove? We are here: calm yourself!"—blurted something.

"Ah, what's with you?"—something blurted.

"What, what? It's—we, it's—we: it's Papa and Mama!"

I, the quiet witless one, I see skinny-minny, Mama, with a wave of hair covering my little breast and with an embrace, bringing joy to me, falling feverishly; and I see Papa, with a little candle: in a gray dressing gown, shaggy, he phooeys, he wrinkles his brow so sleepily, fanatically; the uncovered breast is—hairy; on it barely noticeable is a hang of flab—some sort of halfwench; he—bleets: "You, my little brother, how could it be, as if... yes!"

"You have given yourself up to atavism, brother: to the experience of primitive man..."

"To pile dwellings!"

. . . .

But Mama blew up like a bean at Papa.

"But I am always telling you: here are the fruits of science..."

"The child ought to play! Why do you bother him: all your 'forces' and 'forces'..."

"What 'forces' are there..."

"The child—ought to sing, romp about, but you with 'mathematics'... He even shouts: 'Aphrosim'."

"But what is this, my little one?"

"Who is this Aphrosim there?"

Nightly restlessnesses withdraw, being replaced by restfullnesses.

. . . .

Light-eating night nibbles at all that's mine, even my sleep; and—it appears around; and lets itself blackthoughtedly down into the armchair: to sit until dawn—with the deep glooms saying to me:

"There are no bounds!"

Everywhere is—the unchangeability of the absences of everything there is; and the unchanging faithfulness of darknesses, the unchangeable malice of blanknesses; suddenly—objects dullen; and there bluens between them the presence of morning:—

—inkyblack blues flutter apart into blue blues; and gray demons appear; gray demons have sat down on the little back of the stooping armchair; I know: when they flower,—these will be whites; I will clothe myself in them: thus do all demons dress in the morning,—and they take them off in the morning, in order to run about the rooms:—

—gray demons—

— my doubts—

—they

begin to flower: they lick their lips all over; here is a chair, and on the chair whites, observing with a just deceased puss; the wall stands out already over the little bed in the place of the absences of everything there is; and—darkness takes cover; the nursery is stuck like a little nest to the small bed hanging over the precipice; in the little nest am—I; so that it doesn't fall—the house of Kosyakov was put under, and under it is placed the whole earth's sphere;—

—they flew in from the night again

to the Arbat!

Already white, all white: Henrietta Martynovna stands there like a papillote over the bed.

"Genug!"

"Genug schlafen: neun Uhr!"

"Ah, what kind of 'genug': I lay about the whole time without sleep!"

The apartment stands out like a cliff: streams of events strike, with their foam they lick the impenetrable walls; floor boards squeak under the rocking of the temporal waves; all constructs of events, alas, melt into destructs of non-events: only the walls are left; in the time running by we run inescapeably: I—with a constructo cube, Mama—with a hat carton, and Papochka with a new brochure of his: "On the Radical e— ex"; but the all-eating time gnaws at everything there is, gnaws to death everything there is: there will be nothing to eat! Septipeds of weeks run by impetuously; the floorboards loudly squeak under the heavy foot: that time always passes the same road: it limps by hours on a black leg; and everything settles down under the action of time: the floor, Doctor Pfeffer, living under it; Pils, the confectioner, living under Doctor Pfeffer; the house of Kosyakov has long ago settled down; under it the earth settles down; a blowing wind passes by thunderously along the roofs!..

Yes, everything changes in wind and time: most of all people change; objects are—more stable; but I have no faith in them:—

—the
picture of Marcian sparkles with gilding—the armchair is decorated with
cutwork; but in its little back—a hole with a broken-through tooth of a
spring and with felt hair; beyond the gilted frame—a mound of dust; the
piano, from where sounds—**this is everything**, having moved it,
they saw the boards; but that about which was sung, and that which the
keys shouted under the fingers,—where is it, where? Calico? Yes it is
torn... Playthings in which life was visible to me, like in the
raspberry clown snapping on a tambourine when you pressed on his
breast,—it seemed to have had the stuffing beaten into it: hair, felt,—
—like a raspberry clown
stuffed with this felt!—
—No matter what you break,—you see a
spring which I took out of everywhere, breaking the playthings.
O, gray demons,—my doubts; wakelessly I am stagnating in you!
. . . .
My curiosity comes from the fact that I have no faith in the fairy
tale of objects; and—I know that behind the picture of Marcian is not
the far away distance, but dust on the wall; beyond the pattern of the
wallpaper are the wallpaperless walls; and that which is fastened to
them, flies away and is arranged otherwise, like the study, which
appeared in the same place where the beds had been: two beds in a row;
objects flew about; and Mamochka sleeps in the little room by our
drawing room, spacing out into the drawing room and chasing out from
there Papa, who had just walked in:
"Get out of here: what are you loitering about for!"
I remember:—
—you awake: the dining room is—here, and the
drawing room is—there; this is—Mamochka: she was always fussing
about, she rewiped, changed, screamed, chased me, Henrietta
Martynovna, Papa from room to room and made us hope that now
would come, after all the changes—the magnificent life; it was left as
before: with hair, felt, dust and a doggy smell; the spreadpawed armchair
smelled of a doggy smell.—
—Mama tries in vain to decorate everything
with a complicated construct of objects, delivered abundantly from
Kuznetsky Most; constructs of objects are—destructs: they fell apart!
. . . .
I remember two important events in the life of objects; the satin
furniture had been wiped worn all the way through: it had been worn

out by sitting; ragamuffins dangled about; dirty cotton stuck out; in the places where the professor usually bent his gray spot were designated dark spots of his unwashed hair; here appeared the upholsterer from Kuznetsky Most: and he showed us scraps of material; we liked the blue, with the little eyes; but—we ordered the olive color; we re-upholstered the armchairs with the material, glued paper on the walls; we hung elegantly very dense shades of olive, dark shadings; but the armchairs grew gloomy from the new satin; the exact same wallpaper stared from the walls; there was hung the darkest green lantern, il-lumining all of this with a scattered-about light; elegant, but—sullen; we were fed up with the color: I longed sorrowfully for the crimson wallpaper, for the former upholstery; I remembered the crimson see-through lampshade, with the black beak, with the owlish little eyes; the crimson sparkle smashed to pieces on the parquets,—not this one, a green and pale one; now they come in; and—grow dark with green faces; they look with green faces; it seems to me: with the appearance of the olive armchairs—Mamochka has become gloomy: the red fairy tale of objects darkened into green prose:—

—There tried in vain to com-fort her—Ivan Nikolaevich Gorozhankin, the director of the botanical garden, when he unexpectedly bestowed on us a gift of reeds, rho-dodendron, ficus, palms; they placed pots of flowers all around our apartment; so what—the palms withered from the dumb window sills, reminding: that all is—transitory: all is—felt and hair!

"So—yes: that's all there is to it ... Nikolai Irasovich is also here: dust,—that's all there is to it!"

—This is—Phooey.

. . . . . .

I stare into the little corridor; it—seems to me a suspicious place; already dusk: all the roofs have sat down into darkest niches; gnawers-mice—play all the quieter; from the corridor again has come to us to glance about—Phooey:—

—it exits, sits down on the little back of the stooping chair; when it dawns,—it turns into little trousers; or—it becomes a little shirt, yes, yes: these demons are—clothes; they are put on in the morning; and they are taken off in the evening; they will run about the rooms, hanging like dustcovers and... with a deadly puss; and I shout:

"Aphrosim"—

—an ununderstandable word, the key to a secret, combining fevers and a sphere!

The fever widens out in the nights, the sphere develops quite distinctly—in the morning: with the geography of India, Persia and Scythia; the earth's sphere is—feverish; the nightly fever is—spherical:

"Aphrosim!"

They assured me, comforted me, that there is no "Aphrosim," but there is "Afrosinya," "Petrovich," a "muzhik"; but I know: that very same widening of the organs of the body without skin, in total ungraspability,—comes not from Petrovich, not from Anton (gangrene—Anton's fire—that is something!) no, a **"muzhik"** has nothing to do with it:—

—I know: the gutter which you will not overcome in one hundred thousand years: the backbone; I crawled from worm to gorilla, to... to... the widening of the sphere: of my head, on which I attempt to sit down; and I fall anew: into the antediluvian past:

I heard from Papochka:

"Reincarnation is, Lizochek,—a hypothesis of the ancients, according to which we, so to say..."

"The Hindus—had faith in it and Pythagorus recognized it; and I, you know, so to say!"—

—Tenderly he stared beyond the window: at the Persian colors of peacock sunsets:—

—the universe which was propping up my heels, here was put aside; I—lived without prop; the striking opinions of Papa against Mama, and of Mama against Papa

(—"Reincarnation is—nonsense!")—

—they were turned into shoves of two leaden spheres, quickly set in motion to the right and to the left along the weak five year old body: utter crushings.

I—in a crush of delirium was knocked out into a realm beyond my skin: and a sensation of the grave—strengthened: into a wreck of foundations—of physical, nervous and moral ones; "dependence" in me shook into independence: yes—both blank, and black.

This stalk sticking up into **"nowhere"** is—a transgression.

. . . . .

The raw damp, multidropped gutter—began to drip; and it—drips; everywhere icicles flew out from gutters with a weak crackle; the snows halvahed, they crumbled; sleigh runners, like little knives, sliced straight to the stone; throughwinds started in the windchasing days; snowfalls dampened.

. . . .

Thus I became an independent variable, disagreeing with the laws of Papa that the house does not fly upside down because of the forces of gravity; at night we all fly upside down, widening out: the law of gravity does not work; everything dissolves, gravitating neither to Papa, nor to Mama (I am smacked away by her smacks).

There began—the dissolution:—

—an American sitting above us, sensed himself very strongly, but we,—the dissolved,—fell through the roof of the house onto the flame of the constellation The Great Dog...—

. . . . .

"Aphrosim!"

I awake—

—a glassy, dark blue morning; living fires—on the snows, as if sprinkled by a broken glass—

—I awake with a confused consciousness:—

—reason is not necessary; without a rule, a limit, guilt—I sense myself; all the same I am guilty; in me strengthens the consciousness: "of guilt without guilt."

I recall:—

—why it is that Papa shouts at me when I become messed up from fright in thoughts of Mama, who may awake; if you listen— you are guilty; if you do not listen—you are guilty:—

—guilty without an end; guilty and all alone: guilty—up to the end, guilty—without reason!..—

—And for everything you get a resounding smack in the face!

I tried to please, living in sheer lawlessness; squeaking out with a tiny little mouth made-up thoughts, in order to all the quicker, having torn myself away from the malevolent worlds,—to spin out of the orbit: to sink—

—into development: **of this and that's own**—

—**m y**

own!—

. . . .

Here toward midday an outline is drawn in a goldenstreamed stream, toward midday it breaks up and everything sheds a few tears; and everything—becomes diamondlike, so that it covers evening with a coarsened film; the shiny icy ruddy glow crunches under the feet.

And then—weak February with drizzles and soft sleet slushes the streets; a yellow-raging mist sticks to the little window: and Papochka whispers to Dunyasha:

"That's something for you: our lady—from ill-health, from nerves!"

"It's shameful so!"

"Have patience: that's something for you."

. . . .

And for me the thread of the transgression is clear: these nerves are—the consequences of difficult births; the lawlessness I committed against Mama, appearing before her, and after: I planted dissension between her and Papa: selfconsciousness is—transgressive:—

—to seem eternally unknowing!—

—Yes: and if Papa would recognize this,—he would tumble his head downward with his study: seven shelves, striking into the deaf ceiling, they would break through an opening; Papa would with a volume of Sophus Lie, the Swedish mathematician, tumble down there:—

—into his own black precipices!

. . . .

"Those, who" are—precipices: the dissolution of forces; the "nail" is—lawlessness; I walk up to it, crawling out with my legs: to overturn all constructs, to overthrow rules;—

—Phooey phooeys in me; he was walking past, he was coming: a bigheaded gorilla, a Scythian ("Reincarnation, my Lizochek, so to say!"); he had been employed as the progenital, as a congenital and domesticated animal, he became—the progenital domestic spirit;—

—yes!—

—He, chomping on the Papa in Papa, begins chomping on the me in me; it is evident: the universe is,— "phooeyness!"

. . . .

"Eh, yes the fever has appeared!"

The slush sours; everyone coughs; I cough; they await Smirnov, the domestic doctor; my little body is—burning hot; in the veins, in the ears very distinctly: it shushes, phooeys; I am waiting for Phooey—barefoot, stoutheeled, in patched-up old trousers, to stick out his felt hair from the corridor doors; and it seems to me, that a green and wenchlike stomach, stuck out above the trousers, drummily bleats with a dull, silly navel.

The sound of the bell: two sounds (at the doors, and in the ears)!

This is Doctor Smirnov; he runs in to me: an elderly man—little yellowspots under his moustache, and—how he taradiddles!

"Don't talk"—he waves his bald little head—in spectacles, in golden ones:

"Eh, that's it! Yes-yes-yes, yes-yes-yes, yes-yes-yes!"

The little shirt is tossed up, and— he presses his head to the burning hot little body: he pokes with a pipe; and he goes "rat-tat" with his tiny hammer along the body:

"Breathe in... Again... And again... And again: deeper, deeper; that's it... that's it... Aha!"

He waves his little head, running from the bedside table to the little table: he writes a prescription; having written it out, he slaps his palms very gayly:

"Well now, brother: well you get it; you get the castor oil: castor oil for a start," propping up his hand with the pipe on his respectable waist; with the other he collects a white tuft of his beard, lifts it up to his nose; and chuckles thoughtfully into the tuft of beard:

"And then: a piece of oilcloth goes here; and on the oilcloth, this here, cloth...   We have to fold it in fours, press out the water... And with cotton, cotton on top... Keep it on three hours..."

"And then?"

"Do the same thing!.."

You ask:

"Do I get some of the sour stuff..."

"No-no-no, no-no-no, brother: no-no, no-no-no..."

Here they stand around Smirnov: both Papa, and Mamochka.

"What?"

He—wrinkles his brow, winks and with a shake of the little head with "eh-eh" he sours in a yellow-lemon grimace, glancing up through his spectacles at Papa:

"Eh, rrregular brrronchitis!.."

And—immediately: without any break:

"And thou—what's up, brother?" (He is a classmate: as soon as they meet, they begin to "**thou**" each other):

"I—nothing"—thous Papa—"how are things with thee?"

Having overthoued each other, they come to a stop in front of one another; and they can say nothing, except:

"Thou, brother, thou..."

Smirnov remembers about Bismarck:

"Three little hairs!"

And he lets down his little eyes: he bellows and pants (everything has been said: they have been thoued through and through; there is nothing else to talk about); and he grabs one palm in the other palm, as though frightened, shooting out the exclamation:

"Well, brother, so long: brother,—there are ill patients, ill patients!.."

Grabbing his peaked cap (he walked in a peaked cap), wrapping himself tighter in his overcoat, waving his gray little beard this way and that, as though scalded, he leaps up from...:

"Yes-yes-yes, yes-yes-yes, yes-yes-yes... Don't tell me: three little hairs,—and—everything here... yes-yes, yes-yes-yes!"

I am already more at ease; and everyone is at ease; naturally: "rrregular brrronchitis!"

"Yes-yes... So that the sour stuff: no-no-no-no; so that the oil-cloth, cotton, cloth."

Everything—is fulfilled; and they say of Smirnov:

"Now, Sergei Vasilievich: he's always the same; both gay, and hearty; a bachelor and a simple man."

"Yes, now Sergei Vasilievich: he is the gayest, the simplest; and—a clever person; now that's whom we ought to give our Dotya to in marriage: he was after all interested..."

"Yes, but she—chuckle, chuckle, chuckle!"

They bring me the capsules; you open them,—the capsules are somehow sticky; they look with eyes, in little papers, like from candy; I already know: you touch it: and so—the capsule begins: to turn its eyes around and around!

I recall:—

—such eyes—of Mrs. Doktorovsky; she turned her castor oil eyes around and around at the very handsome Grot; and I oppose it: it is positively offensive; the castor oil eye of Doktorovsky is sweet, and stickily crushes my tongue; I cannot swallow it; and it—burst in my mouth; what was there!—

                    —I took it when Papa, tumbling in with a
new verse composed on this occasion, shouted it into my ear, while I
was swallowing the capsules, smiling with little tears:

> All's in vain: it's horrible after all!..
> Ah, it's only castor oil!
> Why the tears? What look is this?
> All's in vain: it's magnificent after all:
> Kotik—can't you see: this oil
> Will help cure your bronchitis.

It is not in vain that Papochka writes me verses: with them he
creates an enormous power over me; he is—powerful; he is secretive; I
read this secret; and ate that, the forbidden one; a round lump in my
throat pounds: like an apple—in the little throat, becoming swollen at
night, breaking my limits, with the development of the Tree, from the
height of which they eat apples.

I fell, like Adam, calling forth a guess on the part of Mama (she
is—penetrating); here she comes in up to the patient ill "with
development" (she comes to me); and she tests the little brow:

"There is still a little fever!"

And on her is—a wingedhorned hat; and—in a black veil, in her
blackplumed boa, in a black blouse, in black gloves, with a not very
wide bustle she passes into the anteroom, inquiring, where is the
naphthalene: soon the winter things are concealed away; the furcoats are
sent off to Belkin,—for conservation against moths.

It seems to me: Mamochka tests the little brow not because there
is—fever; but because the little brow is growing (this little brow is a
little sphere);—

                    —all of that which appears during the days, like the
round and firm little sphere, that is during the nights—a little fever; and
the little fever is—from **"development"**:—

                    —A little seed of mature
antonovka, smelling like Papa, swells, like a throbbing of the little
brow: it breaks my little brow, my brow is broken by two horned
branches; here—the ends of the branches—

                    —little horns—

                              —slice through!

Ah, it is exposed: the apple—has been eaten!

The branches are—concealed; but one leaf is exposed: it is—a fig leaf; the fig will grow up, will grow up; and it came to be: it's not a matter of the book, but of the fig (under the book).

. . . .

A warm wind blew; the snows softened; the street dripped; the wet walls seemed more ancient, more congenital, tinier; thus Arbat burst into tears, the severe bare icing on the streets strengthened; the month's moon, a simple darkness, became a clear twinkling; drawn out of the air March; drizzles began to drip.

The spring month arrived with an icehardened ruddy glow, which during the day is—overflowing puddles, during the evening—films and little films of ice and fragile wings of glass dragonflies, and the hanging of icicles; in the dryness very dark bald spots dampen more often; and there is no longer any white snow, but—a yellowish-brown, yellowish-dungcolored; they run into three streams—into the entrance gates: little papers, little boxes, the outbearing of sand from the courtyards.

In the end, I recovered: and we go out to take a walk, for the first time... Where is the little snow? O, how everything has changed!

I love to observe the space under the gate in spring—

—and I know from where what flows: from this little courtyard will trickle the purest clarity; from this one—a murky brown swill; they flow together: and the murk enlightens, and the clarity browns; and from Greenblatt's are borne out: the seven colors of the rainbow; if I glimpse a rainbow circle; this—signifies: it had flowed out from the courtyard belonging to the white house, Greenblatt's.

March: yes, people walk on the streets in their new clothes; and a young lady in a bluish blouse heaves clearly her redwinged hat, in a gray little veil, fluttering ahead of its time a raspberry little umbrella; there comes a young fellow in a very yellow coat, in very red gloves and in new galoshes; yes, everything—became short: the fur coats disappeared, although under the feet there is still a chocolate mud, freezing, it becomes a pale firmament; cheeks are rosy; and the noses of young ladies are rosy; the white hares hanging by their feet at the entrance to the meat stores, disappeared: only gray hareshang—they stare with a bloody little puss; the smells of smoke and burning are exchanged for the smell of rotten eggs; little greens shops reek of cabbage leaf; soaked apples are being sold.

In the house they clean out the putty; and—it banged, they crashed: the troubles of tramping, the grumblings of groans of loud cabs flying

by, which are dragged slowly after the flying sleighs; the cabdrivers
have bent backs; and everywhere are smacks: of sticky mud.

And there—a selfwilled smoke passes selfrunning like fleecy clouds
in the heavens; and—the voice of the pedlar:

"Fresh eggs"—

—bursts through the window...

. . . .

Ah, how shameful the act—mine, my very own: to eat on the q.t.
the herring tail: from the sauce boat!

"Where is the herring tail?"

"Dunyasha?"

"Again!"

"A unimaginable disgrace..."

Mama with the ring with the turquoise—hurls the turquoise against
the little table: and here—the turquoise flew out from the ring (the ring
will be given for repair to Raspopov, the goldsmith,—on the Arbat).

"Henrietta Martynovna,"—Mamochka here spread her arms and
threw her head—before herself: toward Henrietta Martynovna:

"You, maybe?"

The little eyes (leeches)—drank in; Henrietta Martynovna threw her
napkin onto the table cloth, having rosened just a bit.

And—into tears:

"Nein, nein!"

"Gott sei dank!"

"I ain't come yet to dis!"

And—she exited from the room; here something in me went pitter-
patter. I had—come to this!—I imagined my fate in this:—

—Mama
comes quickly up to me, and jerking me painfully by the arm, pulls me
up to her, shoves me, waving her hands:

"You little thief: the herring tail—you stole it!"

And grabbing the little comb, she starts to comb my curls, in order
to reveal the big brow; and on the brow—to the right, to the left—grow
tumors, i.e. horns:

"Look!"

"Admire them!"—

—I imagined it so clearly; meanwhile: Papa, began
drumming his fingers on the tablecloth:

"You, my Lizok,—you did it in vain: ai, ai—how could you... A girl from a poor Livland family,—and... the suspicion... A herring tail!"

But Mamochka, pressing her neck, and sticking out her chin—uff: Puff-puff-puff!

"You—make no mistake: she ate twenty-five mandarins recently; I came in—reached for the sack with the mandarins: skin and pits! Where are the mandarins? I searched, searched: swore at Dunyasha, swore; she—confessed: 'I—ate them.' 'How' I said—'could you eat twenty-five?'—'Yes: first one; I—liked it; next another; and thus one after another I ate them: Forgive me, please.' I said: 'How come you are not ill?' 'It's nothing!' she answers."

"Please, don't mess me up: I know, what I am talking about..."

Papa spread his arms, and how he thunders in a peal of laughter:

"How, twenty-five mandarins?"

"Ha-ha-ha-ha-ha!"

"Without Asian cholera?"

"May I say..."

"Yes!"

"An amazingly limited nature..."

They forgot about the herring tail; I—did not forget; and—I fell into Mama's arms.

"I... I!"

"What is it?"

"The herring tail: it seemed to me so tasty!"

"So—you?"

"And—not a word?"

"You prig!"

But Papa, leaping up with a napkin threw himself straight at me; and in his palms he pinched my little head:

"Ah,—how could you!"

"The herring tail!"

"Leave his tail be!!"

"Leave the herring tail be!!!"

And Mama left it.

. . . .

I became a "prig,"—o, if she would know in what measure.

And so somehow she looked askance (a keen one)!

Papa does not know that it is forbidden for us to be friends: we can develop ourselves without Mama—not with Mama: stealthily; and

Papa—does not know, that developings are harmful to me; sinful feelings come; therefore I love to develop myself, understanding, that a clear butterfly turned out her own wings from the cocoon; Papa read this from Baer's zoology, Papa was reading for himself one little book: of visual learning; and having learned to learn visually, he visually teaches me: Baer's zoology appeared at our place; here he thunders off, scratches himself under his lip with a bent finger; and—sucking in the air through his teeth like sweet syrup, he indicates with his hand the little picture of a gigantic oak; and—he becomes a ruddy show-off: he stuck out his head, and looks, placing two fingers under the glasses of the huge spectacles: and—wheezes, and—sniffles:—

—and at the felling of the gigantic oak—a little square; men and ladies dance at the felling...

"Hee-hee" he picks at the air with his nose—"hee: here-here-here!"

"But, tell me please!"

"The tree!"

"Is an American one!"

"Now that there is a tree!"

Turning over the page, he jumps onto the chair, spreads his hands in the air:

"Here is, my little brother,—such a scandal: do you know, the monkey is—chaintailed"—he plays with words.

"Well—repeat it!"

I repeat:

"Chaintailed!"

The nose, like a frog, begins to leap:

"This ram is made of stone: he throws himself about, the rascal, from the slanted slopes, onto his own horns."

Papa's mouth is overfilled with beasts (and I—am bestialized); he is all—a grainery; my head is—a sharp little beak; it—pecked its fill of the grain, the grain of knowledge; Mama from the bedroom shouts:

"Here!"

"Come here!"

She—knows, that this development is—"phooey"; it is—congenital, domestic, domesticated; it walks along my veins, I will be—"phooey"; during the days I will, having put on my spectacles, calculate, and nights—I will have an axe to grind, widen out; I will be a "muzhik"—stoutheeled, shaggy—show a wenchlike green stomach, sticking out above the trousers, and shaggy ribs, where two imageless flabby overhangs are barely noticeable; I will walk looking like this to... Dunyasha, hearing from Dunyasha reproaches, that it is very embarassing for her... with such a muzhik.

I know, I know: "the herring tail" is—the beginning of the end; there will be a more important one—the tail of the "white salmon" from Generalov!

The policeman on duty will grab me; they will—lead me in:

"Look: with the tail!"

Papa sullenly gazes, so as—to hit the "nail" on the head with me.

"Well, and this good-for-nothing, Lizochek, we'll..."

Expelled!

And—"**paradise**" will come to pass between Papa and Mama: they go to a correction home, they go to whip with the copper, belt buckle this "**one's own**" out of me.

When Mama flayed me by the curls, with one side I prayed for this "sinner"; well, but with the other I knew: she is—right that she flays me for the original sin, for "**phooey**"; and—night approached: with a bunch of rusted keys the barefoot one—"stamp-stamp" about the apartment: he appears: sniffs, advances, rustles, suddenly beginning to scratch behind the ear with his foot; and I hear the stomping of the elder's foot, striking the floor, and—the chomps of a slobbering lip, actively seizing onto the fur: to snap a flea by the tail; and with bare feet I stomp into the past; ah,—there everything is fiery: two eyes flare up, like candles: I—am a grabbed nameless one: in wild leaps—through years, through the ages, through the gutter: we crawl, we do not crawl up:—

—but the gutter is—my height; I'm—on the gutter, twitching a hung foot, apparently exceeding the limits—from the stalk (of mathematics)—

—I am falling!..

"Kotik, my Kotenochek, my Kotosyonochek: what's with you? What are you doing, little one? It's we: Papa and Mama..."

And Papa in a housecoat—shaggy (the uncovered breast is—hairy):

"You, my little brother, what is this: is this how you develop yourself?"

And—with a little smack he dropped with a thud backwards, into his own room; I hear—he tosses and turns; and sneezes: he cannot sleep; he goes chiffuchir with a match, stalking about in little tomes of Sophus Lie, the Swedish mathematician; previously, when the two beds stood there in a row—he slept, did not read, always fearing to frighten off mother's sleep, a very keen one; now the study has been turned into the drawing room, the bedroom turned into a study; here he romps going chiffuchir, sneezing and phooeying; gray demons drop in there; I know: the gray demons are—whites.

. . . .

Cumulus clouds, graying, curtain off the heavens and earth; and time, a frightened hare, pressing in its own ears, runs into the yellowing scum.

. . . .

I am amazing: they dress me—in silks, in laces; and coquettishly curl very dark curls on my shoulders; and they cover my brow—up to the future bald spot;—
         —I am—
              —just like a girl.
The curls are tossed back:—
                    —the brow changes me; the little mouth is—slightly enlarged; it—jerks with a half-smile, cunning, with double entendre, and from the sleepless little eyes, screwed up, inset into circles, having darkened, of enormous orbits there breaks through like gigantic eyes—
          —an archgreen: terrifying!—
                  —Locks, a dress, bows—a face mask: an orangutang squats behind it!

. . . . .

> Let's get him a bowler hat,
> Let's get him a new frock coat
> Then some comme-il-faut cloth pants
> In which to thrust his little hands!

. . . .

SPRING

And everyone knows:—

—under the rose house, where white maidens
dignifiedly held the cornice on the solid stone backs of their heads,
bending their torsos, withdrawing into the ivy (under the navel) and
secretly turned into a stand for the torso of white stone, complicating
the widening of a water fountain, between the windows, where over the
glass, from an oval, a ramhorned scoffer showed a round little mug—
—that house they broke apart long ago; in this place rose a huge heap
of stone—

—everyone knows:—

—under the rose house, where maidens held
the cornice,—there flounders about; a white bubbly comb by the naked
pebble—just like seethrough, radiant beads: it blows up with a multitude of clear little bubbles, it bursts; new ones are blown up; the foam
runs from it slobberingly, water thundering in a waterpipe; ah, everywhere—a discharged waterflow; from the space under the gate to the
curb; little boys throw a paper ship into the curly combs; piles of split
pieces of watery snow are plopped up; everything is—soiled; everywhere—the gay **"chirp"** of sparrows; someone, all soiled, runs in a
chocolate-colored bowler hat, crushed and put on aslant, in an overcoat,
hung with old tatters and not covering up the tail of a frock coat,
brushing with a wave of the hand,—I did not recognize the runner: this
is—Papochka, not noticing us;—

—still yesterday I had seen on him the
bowler hat of palegray color (his, the black one,—is lost); he was
holding the crooked handle of a hung-open umbrella; today he has on a
bowler hat—chocolate; and the umbrella has—no crooked handle, it is
turned-in, newish.

March gayens the Arbat, but it is sweeter on Kislovka; the rose
Kislovsky house, like a candy from Felsh; tin cans sparkle in the
window of Retteré (coffee—**"mocha"**): Monsieur Retteré is graying;
we go into the shop opposite: later there was a display here of frames
and splendid pictures—**"The City of Nice."** This was not there at

that time; the green "**Hope**," which opened in just eighty-seven with little notebooks, tracing paper, colored paper and other temptations, was not there at all; the ladies of "Hope" later greeted me amiably (that one, the skinny, blond one —not so much, but the other, the full-figured one,—very much so); the Arbat residents know "**Hope**"; and they knew the "wine merchant" Popov; but who remembers "Burov," who used to buy canes and umbrellas at his place? The house, where he carried on his trade, wooden, brown,—was borne away by stormy time; here is— the Neidhard house, the Patrikeev house, the Starikov house—

—from

where—

—with sausages, tea, and fruits "**Vygotchikov**" teases (afterwards "**Kogtev**" teased from here); I wait; he—pushes through the door: to invite the buyer,—a proud, doublesideburned, snubnosed, bald; and—in an apron; he snaps the abacus; and—looks out for "**the little ones**"; ah, how the selfresounding ear burns, the overflowing warmth of puddles cools off into treasure frames of cold; on a fiery frame someone is borne off into the green heavens. Yes, March!..

. . . . . .

In the month of March all perceptions are—fresh, light, musical; and Mamochka is—too: light, musical, springy—

—she bends with a

sigh over the piano keys—

—grows thoughtful; smiles; and—

—don—

—don—

        —don—

                —don!—

                        —gives out on the keys.

With a bent, tiny pinky the little hand tossed about; and— everything lightened; everything—shone; our dining room was constructed of sound, made of sound; it revealed itself for view:—

—I saw—

—light lilies flying flowingly onto white wallpaper; I heard how with some response the yellow buffet was filled, oakbodied, which was usually crazed, was aroused; and—it answered with a tremble to the stride; how the ringing sounds of glasses melodically answered its sounds; three little busts rose: Pushkin, Tolstoy, Turgenev; the buffet was aroused: the little busts fell; the box rose like a black cutwork tree; it stuck out its jaw, covered with a black lip; the lip opened into a singing whitetoothiness of keys; and here and there the fold-out candlesticks turned bronze: Mama was sitting down to play—

—in the cornflower-blue gayish blouse, throwing fingers into the air and falling with a finger on a key; she was sitting down to play the same thing that she often played, which I am unable to make out,—is all of this good or bad:—

—aha!—

—here it is: what is it? I do not know, but I do know that it is—"**this**"—

—aha!—

—how there are thrown out, how tossed out with powerful sounds, producing disorders, in agreement with one another: all of the world is reconstructed now: and I am reconstructed: not to recognize any of that,—

—which—

—lorded over my soul before this: but Mama will close the piano—

—I will forget everything, I will not recall: it returns back with the return of the roulade:—

—the fold-out candlesticks illumine Mama with burning candles; Mama closes the lip: the black box—the piano; the picture of Marcian hung over it with its withdrawing distances (I withdrew into these distances, pressed by the heavy frame); the wall candleholders lightly turned bronze; and over the oak table from a fruit circle the glass lamp with a seethrough hemisphere was hung resoundingly with a quiet rattling on a bronze chain; the pull-up shades showed through with flying lights from walnut strong baguets; under them the leaves of spread-apart palms lay flat; from the window sills, from the windows, from the white wicker baskets, even from the floor; from the corner, to the ceiling, went out a tossed out rhododendron; and there—a wooden clock head hissed the hours; under it blackened, just like a Negro, amazing one on all fours, a folding card table; along the walls and windows evened out by their bent backs were the chairs with the wicker seats, ready to fly about any way you like; arranged this way and that; and—again to fly back to the walls.

. . . . .

The open door led out into the drawing room; everything here is— olive: the walls, wallpaper, curtains, wall drapes, **brocatel**, or the satin upholstery, of the furniture; the general impression: beautiful, but how—nameless! All the objects keep quiet; here everything is— timeless; everything here is— exitless, atmosphereless, voiceless; everything is—nameless; an illusion: placed up to vision; put aside, it will be—non-illusory; but there is no place to put it aside; the illusion—stands!

And—

—the lantern hangs from a fashioned fruitwood circle like a facetless, dull-blownup; in the evening it timidly emanates a loss of faded light; there stands between white doors, covered with an olive damask, a stocky roundtopped walnut cabinet: on it—two goddesses, two tiny, alabaster statuettes, and between them precisely came through weighty with yellowing gold the bronze of the high stand of the light-giving hexacandelabrum (it—impresses one by its beauty without candles), threelegged touching the cabinet and raising with yellowing from the gold a sacrificial altar (a bronze one) in the shape of the beginning of a fountain, curled with a garland, where twisted heads of bronze, yellow rams clench with their lips assortments of garlands; on the fountain grew a curlygolden vase, from the body of which some kind of degenerates showed their pusses; the leafy metal of its very-very high pivot ended in a flowery golden blow-up, a bronze bend of delicate fivebranches and delicate rosettes of the candlesticks; the top was crowned with a sixth rosette; the interweaving of the capricious curls of metal occupied me;—I loved to observe the candelabrum; and I loved the olive soft divan, raising its back with the high, walnut, cutwork edge; four walnut, cutwork pusses grinned from the edge; among them—a cutwork of curls; I look,—and I want to bite the pusses: they are chocolate colored.

And of such a color is the walnut, cutwork solid dining oval, raised by the bend of firm walnut blow-ups—of the three legs, curled with a garland of fruits and touching with its lionpawed cutwork the carpet; on it plushly dulled the tablecloth, hanging over the legs with fringe and long ragamuffin; yes, I looked—into the motley of this tablecloth, colored through and through with black rustyish background, where three motley colors curled chasing one after another in spirals, com-plicating a flowerlike ornament—orange, rusty and yellow, rarely dis-turbed by a blueeye, there—a redeye, but in general giving the look—a tigery one; the wiped carpet, also tigery, as if of such compositions, lay flat under the table, under four squatting, very spreadpawed arm-chairs;—their gesture was to me a suitably frightening look of four professors squatting on their haunches, their hands placed on their knees; four deans squatted here on their haunches: to sit in conference; and the cutter had carved them out; and the polisher covered them with lacquer; the pitiless upholsterer upholstered their knees with satin: the four deans became—squatting armchairs! And arriving guests sat on them: they composed their restlessnesses from words, their rapid shorthand of incoherent words; here ladies sat like beans;—and leafed through albums under the lampshade, satiny olive, with blonde laces; here through the rustling of skirts and fluttering of little mouths is borne to me the deep bass of a coarse voice: everything becomes lacey; and there waft—perfumy spirits;—

—among the ladies I observed a special, dumb conversation, turned toward one another; and—composed of gestures; they would announce to one another some bits of information which are to me and to the men completely ununderstandable; one lady would cry out to another lady:

"How pale you are!"

The lady—maintains silence, but she pulls up her little head to the lady and raises her brows: with the hands of both little arms one placed in front of the other she indicates the bottom of her stomach, barely sticking out her lips; the other immediately guesses, barely nodding; and she quickly changes the conversation, having received a clarification.

For me there is no—clarification!..—

—I observe in the corner a threelegged cabinet: a sideless cabinet! On it is arranged a white-headpiece of dolls; this is—china: a shepherd, a shepherdess in a straw hat, in a china, in a rose skirt, a gray pug-dog; and—an Italian, painted (brightbrown and with an **ocarina** in his hands) and some sort of Berendei-plaything; and a headless Chinaman;—

—and a multitudinous multitude of very occupying things exist timelessly here; many armchairs, curtains, **brocatels** on the furniture; everything is so beautiful, but everything is so exitless, atmosphereless, voiceless; everything is—nameless, an illusion: placed up to vision; put aside—by sounds; sounds fly in, reconstructing everything and attuning the new.

. . . . . .
"Mrmlya"—gives out here!
"Mrmlya"—

—a very complicated chord:—

—it lies down with a teary, wet sourness on the keys; and with septaccords and nonaccords it is conducted: a black little bone—"re"; "dlya-dlya-dlya" is a triad; "mrmlya"—

—a very complicated chord: shouts out, like... Almochka; no, louder than Almochka: it converses, like... Mama:—

—everything flickered, everything began to wink into my soul; the candlesticks began to tinkle in little circles; the walls are pulled up, they grew; just as if they had widened out to the height of the ceiling; they delved deeply and became impossibly lookthrough—

—already on little wheels one armchair is wheeled to an armchair; on tiptoes, suddenly having flown through and heightening from the bursting sounds,—it stands!

In the music something limitless is imaged: Granny, I, Auntie Dotya, Dunyasha,—we understand; Papa—doesn't: here he exits to howl from time to time in the sounds; and to sing clarifications, setting the limit:

"Yes, Lizochek: of course... Music is mathematics which has not achieved clarity..."

"Leibniz still said"—he attempts to flare up with a green spark, like Mama's faceted earrings.

"Here the very rational clarity of the French thinkers helps"—he attempts to flare up anew with red clarity; but not he flares up, but once again the earrings flared.

"Mist! It's the Germans letting loose the mist!"

But the clarity of French thinkers bursts under the sounds of Schumann: he does not understand music; and—he calls everything that gallops along the keys there—a shooing noise: not Schumann; there gallops not a shooing noise, but—

—a gay little pension of tiny girls; all—in pelerines, and tra-lya-lya-lya:—

—the little girls began to run, the whole pension skipping: quickly they organized in pairs; skipping, quickly they passed into the corridor:—

—the corridor door closed: the piano is closed: the candlesticks go out...

FELLOW TRAVELER

The minutes ran like little girls along the little corridor; with their eternal little pension; the hand of the clock moved, because they ran; on Sunday, having risen, grunting, onto the longtime rocky chair, accompanied by the exclamation:

"You'll break the chair that way"—

—Papa set the time for me, turning the clock spring; and—

—trr—

—trr—

—trr—

—the turning points wheezed, winding: Mondays, Tuesdays, Wednesdays: and—"trr-trr-trr"— until Saturday: inclusive!

A new week began ticking!

. . . .

The days fell out speckled: here—the sun, there—a shadow; here— a little snow, and there—a little rain; the snows were dissolving; and I passed through days muddy from chocolate puddles, the snow mumbling from the speech of shovels and the gay splashing of cabbies; by evening March was—a shining March; it set up a crunching of icy cockleshells; with my foot I step on the cockleshell of a puddle: and under the cockleshell dark spots quickly sweep about; and—a little foot withdraws into the little puddle. Larks flew to the Sevastyanov house; from Sevastyanov's they flew to us: ruddy and delectable; I love to pick out the raisin-eyes; and tastefully snack on the little head: edible and delectable—totally incomparable; you eat a bit—afterwards there rises up to your little throat a "hic"!

The week flew by: and Papa—leads in another one, an April week:—

—in the young spring they picked out the putty; and—in the young spring we pushed through into thundering crashes; dryspots were imaged there, where slimy softspots dirtied; the doughnut man walks about the courtyard; his catchphrase is heard:

"Little boys, I've brought you doughnuts sweet as honey: won't you bring me all your money!"

The pedlar bawls like a throatsplitter "buy-sell"; a water barrel bangs thunderously: and they set up the furniture with the pallid colored upholstery: they beat it with a carpet beater; the carpets slam loudly between two floor polishers; life in the courtyard occupies me! The oakennosed dildo, Anton, is spread wide there not in a sheepskin coat, but in a rose calico; he is hurrying: to swear off into space; a red cock hurries behind a whitehaired chicken; grabbing her by the neck feathers with his pinching beak, he crushes her plumed back with the feathery spurs of his feet, rocking his bloody comb all together back and forth.

At our place—there are changes: yellow moths are borne in the air; in the anteroom are two of Papa's hats—the brown one (an alien one) and a gray one (the same). And Papa crawls up on a chair; and—the third week is lead in; he is a timemaster: a ringmaster! An amazing person!

. . . .

Squeaky and simple, but he is—secretive; he squeaks and hurries at the whole house, turning with a fuss among us, disturbing the order: with a helpless call to order; no, he is not cunning, but... some secret had been inserted into him: he is sealed, riveted, like a barrel, which with a din is thrown down the stairs, can in its turning crush one very painfully, leaping over what it meets, so that when it has fallen, the split wood jumps up and crunches one.

There is no turning away from the momentary run-outs with a pencil stub into the dense thicket of domestic cares, understood by him in his own way with lightning speed (and not at all from the right side); and immediately resolved in the wrong direction: Papa—short, an oaken barrel, began to crash, puffed out he throws himself with his brow stronger than strong coconuts; and breathing out smells of felt with his harsh stubble, he rolls off with very hurrying little eyes into your idea from spectacles, raised by fingers, from which is borne sealing wax, with a shouting, somehow shrill, wenchlike, and somehow obtrusive, mouth—all shaggy, browless:

"What are you doing?"

"Allow me!.."

"You're doing it all wrong..."

"How can that be?"

"Like this..."

You roll back: the moved table passes very heartily in the wrong direction on little copper wheels, banging into Dunyasha's hips with its walnut edge:

"Ouch, Sir!"

Having banged his clumsypawed act on the white wall, where the lightest lilies pour out, and borne off, like an oaken barrel under the yellow buffet, he stumbles; and wooden masses answer in a seethrough tremble with ringing sounds of glass.

"Ah: you've messed up everything!"

"You ought to get out!"

Papa, falling, jumps up and crunches, falling to pieces on the squared beam—helplessly, running across frightenedly with eyes exchanging glances:

"Ah, as a matter of fact..."—

—you wait: in the barrel is cooped up the mould of slimy herring, or bunches of grapes, sprinkled with sawdust, but out falls:—

—a soft raspberry outpouring of dear muslins, of magnificent moires and shiny fires of Arabic materials; you—are amazed:—

—flights off into the dense thickets of cares are directed by the norm of practical philosophy of the Stoics, which is—in the Diogenes barrel; they riveted it into oaken forms and into a very wide jacket, blown up by the vanity of puffs:—

—and the fingers jump like a pea; from under the vest the half-belt of the shirt shows itself:

"You should pull up your belt!"

He pulls it up, and—the former is exposed: the half-belt of the shirt; thus he retreats with the half-belt straight into his study from the dense thicket of cares: into—the carelessness... of integral computation...—

—Yes, in the Diogenes barrel sits "**content**": with a sunny dance and a sunny ruddy glow; and the barrel thunders, but Diogenes is invisible in it; he jumps out suddenly from the crunched barrel with a lantern; and he begins running in a commotion with the tenderest of eyes:

"Where is the man?"

The eyes seem like tiny little swindling mice; from the thicket thunderously is given out only the "**belch**" of everyday occurrences: just like in the belly:—

—from above it aa-oos with a delicate weeping:

"Aaa-ooo!" On a floor lower, how it belches; and the "**belch**" goes like a roll of thunder: from top to bottom: from right to left!..—

—Already a cloud has become solidly swollen behind another cloud; May thunder clouds roll into the swelling of dumb smokeheads; the glazed green roofs sparkle; and—the self-flying fluff frizzes; the thunderbeating street ohs; I know: very soon the lightflying swallow will fire a shot in the window ...

. . . . . .

Papa passes by stealthily, on tiptoes, hunching without a murmur from the inconvenience, borne by him, all in pranks, childish and sparkling; he is—expelled from the rooms; trying to be the equal (a professor—with a professor, with a yardman—a yardman), he lowered himself into a halfsquat before the nose; and because of this all the "tiptoers" measured Papochka from above with haughtiness:

"He is—lower!"

And Papa jumped up here, chucking,—the scoundrel, the professor, the buffoon, the minister! They did not understand these Aesopian appearances in domestic life: to bitch about prejudices with Stoic thought, complicated from the reduction of the denominator and numerator of the fraction of cares, and being a new **means**, as for example: the **means** of peeling a potato:—

—"First"—he bends the pinky, drums out, throwing up words with a pen knife with a very loud click of his heels—"the potato, yes, yes, it was very difficult, believe me, to transfer it to the Old World..."

"Second"—he bends with a bow the next, the nameless ring finger—"it was very difficult, you know, to introduce it among us!"

"Third"—he breaks for some reason his big, own naily thumb, left with the third and index finger; and raising his hand with two fingers over the kitchen's offspring-fumes, like the schismatic priest, Pustosvyat, he walks like thunder about the little kitchen...

"Third: you have to pass from the Flint Age to the Iron Age, in order to get to the knife, Afrosinya; the union of the knife into the matter of potato peeling is, Afrosinya, a sum, the integration of very complicated questions of culture"—

—here start "**ahahs**," here start "ahohs"; and the much-steamed kitchen strikes a sound: Afrosinya, Dunyasha, and I—

—on the q.t. I snatch a savage radish: a savage radish!—

—And from the stove door the fire runs in combs; and a log snaps; it is clouded with smoke and spit upon with saliva; and hissingly sang out, twirling, a luminous unclarity; sunflower seeds were thrown about everywhere on the floor; that signifies that Anton had been sitting here; and he grabbed around Dunyasha; here there were chuckles and scuffles; there sat at some distance on the chair a familiar old wench,—a biddy; this very stout biddy was called a bitch (a foulmouthed beldam!) I know: the witch-bitch was biting on her juicy chomps; yes, and she yawned wide now her yellow mouth; and sat bigbreasted and sweat bigpussed, puffing out her belly; she was greased over in yellow lusters—

—Papa, not seeing the smirks, hovered over Afrosinya and la-la'd his own:

"The peeling of potato clumps is, so to say, an integration of actions; and you—peel the wrong way..."

"Ai-ai-ai-ai: can you really peel that way?" impetuously (Papa's actions are impetuous) tearing a light brown clump from the hand of Afrosinya, crushing it between the fingers, so that, thrown into the air, the potato fell, he took it up from the floor, set his feet apart; and...and...—

—according to the rules for sharpening a pencil stub, he himself began to peel:

"This way—this is the way... Not away from you, but towards you..."

"Sir!"

"I'm telling you: you sharpen a pencil stub, peel a potato,—like this; using these means"—the breast, like a bellows, blew out fire from the nostrils.

"Sir!"

"Yes: everything has its own means..."

I noticed that the woman had snatched a carrot; Papa exited from the kitchen; and everything began to gackle, everything began to cackle: a friendly **cackle** was borne in; but Papa, like a peripatetic loudly, oakenly strode into the corridor, grumbling that the **method** of peeling a potato—is: rational.

. . . .

"Where is the man?"—exclaimed Diogenes.

Space answered; with a downcast "hic."

If Diogenes would appear amid the marble curia of Julius (the Holy Father), Moro, or Este, amid Leonardo-da-Vinci, all embroidered, frizzy-haired in a fiery tunic, the ladylike Raphael, Lorenzo, or Valla, or Poggio,—would there have occurred a scandal in the genteel family of the century: and they would have burst out in a peal of laughter, as they burst out in laughter at Papa's exits, his half-belt up, into the rituals of domestic cares.

Papa was not in the fifteenth century; therefore he was coarser, like... a Greek; but he was healthier; not with the tender cruelty of Borgia, with the coarse, Attic salt he guiltlessly danced on the parquets his "**billygoat hops**"; one "**billygoat hop**" was especially successful—with "music"; I think: Papa, the joker, constructed this spectacle on purpose, in order to amuse us (he is—secretive); he played out the spectacle, as if according to notes: I used to see:

—in the dining room over the chess case, he chomps his tea, moving about words like figures over the chess case,—very prominent cheek bones, bigpussed, sooner a shorty; but: a tosser and a turner; his strong starch snaps, he thunders words like pawns in the chess case; Mama looloos sounds over the whitetoothiness of the keys; Papa bothers her—with words and "chomps"...

"You, Mikhail Vasilich, do not hear music: you hear a shooing noise? Well—admit it..."

"No: why should I!.."

He hears—military marches; and—Glinka, now and then he hums under his nose jerking sounds like a billygoat; and hums are heard by him instead of Schumann; instead of Beethoven simply—some sort of "beating" there; but rising with ardor, he bangs:

"All composers are poor in melody; there are no original thoughts: I would—think up..."

"Well, then, try it?"

"What, why should I?.. And rising from the chess game (he used to play with himself), he bends himself over with a loud puff onto the stool, all grayish, singling out something on the black searched-out lacquer of the piano board; and over him the wall candleholder turned bronze. Taking aim with his finger at a note,—he bashes: against a note.

"Well, what next?"

"Bash, bash!"

"Ah, monstrous!"

"Why: it's not bad!"—and hooting a hahoom and thumping tatoom, drumming dadoom, booming baboom: he reminds one with sounds of that which now and then goes on in the stomach, where—
—something is given up with a fallen grumbling, where "thossse," who roll down, remind one of the secretive thosss—

—sss—

—sss—

—e!

Papa stands up on top of the card table; he beats, as if on the back of a Negrito, covered with lacquer, with his autologue:—

—he drags his study everywhere; he drags it in and—sets it up, like little screens.

No: he is—a nailbeater; he doesn't know how to beat on the key board.—

—But an outwind of smoke is borne into the totally selfcolored windows; and a black Miss Modesty, a shadow, sits down; the covered distances are becoming tired; and they became sunset; and there a redheaded cloud is—twoheaded; and here, headless: flattened in velveteen: the borne-by night wafts; and—they rose: the septilegs of shadows like a handleg of days; we do not screw off: in front of all stand conversations with the week; "toook"—horror scratches with a paw: it brings into the anteroom a smelly doggy smell; from the corridor multipawed shaggy terrors beat again with smells of methane and smells of peptone.

The gripping terror ran from the same place where Papa had been bashing.

I am afraid of Papa: he is dreadful at times.

. . . .

The demon of Socrates, the unheard Leonardo-da-Vinci, lives in him; and from him spins out a delicate atmosphere—not an outpouring of soft muslins, raspberry woven velveteens, but the content—

—of a life
of spiritual existences, the bases of which he subsequently substantiated in the tiny brochure "**Monadology**," given to a philosophical collection at the request of Grot; he preached "**Monadology**" in the rooms.—

. . . .

Once he narrated a dream—an arch-serious one.

"Yes, you know..."

"I saw in a dream."

"An arch-curious one!"

With a hanging wide-nostriled face he came up against the word, which he served carefully, like a very strong-smelling dish of jasper berries, trying not to break up, but showing, that—he is joking: "Yes, you know, I saw in a dream—an arch-curious one" there wafted to me little branches, wafted to me abundances.

"The dream is—an arch-curious one"—he raised his upjerked nose somehow aslant, downwards and upwards; and—wheezed with a goodpuff.

"Of course, dreams are—dreams, hmm... nevertheless there are some dreams, and then others—**this kind**"—he sat, as if breathing in the spirits of linden, in blissful heat exhaustion, waving under his nose, as if we were in the days of Andrei the Filler, in the days, when the winter crops fill to full ripening.

"It's as if I see in the dream that there is placed a Kasyanov, you know, little table, oakeny"—he pronounces with his spectacles. —"And on the table are—strawberries"—his eyebrows jump up, and the spectacles fell down, and his arms spread.

"With me is—an unknown person with such a sympathetic"—his goodcheeked face drove apart—"a sympathetic and honest face; and we are—eating berries."

"I start to lay out for him very hurriedly the bases of 'Monadology,'—not the Leibniz one at all, but my own: point by point"—he tossed himself back, looking at the baguet, and sat in great tenderness—thus: neither this way, nor that; and was embarrassed by the word.

"And the unknown one, taking a berry, listened very attentively to my first point about monads. 'Yes, you know,'—he says to me, smiling:—'I agree with you, Mikhail Vasilich: that's it exactly, exactly; the definition by you of the monad is simple, and exact, and—the main thing is: it gives the essence of things.'" Papochka clicked his heels under the tablecloth, bowing his head low, presenting to us the gesture of the unknown one; he sat and breathed... Yes and he jerked all across the table with a pencil stub:

"I tell him—the second little point!"

He stopped suddenly in exhaustion and tenderness; and—tossed himself all the way back.

"He says to me here too: 'I agree: that's it exactly!'"

"Suddenly I understand here"—he scratched himself,—"eh, eh, yes somewhere I saw an imaginative young philosopher"—and spread apart an eye from... terror, although he tried to scream with his whole appearance.   "Never mind, never mind, calm yourself, Mikhail Vasilich!"

"Eh, eh! These curls, the little beard—eh, eh... Hee-hee-hee... After all this is... Christ?.. How's that for a joke!"

"And I tell him little point after little point. I tell him!"

He stood, extending his arm.

"He stood up. He—said: 'Yes, I agree with you.'"

"Then I tell him"—here Papochka became like a child, clumsy-pawed and eyes screwed up from tenderness: "It's horribly pleasant for me that you, so to say, the World Monad—the Central One, you know,"—he added—"and of the highest orders in relation to our, that, so to say, you accept..."

"We kissed each other!"

"I tell him"—he snapped his fingers—"I—say: only, you know 'Our' here 'Father' is—unequivocally monadologically, I do not dispute, but—all the same"—he began pugnosed over his fingers to bend his point of view—"we should first replace the words 'Our Father' with the expression"—and for a minute deeply in thought; and he boomed in a bass voice suddenly enraptured:

"Thus for example: 'O'"—he boomed in a bass voice—"'Source of Purest Consummation'."

He stopped.

"Or for example: 'O'"—again he began booming in a bass voice—"'Absolute, so to say'..."

Suddenly he was completely amazed—to the very edge of his bounds, almost... to vexation.

"But he answered me to this: 'Yes, you should, Mikhail Vasilich,—without the so to say "O, Absolute," and not "so to say, O Absolute!"' I to him: 'Yes, have mercy, that you, really...'

And he"—amazement, pain and vexation were now written above
Papa's nose, below Papa's nose—"But he..."

"He just, imagine—disappeared!"

And he spread his palms savagely.

"Now that's a story!"

Boomingly he went to spread stomps with his feet on the plates of
parquet; and it seemed to me, that Auntie—livens up, Granny is—pale
white, Mama is—totally an aromatic; we all were pineappled with the
spirit; and into the open windows passed a little wind from the
Heavenly Empire, where Chinese satins were laid; thus the heavens
covered us all with its head; for sure, Papa, is—a Christened Chinaman!

. . . .

"Lizochek is now having a gay time at the Usovs': I, here,—where
to: I am so unhappy, I want to live; but there is no life"—Auntie used
to complain.

And Papa at this exits like such a bigbrowacorn, tossing his
stubnosed legs, not bending his knees, his hands rolled up behind his
back: he does not bend with his ear, but he hears with his spirit, his
eyes closed and trying to place one foot after the other.

"That's enough from you, Yevdokia Yegorovna!"—

—and now there
begins to thunder from him: an outpouring of words, breathed out; there
thundered the freshness of light; a clear glance exploded; and—it ignited
the sunsets; everywhere around the dining room sparklers were tossed;
in him thundered, slicing through in the features of his whole senseless
head, as if sitting aslant, a raspberryish somehow not-flowering mouth;
with an azure look he grabbed out of himself assurances of the fact that
the dignity, yes!—

—of man is—enormous, that...

"You know, Yevdokia Yegorovna, you are after all—the universe:
an intersection of monads; and a monad is the world!"

"What are you crying for?"

"Eh, look more hearty: walk with your brow raised high!"

And she begins to walk with a brow raised highly, all whiterose,
whiteluminous, on stout legs,—through the years, to glance into the
adjacent room, as if into the coming era, where—

—yes!—

—Yevdokia
Yegorovna, do you know, in the end the assurance will turn up anew:
to bear her lot!

And tossing apart his palms, he collected in his good-accepting
bosom the damp raw material of cried words, turning them, like the
Lord, into turquoise downpours, into pearly clarities; just like some
blue-ocular, it used to come to him in the eyes; and—with his spirit he

descends on us: onto the parquets of the apartment, reminding one of
Socrates, before the poison; and he falls with his whole corpus onto the
chair; and they whisper: Granny and Auntie:

"That's—a man!"

"A golden one!"

"A diamond one!!"

We see: from sliced-off little clouds blindingly splashes light:
edges, ridges; here they've already—purpled, ashened, darkened; the
glassy heavens, exceeding themselves, withdrew into heavenlessness;
below shone clearly a strip: of Chinese silk...

. . . .

It is known to me: the **"forces"** living in him, after the fall from
the great cosmic into the thunder of the comical, were invisibly widened
by palms of light; and—**"paradise"** rose up: a dense atmosphere;
Mama voiced; with enormous seriousness:

"Yes, Mikhail Vasilich..."

"What?"

"Yes he is—a 'force'..."

Thus in the weak dimness of the study, the gray-green, gray-coffee
one with the slits of bright-orange patches of light (from the lamp) was
secreted a powerful gamma of Persian motleys, thundering out with the
voice of Trinity Monday.

Yes, thus such a **"force"** made itself felt to me, made radiant by
him; and—yes: **"those"** are—penates: they penetrate me; the apartment
is penetrated by them; the walls stream—current; the etageres, chairs,
armchairs, tables stand in an immovable thunder storm,—charged; if I
had known of "electricity," then I would have said that Papa had placed
a Leyden jar among the rooms: oh, oh! Don't touch the little sphere of
the jar: it will bite! Oh, oh! Don't tease it: it will shoot a needle (the
spherical surface of his head takes after the sphere of the Leyden jar);
and **nails** flew; and the air of the apartment, as I remember it,—was—
"naily,"—

—wideshouldered, short my Papochka was like... a big ink
pot...

"Those" (Elohims!) sat deeply and silently; knocking into base-
ness, thundering with a "bash;" and growled out, like... at Delyanov, at
the Minister, in the hotel, in the room where he had placed his suitcase
upon his arrival in Petersburg, where Papochka was lowered by the
corridor servants, to whom he seemed pitiful (he joked with them),—
until the minute when they served the calling card to the tiny room: the
Minister of Education had arrived on a visit; and Papa had clicked his
heels to the Minister; and he presented his hand to him in greeting;
within a second he had already begun to fidget on the chair and, half

jerking the table cloth off, suddenly fidgeting in the air with his hand,—he fell upon Delyanov with "**bashes**";

"How can you, old chap?"

"Ehhh?"

"Eh!"

"Leave it be!"

"Yes enough; enough!"

"Yes where to here!"

"Eh!"

And as the Minister departed in the ministry carriage, everyone was drawn up before Papa—at attention!

Papa shouted: at students, docents, professors' wives, professors, literateurs, babblers, liberals, ministers; and in "**influential spheres**" they respected him:—

—I imagined to myself these "**spheres**" as "**cosmospheres**," not firmed into little spheres: the earth's sphere is—such a firmness—

—his coworkers and timid handshakers (respected and "**shaken**") afterwards passed on to there: to ministers; and he remained a "**dean**," spinning his wheels as he wished,—

—(about which I thought that these wheels.. are some sort of... Ezekiels)—

—of the department!—

—Yes, yes: they did not permit him into the "**cosmospheres**," fearing, that he would begin to turn such "**cosmospheres**" in his own way,—

—just like they turn the creaking handle of the coffee grinder, or like they turn the wheezing street organ, the grieving Traviata—

—I imagined :—

—surely, he in his uniform tailcoat conducts grave arias: in the university, in the court yard, straight under the window of Maria Vasilievna Pavlova; lifting his bowler to her:—
—and to him from the little window, right under his feet, she throws a copper which was wrapped in paper: there Papa turns "**everything**"!

But "**spheres**" do not like to be turned; they do not give up; and Papa lives far away from the "**spheres**":—

—in the end the imagination of a "**sphere**" firmed: it is—

—a hollow sphere illumined from the inside by light; there they permit an invisible spirit—from the gut; and here— a blown-up "**sphere**"; it is possible to fall into it: for this it must flow from the gut, turn itself into an "**absence**" (everything there is—

"absence"); Papa was **present** everywhere; and he would have gone into the "**sphere**" with a stuck-out half-belt, not pulling up and sticking out his solid stomach: everything would have burst, just like a bubble, sparkling with its luminescent shell... of soap;—

—for   Papa such blown-up "**spheres**" are—bubbles: he blew them up from soap; amusing me; he blew them out to me: he blew them up from the fire; and he watched them flying; and poked at them with a finger; others of them became firm; and—yes: we live on one (the earth's little sphere is—a "**sphere**"):—

—and our Papochka, blowing out the little sphere— earth's, calls up in me rapture and trembling; he—constructs "worlds" letting himself down, where necessary, to them and wandering there as a fellow traveler from an Andersen fairy tale, unrecognized by those whom he is leading to the goal,—with an enormous umbrella, with a bowler hat, beaten by someone's malicious hand onto the brow; he would meet with us; and having led us, he tosses us aside, waving his hand in parting in the air:—

—he tossed us aside: some eighteen years have passed since he withdrew to himself: into his own luminescent cosmospheres!—

—I know: in the centuries he disguised himself a multitudinous multitude of times; he visited Abraham; he bowed in parting: he is no more! But Abraham fulfills the testament, because he knows: Papa will appear: and—he will ask for an accounting:—

—and I fear: that with puny actions my anemic life is turning an apparent yellow: a mouselike green is in the eyes, under the eyes!—

—afterwards he already, not noticed by anyone, lived in the apartment, in Sodom; and just, like we, the Sodomites mocked him: he—quietly, submissively bore it:—

—(Our Mikhail Vasilich—yes, yes: a man without character; he is—boiling water, he is—a hot-head, but—such a rag)!—

—Mama   does not know, wherein is the "**force**": I know:—

—and the covered-up "force" holds me.

. . . .

I know: I concluded a testament with him; on Sinai, on his knees, he gave over the contents of two little books (a small green one and a small lilac one: they were—the Old and New Testaments); if I, like the Jews, violate the testaments, following the call of Mamochka shouting at me ("Kotik, come here: don't you dare listen to your father!") if I run behind the alcoves to create with her little calves from little candies, ribbons, bands, clasps and elastic, the whalebone, the corset one, then I will be grabbed by a panicky horror; it will be not a "**nail**," but purer than a "**nail**":

The tablets of the "**testament**" will be loudly smashed apart!

Oh, no, better to be boxed on the ears, tortured by Mama; what the heck: Christians were tortured, and lions were let out of the cages; so am I: locked by Papa into the dumb study, like in a cage,—I learn; he—withdraws from the cage; into the open door flies a growling Mamochka, a lioness, but this is—an ordeal; the lioness—a mask, a likeness, all the same: the "**symbol**" jerks very painfully; but the "**force**" of the testament is—with me; and I do not go with Mama to feast as a pagan: I reject with my hand the chocolate of Kraft, pressing the dry, dumb tablet: I will be a "**force**"!..—

—Because I had seen the "**force**" of fire, because I had heard the sounds of the "**nail**"; and the fate of Sodom is known to me!..

. . . . . .

He rented an apartment there, manifested a laughable weakness; eccentrically, scatterbrainedly he calculated together with Lot, a talented young man in spectacles, being led through the reviewing line of the Sodomites: to a "**docentship**"; and the Sodomites shouted like Mamochka:

"No, he reeks of trash!"

But he led out Lot; and returned again to our place: and they threw very rotten eggs smelling of peptone at him; placing into the open window a "**nail**," how he began to growl, instantly constructing with it the Dead Sea; and he moved to Greece, suffering misfortunes from a very shrewish landlady, Xanthippe; there, having drunk the poison, he appeared in the sixteenth century—a wanderer all in patches; with the same enormous umbrella, with a little bowler hat, in a lapserdak frock-coat; he knocked under windows; when met, he quietly sat down at the table, began to narrate just like to Dotya—"**Monadology**"; here unnoticed he got messed up, seeing those whose hopes had been lost; and he renarrated his personal experiences of events occurring under... Caesar Augustus and under Pontius Pilate; there, hiding behind the debris, he was not seen at all by Mary, but—seen by Him,—

—from Him he directly received indications, on how to act and what to do,—in the millenniums of time; here, passing through the centuries, straight out, slicing through the big road, he appeared to sound the bell: to us in the room,—with a rather stuffed portfolio, stuffed with "**Testaments**"; now—invisibly he serves and secretly he images to all of us:—

—he met with Mamochka: Mamochka, Granny, Auntie and Uncle were already hungering, when Granny had squandered **"everything"**; twenty-three suitors, like dogs, sat around, proposing marriage; but Papochka gave them a hand, leading Mamochka by the hand and leading her to the house of Kosyakov (and the suitors ran away)—

—and Mamochka knows: she knows **"everything"**; and she knows, that Papochka allowed her to swear at him, but... up to... up to: up to the **"nail"**; and up to the **"nail"** she swears; and after the **"nail"** there comes to pass a majestic severity and clarity of **"simple relations"**: mirrorlike, crystally, like on the day of the creation of the world!—

—if we transgress the **"nail,"** once again the **"red downpours"** will break through, and—the Dead, bitter Sea will immediately be revealed in the rooms .

. . . .

The spindle of days turns around and around: in the shadow of shadows!

O M

Paradise is—a sparkler.

From a little branch it separates with a burst; it stars; and—the tail pours out; and plumes drip through like a comet; and—it huffs its wings:—

—the bird of paradise!—

—And then from the fires and the shadows striping boils through; and—it roars: this is—a tigrish beast, named by me a tiger for plays of shadows and fires, imaging its luminous membrane: "**tigress**"... Here—

—the World Tree raises up a wingplume; in the middle puffs up the Disk, bending its biwings and falling as a rain of luminousrose plumes, imaging a body:—

It bursts and	——————	He bursts his breast
beats out an enormous illum-		beats out with a Sword;
ating geyser, shooting a		borne past by Love:
pillar, like a Sword,		by Fire, like a Sword
into the world's		into the world's
Nothing!—		—Everything!

—I recognize, that that Sword is—
the Archangel; they call him Ra
phael: Raphael
Sound
of the
burst
ing!—

—Yes, Paradise is a sparkler!—

—Trees,
are grabbed by a hungout lampglass, by a clear seethrough silversheet in a thousandbranched Candelabrum of Light, penetrated by the golden warmth of cannetille and red luminosity; everything there is, grabbed onto itself with the luminous cannetille; everything is—threads and beads; flowers, like little lanterns; and not fruits, but spheres gamboled

in sparks, in play: tigers! From afar, where the Seven Rivers began—a palm forest is begotten from the melting of corals (trunks) and it moves with coronas of luminousplumed palmettos, imaging the just beginning to breathe, motley, striped heavens:—

—yes, in Persia these colored carpets are—a solidification of the ancient heavens: from Persia they saw (from afar) the illumination from the Tigris; the flying fireworks of Paradise; to there Zarathustra, perhaps, was invited at times!..

In the firmament labradorite soils, intoxicated, foams the Euphrates, striking the shore with a pearly bead; and the Tigris—roams around: into the steep Labrador (somewhere afar); above the Labradorite lump, raised up higher than the heavens, there burst,—as if trumpets: tambourines:

"O!"

"Om!"

"Miramma!"

And—it is repeated: "He, the world,—Brahma." And it is written : Mahabharata:—

—I consolidated in continuations of my life
the rising sound:—

"Om-mir-mira-am-amo-!" ——"Ineffable World,
marvellous one,—
I love you!"

"Amma-amo-mam — "O, nurturess, mama!
mama" loving: you—are *mater*
of matter!"

"Ram-rama-brahm- —"Hero, dedicated,
brahma!"— —like god!"

—And we here fell apart into exclamations: and from the exclamations collected a responsorial exclamation:

"O!"

"Om!"

"Ommiramma!"

. . . .

We knew: Ommiramma is walking in the garden—the Invisible; I remember—

—we see the composition of the Candelabra of Light, crossed, stormily bursting flames, in which he walks,—

—and the flame, like the Bush, blazes, at its summit, from here, from the Lamplights, he pours out a pearly beard (and the waterfall of the beard is called god); boiling imageries pour down into the cupped hand of the palms placed by us, **astras** (or stars); we insert **astras** into the storm of the luminosity; and the cannetille collects into a body: into the astral; thus we image the circle of the Life, or animal life; this is the act of naming.

The Bearded Stream is a collection of Luminaries, or of Beginnings: the Beard, poured out from the Stream,— the Beginnings: of Time.

The luminous bifinger rarely shows itself in the Candlelights; and—a strange occurrence, the strange Composition of Candelabra of Light, moves: further!

. . . . .

This was a live passing Tree, from whose fruits we were sated; the Collegium of Candlelights, or of Beginnings—of Time; they are—a circle. But one of the Candlesticks, Dykirion, fell,—a candlestick of the Composition, crawled like the staff of a candleholder; having placed out the candles like horns, having appropriated the name of the enormous circle of Beginnings: thus appeared the Serpent—endless Time, which had lost its own beginning; this **"beginning"** was left in the Composition of Beginnings.

Very soon Dykirion fell apart into Dy and Kirion; thus appeared in paradise an imposter, calling himself the Marvelous Leader; he taught us to taste the stars of the Stream, which solidified in our throat like the sinful apples:—

—I remember, how, sweeping me out of paradise with a storm, the golden cannetille was borne, at one time sacred—was borne, flying about: amid the soils and the lands, near the Tigris, where I poured out all my working perspirations: thus I sowed near the Tigris the expanses of swampy places with **"culex,"** infecting me with malaria—

—ah, ask, please, a Mesopotamian: are the places of the Tigris healthy; he scratches himself under the turban, confused:

"Not very, sahib!"

. . . . .

Occupied with the complication of stone, the firm pillars, from which later our Babylonian captivity was complicated, I was not very...; however: it was still bearable for a while:—

—while the patriarchs led, I understood: they are the Fathers from the Beginnings, or

"Papas"; I guessed their meaning: a patriarch—disguised as a Candlelight of Compositions, wrapped in chausables: like the old, Nativity Ruprecht, he put on the gray, curly beard, he sprinkles it with salt, so that it sparkles, and he puts up to the Countenancelessness his nose (from cardboard) and, clothing himself in fine linen; sticking out golden humps, like a priest, he gives up his life only with ends of uplifted fires of lights,—first the jagged corona, then the diamond miter, reminding one of the patriarch's universal miter; and he places on the small table a cup: with the testaments, clarifying to us the period of his appearance;—

—The patriarch reveals a period, he leads one through; then at the threshold of another, suddenly he becomes "Enoch": he is taken to heaven, leaving: blank fine linen, an enormous beard, a nose!..

Today Papa leads us: Methuselah led formerly; Abraham led, who else—will lead?—

—Thus it was revealed, that the patriarchs are— "Enochs"; Methuselah was—"Enoch"; Melchizedek—the same; that is, one who is taken alive to heaven, arraying himself at the descension from heaven to earth in venerable, patriarchal, elders'—chausables and reliquaries:—

—yes, yes: "elders" image a union: **"elders"** firmly know how to be crabby and quarryfaced: they quarry in the heavens, where all elders, imaging one **"elderness"**—thunder out testaments with a mumbling roar; and pshaw sanctitites; you do not hear the words:—

—but you do hear: sheer incomprehensibility, toothlessly reprimanding with a whisper:

"Bff!"

"Bff!"

"Beff, beff, beff!"—

—in peals, where—

—th-o—

—ss—

—ss—

—ss—...

Those, who!

"They" are—in Papa; and "they" are only "he": electricity, patriarchy; "those, who..."—in Papochka—

—Papochka is—also Enoch: having tied on his beard and tied on like a live frog, his nose,—from under the nose he "**enochs**": a sacred testament! He is—in his morning, gray housecoat, sewn with velveteen trim, with tassels, sewn with raspberry velveteen trimmed sleeves, reminding one of the patriarchal vestment,—he inserted into my little breast this fateful knowledge; frightened by the fact that Mamochka often burst into the dining room, he began to lock me in the study in the morning and narrated on the go to me, washing and chuckling with splashes, about the patriarchs, forever binding us with him, performing a religious rite before the faucet, knocking his toothbrush against the tin plate of the hand washstand, behind which on the little wall, I know, hung the secretive "nail"; all of Papochka's acts reminded me of the acts of a bishop, in a gleaming miter in the middle ground of the gleaming spaces behind the iconostasis—over the altar, the cliff of Labrador; he "**enochs**" with the nose and he lifted up his sleeves over the porcelain cup: the washbasin; and from screwed-up eyes, wet, of the widenosed countenance,—he voiced:

"Yes here, Kotenka: here…"

"My little brother!"

"Here: the wanderers appeared to Abram," that is, once again, "Papas"…

"They appeared, saying: Abram: you will be Abraham!"

"Do you know…"

"And you will give birth, you know,—to Isaac!"—me!..

And when it came to the sacrifice, then we came up naturally against the dense thicket of domestic cares, because my domestic care was exactly that—a sacrifice: to lie up on an enormous stone dignifiedly, so as to be sacrificed dignifiedly: by Mama!

. . . . . .

I see in my dreams, it's as if Papa crowns me as king with a lesson; he comes with gifts of knowledge, as with a cup, overfilled with precious stones, brocades and tasty fruits; he stands wordlessly like a brocaded alta-relief, stands with a pineapple, an Oporto apple, or goose apple, even with an antonovka, spirit apple; day begins; and a little star rolls down—with a luminescent little trail, toward morning they will lay out atlases, satins, Chinese satins; nature, like an ancient Chinaman, grows ancient with its overgrowths; and from the Heavenly Empire wafts into the little window an azure air.

RED ANISE

During the evenings of April come a light blue expanse and crimson dusk; clouds are—golden; they complicate themselves: into blue-crimson, into blue-golden, into golden-crimson; August is—lilac; July—gray-blue, oppressive with a feverish heat; in June: the sunset is—a gilder's shop, the sunset is—a goldsmith's shop; Marusya-dawn, goldenbrowed, walks the streets of the world; goldenstreamed she sows rain on Razvanya; Dadon, begins to crawl, a rather stout cloud: bells clang!.. Thunderously!

. . . . .

A May morning, a shepherd, like a cock, begins to beat on the window from a stern horn—from the stone curbstone of the Arbat; through a dream I hear the beating: six! The little bell of a cow ding-dongs; to the gate come the cows: reds, motleys; on the streets it is rather peopleless; only the blankety-blank of the yardmen is chased by brooms.

I sleep...

. . . .

A cornflower-blue sky—with a brown kyte; the kyte darts from the sky to the earth—behind a roof; goldencrested chickens began to bustle about, banged about; the kyte—is borne back over the roof; and Papa is heard, kyrie eleisoning kyrielle; yellow moths are borne about; and we walk along new paths: along Prechistenka, Stozhenka; dragged through the buds by a caressing May; and there can be seen a chocolate-colored house (someday headquarters will be here), the house of Ganetsky and the colonnade of the Mariinsky Institute with the deaf Chertova, Dame of the Order of St. Catherine—deaf, but not a spade; the Kister house; here a military man, he comes out from there: Kister himself.

And we return: by Levshinsky!

. . . .

Once we were beyond the Moscow river: there beyond the river Moscow squats, solidifying with houses; there little houses stand around houses; bone-houses crawl out, little houses droop stonily; and the Kremlin glows ruddy, placing under the heavens Ivan, its finger in a thimble; the Redeemer grows enormous like a gold melting pot; bells like paschas; and towers, like... wenches: exactly like a little snack table?

Moscow!

. . . . .

Mornings we stealthily run through the "Testament," the little greenish book: the fall, the deluge, the patriarchs, Egypt, Sinai, the division of the kingdom, prophets, kings,— are behind; a new little time rolls up with a decorated red egg, a snack table, pascha, a chomp, and the common saying: "He is risen, truly!"

And the booming of thunderous, thundering boots—into open windows; and then the God who has—the beard is abolished; there begins: the Son of Man, who had suffered before me; and by that having atoned; and it is required of me to atone; who has not yet been atoned for?

Mamochka!

This was narrated by Papa, extracted from the lilaceous book with the snowball tree little sun of the New Testament summer.

O Mamochka, angellikeness-whiteness, you seem a lioness, preparing for the purest fate: to torment me! And I am tormented by the thoughts, standing under the window: am I pure, am I purified;—

—and

into the cornflower-blue sky a serpentmug, a kite of paper, how it jerks, drawing arcs, with an extended tail of bast; but the wind falls off,—

—and—

—jerking like a battering ram, the kite rustles its paper: the yellow mug was exposed over the roof!..

And behind the back it grows feverishly hot—from the bottomed body, from the sailcloth mended-jacket: this Papochka presses to his breast, just as if foreseeing my fate; it grows blue to my eyes; a goldspark, goldgleam goes from me, from the crucified one... Madam Hornung,—

—whom they invited from her chattering establishment for the consummation of all this: Kotik's crucifixion,—hey, you listen!— the time will come when, having prepared himself, Kotik will give you his little palms; and Papa will bellow:

"Behold, the man!"

Under the spectacles two little turquoises gleam: Papa's little eyes; will he cry?

. . . .

Yes, he broke out crying when the scandal got rolling; Mama anathematized and beat me for entering into the New Testament; Papa glimpsed this; crested, he threw himself with a bright facial crimson, and oakensided he tore me out, put the castor gray cap with the very slicing elastic on my forelocked little brow and bundled me out with force; we abandoned forever the native den; and after us ran the wow-wow—ow-ow; and—yawled yowled: Herod's warrior.

We threw ourselves to the first flying span; it banged; Papa covered me with a strong embrace; this old walrus face fell with its lips toward me, Papa howled arch-heavily: it is impossible to live like this; we have—endless malice; much had been compiled: doggy smell, and malsmell; one could become totally doggish—in such malicious-imagery;—

—and the span banged the very same way with the discolored color, jumping up with a hop under the red calico curtain which was tossed into us bubbly from the little window and under which the lamina of a green ficus, as if greeting, lapped;—

—and I answered, but do not remember what exactly; thus we entered into the testament, in a cab, for the purification of our house from doggy smell and dust;—

—but the dry dustflight jerked like a gate post of rolled papers, quickening like screws; there started up a windblow, windburn, windwhistle; again the kite jerked from the chimney into the dusty and pull-down heavens; but, catching on the net of telegraph pillars, falling, with a shiny paper puss,—it hung flabbily;—

—here I thought: yes, yes: I am like a flatterer under words,—like a serpent under flowers; and I began to want: to be crucified...—

—the pillars of dust of Devichy Field turned brown; through them came toward us a gallop of white-gray and marble horses; the galoon and the wiped worn sables of the dragoons sparkled, these rushing warriors of Herod, made by Mama—

—there—the parade ground for learning; now, behind the little square, there are clinics!

. . . .

I do not remember what was going on at Uncle Yorsh's, where Papa brought me, beaten: it was—crowded, multifamilied; from a teeny-weeny bed onto the carpet hung toward me with a constructo cube a very importunate pest, my cousin, completely forceless; I attempted to heal him: he would not heal; in a circle collected little mouths, milksops-kids,—

"We'll 'hang' you!"

I was deep in thought—all day long;—

—once I saw: Dunyasha, spitting out of her mouth a little nail onto her callous, she stuck the head of a piece of iron, placing the little nail in the baguet; they hung a weighty damask shade:—

—here on the table I lie down; at first everything is hellish; the stove vent begins to breathe its own coal gas-blowing; and the spirit of peptone is revealed; and with stamps of the inescapable they exit from the door with the walnut strong baguet, breaking my little shoulders; there will be a procession: through the drawing room with "**Giftbearing Hosts,**" with the dress maker-chatterer, called for by Mamochka, my Caiaphas,—with Madam Hornung, who pins me up with the seamstresses to the nursery, where darkness spreads about:—

—space is—squandered; time is—slandered; and causelessly causality executes and effectuates the laws; they take down the icon images and give the laws, where the chasers chase—prehistoric horses; they dig their hooves into the floor, and...—

—"Let this cup pass from me"—

—then the rhinocerousy Hornung, enormous, black, in a hellish dress (behind her—the seamstresses) appears, extending her arms; and they cackle loudly, like black jackdaws:

"Crucify him!"

"Crucify him"...

And—the soulsmotherer: a bent baguet! Everything vanished into an angry cloud; it was covered by a malicious creature; my Henrietta Martynovna—into tears! I know, I know: it will be hellish before the dining table, where they will undress and laugh over the bare me; and Hornung, swallowing slobber, spreads out my arms in layers; she orders the seamstresses to wave about their little hammers: against the little hats of the nail the little hammer irons ding-dong—to the baguet! Already my tenfold fingers are bloodied; I will hang on the baguet, giving my admonitions to Dunyasha sobbing—right up to the hyssop.

In the apartment of Professor Pompul will be a strike—an extra heavy, oaken one; into the cleft of the walls will bustle Pompul, doublecrested and deafened, witnessing: it has been consummated!

Then:—

　　　—the heavens will enlighten with such a velvety-blue; there fly up clouds-velveters;—

　　　　　　—completely persicans!—

　　　　　　　　　—And with alta-relief, with Persian brocade, the heavens will be wind-beaten, in order to be amianthine, dimming into a golden-crested cloud;—

　　　　　　　　　—they will take me down: and wrapping me hastefully in a twenty-length of demicotton with the bloody mark "**Elizaveta Letaeva**," they will bear me off to the chest, where the groats are concealed, from where they once extracted a dead mouse; and they will sit and keep silent, someone will curl up to the chest; someone will say a lament over the dead Kotik; and already around the room ding-a-lings a cooing; and all—listen:

"What is this?"—

　　　　　—Whitebells: I —coo...

And everyone caresses one another dovelike; to everyone shine: all the candles, all the lamps, all the sounds, all the words; and Papa, rising as the head of the family, anxiously informs them:

"Kotik is risen!"

. . . .

In these thoughts I spent all day at Yorsh's: I thought of the torments standing before me for tomorrow, until beyond the little window the greenish cold-stone lit up—from the heavens;—

　　　　　　　　　　—from the little courtyard I saw:—

　　　　　　—a wettish little bush—some sort of marigold; from there—it smells (and yes: goldenrod, and that one does not come here); there were goldensnouted swine; and—they chomped, chomped on gold; but in the heavenly sky paleblue spars of some sort of moon color are laid out;—

　　　　　　　　　—those are—amianthi—

　　　　　　　　　　　　—a mosquito buzz buzzed: it began bizzing in my ears; they carried me to the divan—with a yawn.—
—Thus I remember the evening!

. . . .

I awoke in the arms of Henrietta Martynovna: Mama had sent her after me:

"Kotik, komm!"

Mama met me, opening the door, with angelcountenance: she covered me with the wings of her shawl; and—she cried together with me:

"My dearest, my little one: forgive me, for the sake of Christ!"

I was like one arisen: I walked into the goldacceptings of dawn and watched how over the iron roofs, swelling up, boiling greengifts of leaves stuck up: I wanted to sink into the olive twilight of tree trunks.

. . . .

It was as if this spring I had arisen, having been bodiless (both night and day) in the events of the Galilean apartment, transsubstantiating its sinful Arbat life:—

—Judea is—the drawing room; and Galilee—the dining room; outflows, hangings of light lie like luminouspraises on the alebaster bust, or—the apostle: from the Sea of Tiberias, the carpet, I wash my prim hand; from the armchair balding Papa, a winterer, ran along the water,—to meet me, placing his little palms (such a giftreceptacle) after the sunny, thrown sunbeam; I—

—no longer am!—

—I walked through Galilee; I measure with little legs the tiny little squares of the parquet floor:

"Right here, here on this parquet square—will be the descent of the Spirit; and here on this one—it will not be consummated!"—

—Already on one—a luminouscurl, luminouspraise, luminous-blow! On the other—

—a mumbo-jumbo of dust!

. . . .

One inescapable sun fell to the earth; it sits down on the earth; it sits down behind the earth!

Another, one capable of rising, appears in the morning: blown up, purple; it passes on the run; and—shows itself—

—tiny: here it is, a yellow sparkle! Here an eeny-weeny, raging circle galloping in the little eyes, twinkling to—blue; afterwards:—

The old sunset is—goldenmouthed!

. . . . . .

Or here, I imagine:—

—At the tea ta-
ble col-
lect—
—Papochka,
—Mamochka,
—Grannny,
—Uncle and,
—Auntie—

—but Hen-
rietta Martynovna is—not here,
because she is a Luther-
an;—

—I spring up
on the little table before them:

"My peace—I give you!"—

—and extending my little palms, I show

the two crimson marks on them: they howl (blisters, nailed through);
they begin to separate from the table cloth—

—under the ceiling!—

—where I sparkle with an outflowing of light; I run like a
little fire over Papa, Mama, Uncle, Auntie;

I—

—hang above now, unsoldered on the motley spots of the newly
arrived light, on the crimsoning of the window

sills,—

—before which soon Gran-
ny will light the
icon lamp; the
lamp burns;
I'm—invisible,
inaudible,—

—like a word un-

spoken; here at nights I pour out lilac; and Mama recognizes her own
gospel in it, when, recalling Kotik, on a very sleepless night she lets
herself down into the creases of the taken-down shades; from the creases
I incline my angelicountenance, my silveriness…

. . . .

—And I see—

      —Papa crowns me king: he brings gifts in a gift-
      bearing ciborium; before me he stands with brocaded
      alta-relief, stands with pineapple, with Oporto
      apple, or with goose apple,—even: with antonovka,
      spirit apple; and—he affirms:
      "By Andrei The Filler—you will
      be filled full with knowledge!"
      "You will be—a mature fruit!"—

             —And this occurs in
Kasyanov, where I stand in spiked seedlings, in timothy grass, in other
aromas. Already with goldfilament, a golden thread, the old woman—
dawn has begun stitching her sarafon into the entire heavens.
Kasyanov—the crucifier, the owner of the estate where we spend the
summer, passes into his pineapplerie,—there among the green copses;
and he is a marquis with a very-very un-Russian speech, which
everyone so respects.

"Isn't it time for you, Kotik—to **harquebus**: to shoot my
harquebus?"

Among the pineapples it's—a red hot oven; pineapples are chased
out to us; there, Daniel, I can be cast into it!

I know in the dream that it is not here, on Arbat, my cross, but in
the Kasyanov meadows, in the gladelike pastures, where the gladelike
ryemarsh quietly purls, bubbles and an irony, watery azure grows cold,
where at dawn—it is Nazareth, where a gray old man on a gate blindly
chews **ryebread**, covering his brow with an earless and roundtopped
askew, a cap, where dawns, dignified wenches, putting on their sarafans,
the golden ones, prepare my path to the heavens, like for... Elijah,
and where all are treated with a red anise apple.

Papa here rises before me, he rings out deafeningly:

"There will be—the raising of red anises!"

. . . .

And I awake; and I see in the window, a star skips along—with a
luminescent trail; toward morning they will lay atlases, Chinese satins;
nature, like an old Chinaman, grows ancient with its overgrowths; Papa
is—the Christened Chinaman!

NOTES

The Study

Mittag-Lefler, Magnus-Gustav. Swedish mathematician. (1846—1927). In 1877 he becomes Professor of Mathematics at the University of Helsinki. In 1881 he moves to the University of Stockholm, where he works closely with the Russian mathematician, Sofia Kovalevsky.

Poincaré, Henri. French mathematician. (1854—1912). Professor at the University of Caen from 1879, and at the University of Paris as of 1881.

Klein, Felix. German mathematician. (1849—1925). He does work primarily in the field of geometry as a Professor at the University of Erlangen from 1872 and later at the University of Göttingen from 1886.

Scythian. Horsemen and nomads who were the first occupants of southern Russia in the 7th century B.C. The Scythians served as connectors between the Greeks and Mongols and Chinese, according to George Vernadsky (*A History of Russia*, Yale Univ.: 1929, pp. 6,7). The word "Scythian" has connotations of barbarism and a lack of civilization. As such it was used by the Symbolists as a keyword denoting the "Eastern" and less cultured and irrational aspect of the Russian people, who were culturally descendants of Byzantium but geographically descendants of the Scythians. One example is the poem "Scythians" (Скифы, 1918) by Aleksandr Blok (1880—1921).

Eccentric. One of Bely's other autobiographical-fictional works is called *Notes of an Eccentric* (Записки чудака, 1919).

Darboux, Jean Gaston. French mathematician. (1842—1917). In 1880 he assumes the Chair of Higher Geometry at the Sorbonne.

Chebyshev, Pafnuty Lvovich. Russian mathematician. (1821—1894). From 1847 until his retirement in 1882 he teaches the theory of numbers at St. Petersburg University. A member of the Petersburg Academy of Sciences and of several foreign academies. Bely uses one of his infrequent footnotes to identify Chebyshev to his readers.

"scorpions...bookish ones." Anton Hönig (*Andrej Belyj's Romane: Stil und Gestalt*, Munich: Wilhelm Fink Verlag, 1965) thinks these are mathematical symbols mistaken by Kotik for scorpions. More likely Kotik sees a book-scorpion: "an arachnid insect (Chelifer cancroides) resembling a scorpion, often found in old books." (*The Compact Edition of the Oxford English Dictionary*, Oxford: 1971, p. 249).

Lagrange, Joseph Louis. French mathematician born in Italy. (1736—1813). Teaches first at the University of Berlin (1766) and finally becomes Professor of Mathematics at the Ecole Normale Superieure in Paris in 1787. He is best remembered for the establishment of the metric system.

Tatar. The name of a Central Asian people most commonly known in the West as the pillaging army of Chingiz Khan. Ten years after the first raids, Russia was again invaded in 1237 and subjugated to the harsh "Tatar yoke" for the greater part of two centuries. The beginning of Russian liberation came in 1380 when the Moscow Prince Dmitry enjoyed the first major victory over the Tatars at the Battle of Kulikovo. The Russian word "татарин" "татары" is related to the people's name for themselves. The more common English and West European spelling "Tartar" apparently comes from association with the Latin "Tatarus" meaning "hell." (*OED*, p. 3238). The saying "Scratch a Russian, and you will find a Tartar" derives from "Scratch a Russian, and you will wound a Tartar." This has been ascribed to Napoleon, but can be found in *Soirées de Saint Petersburg* by Joseph de Maistre.

antonovka. A popular sort of Russian apple which is mostly yellow and somewhat sour. This word also leads to the association of Anton, the yardman. He was an actual person finally dismissed for his dishonest dealings. (А. Белый, "Арбат," *Современные записки*, XVII, 1923, 161). This associative process in which the logic is verbal and spatial rather than sequential and temporal is an important device in the novel.

"his little eyes would become imperceptible *points of view*." In *Kotik Letaev* (1918, trans. by Gerald Janecek, Ann Arbor: Ardis, 1971, p. 53) Bely writes: "I understand metaphors exactly..."

lapserdak. A Yiddish word meaning "a tattered garment." Nora Szalavitz in a translator's note to Konstantin Mochulsky *Andrei Bely: His Life and Works* (Ann Arbor: Ardis, 1977, p. 229) defines "Lapserdak: A long dark coat, such as that worn by the Hassidism."

"to facet the means of life; and to limit us, to cut us down to size..." This passage revolves around the Russian root "гран" meaning "facet," "limit," "cut." It is one of the major leitmotifs of the novel connecting the "faceted" and "cut-glass" world of the mother with the "limiting" and "limited" world of the father.

Lie, Marius Sophus. Norwegian mathematician (not Swedish, as Bely later notes in the novel). (1842—1899). From 1872 he is a Professor of Mathematics at the University of Christiana (later Oslo). He is best known for his research with Klein on sphere geometry.

potassium permanganate. This was a popular disinfectant of the time.

genteel tendency. The central theme of the novel is "род" meaning "genus" or "gender." The Russian word used here is "благородная" often translated as "noble" but more precisely meaning "noble-birthed." In English the use of "genteel" remains faithful to the etymological and morphological origins of the word. This attempt to choose the one word most closely related to the Russian by etymology and interrelated by the root to other English counterparts in the work is a major organizing feature of my translation. Indeed, Bely himself exploits the multileveled meaning of words in exactly the same way.

Westerner. This represents an attitude among some Russians, dating back to the reforms of Peter the Great, that Russia should look to Europe for inspiration and a cultural heritage. The conflict between East and West dominated Russian philosophical thought in the nineteenth century and became one of the major themes of Bely's most famous novel, *Petersburg* (Петербург, 1914). Both *Petersburg* and *The Silver Dove* (Серебряный голубь, 1909) were intended originally as parts of a trilogy to be entitled *East or West*.

Kant, Immanuel. Prussian philosopher. (1724—1804). From 1755 he teaches physics and mathematics at the University of Königsberg. In 1770 he is awarded there a Chair in Logic and Metaphysics. Best known for his *Critique of Pure Reason* (1781), Kant is influenced by the rationalism of Leibniz. He is also intensely involved in the philosophy of mathematics.

Spinoza, Benedict de. Dutch philosopher. (1632—1677). His main work is *Ethics.* "Knowledge for Spinoza is a state of clarity of the intellect..." (*The Concise Encyclopedia of Western Philosophy and Philosophers*, ed. J. O. Urmson, New York: Hawthorne Books, 1960, p. 369).

Leibniz, Gottfried Wilhelm von. German mathematician and philosopher. (1646—1716). Leibniz is acquainted with and corresponds with Spinoza. Leibniz is known for his mathematical invention of a calculating machine which could add, subtract, multiply and divide. He is also the originator of the "theory of the monad."

Professor Letaev. In this fictional-factual autobiographical novel Bely readily mixes fact and fiction. Professor Mikhail Letaev is the novel's hero. The surname is related to the Russian "летать" meaning "to fly" and the root "лет" becomes a leitmotiv in the work. In the "Instead of a Foreword" published with the text in 1921, but omitted in the 1927 version, Bely notes: "in part I used in the depiction of Kotik's parents some (just a few) features, taken from my own parents." But he goes on to warn: "he, who would draw a parallel between the childhood of the author and the childhood of 'Kotik' would fall into a profound error, based on the fact, that not one artistic detail, not one of the *dramatis personae* is an invention out of nothing, but rests upon what has been observed in one's self and around one's self; art is contained in the free composition of traits, one or another character trait of Kotik's father, for example, passes through a series of people observed by the author; to return: the character of Professor Letaev is composed by the author out of a whole group of people, each of which possessed one or another peculiarity..." (p. 23).

Perhaps Bely recognized the futility of his remarks in removing the passage with the reprinting of the novel. In fact, in his own non-fictional autobiographical work *On the Border of Two Centuries* (На рубеже двух столетий, 1930) Bely uses direct quotations from *The*

Christened Chinaman to describe his father, and he goes on to state: "I won't stop for a physical description of my father; I described it in 'The Christened Chinaman'..." (p. 65). He also recalls as fact, not fiction, several episodes of the novel. While it may be impossible to separate fact from fiction, there is obviously a clearer, more accurate portrait of his father and his family life than Bely was originally willing to admit. As such a few words of introduction to Professor Bugaev are called for.

Professor Letaev is modeled on Bely's own father, Nikolai Vasilevich Bugaev, the famous Russian mathematician. (1837—1903). He completed Moscow University in 1859. After a short period devoted to applied mathematics at the Nikolaev Engineering Academy, he returned to Moscow University to receive his Master's Degree in 1863 and a Doctorate of Pure Mathematics in 1866. As a Professor of Mathematics and Dean of the Division of Physics and Mathematics (1887—1891) at Moscow University, Professor Bugaev authored over fifty books and articles, including extensive work on the theory of numbers, game theory and monadology. He also served in the positions of secretary, vice-president and president of the Moscow Mathematical Society.

satyr. Deity of the woods and fields, part human and part goat, who is frequently an attendant to Bacchus.

Zhukovsky, Nikolai Yegorovich. Russian mathematician. (1847—1921). A Professor of Mathematics and Mechanics at the University of Moscow from 1886; also a member of the Moscow Mathematical Society. He is considered the founder of Russian hydromechanics and aeromechanics, and would later be instrumental in the birth of Soviet aviation, including work on a theory of bombing from aeroplanes. In *On the Border* p. 242, Bely recalls that the professor "was always inventing some sort of flying wings;..."

I ching. (The Book of Changes, 2nd century B.C.). One of the five books of the *Wu ching*, this was a collection of the major scriptures of Confucianist thought. The *I ching* is a diviner's manual which gives sixty-four patterns for human behaviour.

Papochka

"**Confucian wisdom.**" Confucius. Chinese philosopher. (c. 551 B.C.— c. 479 B.C.). He preached a philosophy based on reason and a social order meant to govern human relationships founded on the principles of humanity and goodness. The wisdom referred to is found in the *Chung yung* (The Doctrine of the Mean or The State of Equilibrium and Harmony) supposedly composed by K'ung Chi, a grandson of Confucius. Much of the theory rests on the word "chung" signifying "middle" or "central" and was used by the Chinese to designate "China" the "central realm" (chung kuo). Thus one reads: "When the passions, such as joy, anger, grief, and pleasure, have not awakened, that is our central self, or moral being (chung). When these passions awaken and each and all attain due measure and degree, that is **harmony**, or the moral order (ho). Our central self or moral being is the great basis of existence, and harmony or moral order is the universal law in the world. . . . The life of the moral man is an exemplificatiion of the universal moral order (chung-yung, usually translated as "the Mean"). (*The Wisdom of Confucius*, ed. and trans. Lin Yutang, New York: The Modern Library, 1938, pp. 104-105).

Rizzoni, Alexander Antonovich. Russian painter (1836—1902). Especially known for his miniatures. "I love Rizzoni: now that's an artist; you can discern him through a magnifying glass," says Professor Bugaev in *On the Border*, p. 23.

botvinya. "Green vegetable soup with fish" made with a base of kvas, a Russian beverage made from dark bread which has been allowed to ferment. (*Russian Cooking: Recipe Index*, New York: Time Life, 1969, pp. 18, 19).

Clytemnestra. The daughter of Tyndareus, King of Sparta, and half sister of Helen. She marries Agamemnon, then murders him. He, in turn, is avenged by their son Orestes.

Pythagoros of Samos. Greek mathematician, astronomer, music theoretician. (c. 560 B.C.—480 B.C.). One of the earliest philosopher/mathematicians who works on the theory of numbers and declares "All things are numbers."

Lao-tzu. Chinese philospher. (c. 560 B.C.—480 B.C.). Writes the *Tao te ching* (The Classic of the Way and Its Virtue). A contemporary of Confucius best known as the founder of Taoism.

Bykaenko, Vasily Ivanych. Formed from the Russian word "бык" meaning "bull."

Badabaev, etc. While most of these names are untraceable, "Berendeev" prepares the reader for the later appearance of the Berendei doll.

Bugaev. Here Bely introduces the real surname of his family, identified in the novel as the Letaev family. Andrei Bely (Andrew White) was the pseudonym which the young Boris Bugaev chose in order to avoid confusion with and embarassment for his famous father.

Austriophile. Supporters of the Austrian position versus the Russian position of support for liberation movements of the Slavic and Orthodox peoples in the Balkans. Professor Letaev was most likely upset by the Three Emperors' Alliance of 1881 in which Russia, Austro-Hungary and Germany recognized legitimate spheres of influence in the Balkans and pledged restraint in the area. The treaty was largely the work of Bismarck and resulted in a reversal of the traditional Russian messianic Slavophile claim to be the protector and liberator of all the Slavs.

Antonovich, Vladimir Bonifatevich. Ukrainian historian (1834—1908). Professor of Russian History and Dean of the Historical-Philological department of Kiev University.

Grushevsky or Hrushevsky, Mikhail Sergeevich. Ukrainian historian. (1866—1934). A student of Antonovich, he first teaches history at Kiev and then later is a Professor at Lvov. He is also known as a leading Ukrainian political activist of the time.

Bukreev, Boris Yakovlevich. Ukrainian mathematician. (1862—1965). Professor of Mathematics at Kiev University from 1889. One of the founders of the Kiev Mathematical Society and an honorary member of the Moscow Mathematical Society.

Zakharchenko-Vashchenko. The wife of Mikhail Yegorovich Zakharchenko-Vashchenko, Professor of Mathematics at Kiev. (1825—1912).

Kostyakovsky. Actually Kistyakovsky, Bogdan Aleksandrovich. (1868—1920). Son of Aleksandr Fyodorovich Kistyakovsky. Russian criminologist. (1833—1885). Known to be a Ukrainian sympathizer. Here as elsewhere Bely frequently alters the name. Nina Berberova in her commentary to Bely's *The First Encounter*, trans. Gerald Janecek (Princeton, 1979, p. 117) notes that this alteration of one's name was a favorite device of Bely for showing disdain for a person. Another function is to add a new association from the distorted name. Thus rather than being related to "tassel" (кисть), the word reminds one of "bone" (кость).

"the opponent of an independent life for those at the extreme edges of the country." Bely uses several words formed from the root "край" meaning "edge" or "extreme." The mention of an independent life for the "outlying districts" (окраины) is a subtle political statement against independence for the Ukraine (Украина) which could be translated as "at the edge" of Russian territory. In his fervor, the father is likely to go "to extremes" an association with the Russian word "крайний" (extreme).

Shevchenko, Taras. Ukrainian poet. (1814—1864).

Gogol, Nikolai Vasilevich. Russian writer. (1809—1852). Born in the Ukraine in Sorochintsy of Cossack petty gentry, Gogol went on to become a famous writer of stories, novels and plays in Russian. His earlier stories were on Ukrainian folk themes, *Evenings on a Farm near Dikhanka* (1831) and "Taras Bulba" (1835), well known to American audiences through the film starring Yul Brynner and Tony Curtis. He later turned to Petersburg and the Russian countryside for his inspiration. Among his most famous works are *The Inspector General* (1836) and *Dead Souls* (1842).

Jesuit. The Society of Jesus was founded in Paris in 1539 by Ignatius Loyola. This Roman Catholic religious order had a history of involvement in intellectual and political matters. The Jesuits were originally expelled from Russia by Peter the Great in 1719. After the 1772 partition of Poland, which was predominantly Catholic, many Jesuits found themselves on the territory of the Ukraine and White Russia. When the Order was dissolved in 1773 by Pope Clement XIV, the Jesuits were warmly received by Katherine the Great and her son, Paul I. For some time Russia was the actual headquarters for the Jesuit order. By 1815 they had worn out their welcome and were forbidden to reside in St. Petersburg or Moscow. In 1820 Aleksandr I ordered an end to all of their activities in Russia. As representatives of the Roman Catholic Church and as self-proclaimed soldiers of the Roman Pope, the Jesuits and the term "Jesuit" came to be despised by the Orthodox Russians. Thus the use of the word here is perjorative.

Erasmus, Desiderius. Dutch scholar and theologian. (1466—1536). A famous "man of letters" who edited and translated the *New Testament*. "In the annals of classical learning Erasmus may be regarded as consolidating an intermediate stage between the humanity of the Latin Renaissance and the learned men of the age of Greek scholarship." (*The Encyclopaedia Britannica* 11 ed., 1910, Vol. IX, p. 732).

The Smith and the Bear. This is a carved wooden toy with the figures standing on a wooden board. The movable parts are controlled by a set of strings tied to a wooden ball. As you swing the ball dangling below the board the arms and heads of the figures move.

This and That's Own

"icon image . . . Deogenetrix . . . Silvergentleness. . . icon frames of cold: framed treasures..." This is a good example of the multileveled word play in the novel, in which one word or root gives rise to an entire series of associations. Having mentioned the icon of the Mother of God "Deogenetrix" (богородица) Bely continues to expand his use of words with the root "род" by a neologism "сребро́родие," which bears added religious connotations by the choice of the Church Slavonic form "сребро" for "silver." The word also calls to mind the title "благородие" your "Nobility." The translation "Silvergentleness" is meant to call attention to all of these aspects. Bely, however, is not finished; he turns to a new root "клад": the snow "will pile up" (накладет) and the puddles become "icon frames" (оклад) which are "treasures" (клад). Thus Bely completes a revolution returning to his starting point of the icon.

"Henrietta Martynovna, a German. . . but dumb, dumb..." This comment springs from the words "немка" (German) and "немой" (dumb). In fact the two are related etymologically with the Russian word for German, at one time applied to all foreigners, coming from the fact that unable to speak and understand Russian—they were speechless or "dumb." Later on we will learn that Henrietta suffers from "greensickness" (немочь).

Starikov. From Russian "старик" meaning "old man or elder."

Herr Zett, or Herman "Zett" is the German name for the letter "z." "Herman" transliterated from Russian would be "German." Herman is also the hero of Pushkin's famous story, "The Queen of Spades" (1836).

Glinka, Mikhail Ivanovich. Russian composer. (1804-1857). His name is identical to the Russian word for "clay." The word play may even extend to one other meaning of the word "глинка" (wild pigeon). Glinka is best known for the native Russian quality of his compositions. One of his best known operas was *Ivan Susanin* formerly known as *A Life for the Tsar*, in which Ivan sacrifices his life to protect the Russian land from the Polish invadors during the "Time of Troubles" in the early seventeenth century.

"walks the streets. . . streetwalking..." Kotik is still a child and it is easy to understand his confusion when words are used with more than one meaning. In this case "гулять" (to take a stroll) is used colloquially in the sense "to fool around," sometimes with sexual overtones. I have chosen the phrases "walks the streets" and "streetwalking" to create a similar, but not identical association which is verbal rather than logical.

Kotiks. "Kotik" meaning "kitten" is the nickname for the boy in the novel. There is some ambiguity here, a sign of the boy's ignorance, as to whether "kittens" are "little cats" or "little Kotiks."

"We demolish everything..." An echo of the nihilist philosophy of Bazarov in Turgenev's novel, *Fathers and Sons* (1862).

Volodechko, etc. All of these names end in the letter "o" which is characteristic of Ukrainian surnames.

"a bathhouse splasher, even a gangster, and this is filthier, than a robber." Antonovich is associated with bandits and the bathhouse because of the homonym "шайка" meaning "gang" or the "bucket" which one uses for washing at the bathhouse. Actually the two meanings represent different historical developments from a single Turkish word meaning a "wooden barge." In one case the meaning of "bucket" developed in the sense of a "vessel," whereas "band" came from the tconcept of a "pirate barge." (Н. М. Шанский, *Краткий этимологический словарь*, М:1961, 376).

Mrs. Malinovsky, Varvara Semyonovna. Wife of Nikolai Irasovich. Actually Bely has used the Lyaskovsky family as his model. Maria Ivanovna Lyaskovksky nee Vargin is the wife of Nikolai Erastovich Lyaskovsky (1816—1871) a chemist and the resident pharmacologist for Moscow University from 1846. In *On the Border* (pp. 85 ff.), we learn that Maria Ivanovna is the boy's godmother and that she "turned this 'connecting link' into iron shackles," visiting the family twice a year, once on October 13, the eve of the boy's birthday, and December 6, the father's nameday. Malinovsky is derived from the Russian word "малина" (raspberry).

October Boris Nikolaevich. Bugaev was born on Oct. 14, 1880 (Old style) or October 26, 1880 (New style). "October plays a major role in my life: 1) I was born in it (1880), 2) I became conscious of my self..." (*On the Border*, p. 169).

Solovyov. Bely is referring to the famous Russian historian, Sergei Mikhailovich Solovyov (1820—1879). He was the father of the Russian philospher Vladimir Sergeevich Solovyov, who in turn was so influential for Blok and Bely among the younger Russian symbolists. The Bugaev family had very close contact with the family of Mikhail Solovyov, another son of the historian, after they moved into the same building in 1893. See *The Frenzied Poets* by Oleg Maslenikov (Univ. of California: 1952, pp. 45-64).

Uncle Yorsh. Actually the brother of Bely's father, Georgi Vasilevich Bugaev. He was nicknamed "Yorsh" meaning "ruff" or "hair sticking up" by his sister-in-law, Belyj's mother. (*On the Border*, p. 86).

Arbat Square. It is in the Arbat region of Moscow that the Letaevs (and Bugaevs) live. The names of the shops and shopkeepers are factual. Both a residential and commercial district, the neighborhood underwent major reconstruction after the burning of Moscow in 1812. Located not far from the University, the Arbat was a popular area for professors. One ironical historical note is provided by P. B. Sytin: "The Crimean Tatars more than once broke into the center of Moscow along Arbat [boulevard]." (*По старой и новой Москве*, M:1947, 112). Bely wrote a long article describing the region, "Arbat," in 1923.

Karl Morà. Kotik's dislike for the sign apparently has to do with the limits of his own childhood world. It was as Bely notes "an ocean of the unknown" beyond this sign. The concept of ocean springs from the proximity in sound of "мора" and "моря" meaning "sea." ("Arbat," p. 178). Another reason for Kotik's fear may be the association with the Russian word "кикимора" or "goblin," coming from the Church Slavonic "мора" meaning "witch."

Maly Kislovsky Alley. Russian "кислый" meaning "sour." This is now Sobinovsky Alley.

Nikitsky. Now Herzen Street.

All Russian Central Executive Committee. The supreme legislative and administrative organ of the R.F.S.F.R. from 1917—1937. In 1937 the new constitution designated the Supreme Soviet and the Presidium of the Supreme Soviet as the highest organs of power.

Granny, Auntie, Uncle

Granny. The maternal grandmother, Granny Yegorova nee Zhuravleva.

Blackroach. A Bely neologism for "cockroach" using "чернокан" instead of "таракан."

Auntie Dotya. Yevdokia Yegorovna Yegorova.

massicot. The word used in Russian is "масака" which is derived from the French word "massicot." However, the word "massicot" refers to a yellowish pigment, whereas the Russian word has acquired the meaning of a deep reddish-purple.

"one foot in the grave..." The Russian "в три погибели" literally "into three ruins" comes from a saying meaning to be "hunched over" or "cowed in submission." Kotik is unable to draw distinctions between literal and figurative usages of words and expressions. The translation attempts to preserve the identical key word (bent over), but to offer a literal and figurative association common to English.

Uncle Vasya. Vasily Yegorovich Yegorov is the maternal uncle. In the little ditty "Vaska Pazukhov" the word "пазуха" means "bosom."

Mathematical Bulletin. Professor Bugaev was one of the founders and a frequent contributor to this Russian journal begun in 1866 as the voice of the Moscow Mathematical Society of Moscow University.

bouser. Here is an almost perfect example of parallel historical development in English and Russian. The basis for both words is "boza" the Turkish word for "a kind of thick white drink made of milk fermented." (*OED*, p. 260). From this comes the English "bouser" or "boozer" and the Russian "бузыга," all of which mean a "guzzler" or "drunkard."

Roulade

Bobynin. Related to the Russian word "бобыня" (bean).

Sofya Dragonovna, Anna Gorgonovna, Anna Grinovna. The patronymics here are translated rather than transliterated, but the resulting strangeness in English is similar to that of the Russian.

Sleptsovs. From Russian "слепец" (blind man). There were several notable families in Russia bearing this name. Bely mentions the family in *On the Border*, p. 96.

Tintoretto, Yakopo Robusti. Italian painter. (1519—1594). Known for his frescoes and works on religious themes. The name "Tintoretto" derived from the Italian "tintore" meaning "painter."

Kislenko. From the Russian word "кислый" meaning "sour."

"force"... Firs. The word play in Russian revolves around "сила" and the nickname "Сила" from the name "Силантий." In order to find a close sounding name to the English "force" I have borrowed the name of the famous lackey in Chekhov's *The Cherry Orchard*. It is interesting to note the meaning of "sila" in Budddhist mysticism: "Right discipline or sila means the desisting from the commission of all sinful deeds." (S. N. Dasgupta, *Hindu Mysticism*, New York: Ungar, 1959, p. 87).

Makovsky, Konstantin Yegorovich. Russian painter. (1839—1915). The painting referred to is called in English "A Russian Wedding Feast" or "The Wedding of a Boyar." Dated 1883, the painting was awarded the Medal of Honor at the 1885 International Exposition in Antwerp. The painting was purchased by Charles W. Schumann of New York and later sold in 1936. The beauty of Bely's mother, Aleksandra Dmitrievna Yegorova, (Elizaveta Letaeva in the novel) is also noted in *On the Border*, p. 78.

Transgression. The Russian word "преступление" normally translated as "crime" is actually a calque with Slavic translations of the two roots. The original title of the work was *The Transgression of Nikolai Letaev* (Преступление Николая Летаева). Bely later wrote (*On the Border*, 331 ff.) that this "transgression" was intended to refer to an episode in his schoolboy days when in the fourth grade he began to spend time in the library instead of attending classes. Thus according to Bely and most critics the original title became meaningless when the work went uncompleted. This explanation, however, fails to account for the words of Bely in his "Instead of a Foreword" to the first edition: "in it [*The Christened Chinaman*] is depicted the childhood of the hero at that critical point, where the child, becoming an adolescent, by that very fact commits his first transgression: the original sin, heredity appears in him." If we are to take the word for "adolescence" to conform to the Christian sense of "age of reason" we have a youngster about the same age as Kotik.

Turgenev, Ivan Sergeevich. Russian novelist. (1818—1883). Best known to Western readers for his novel, *Fathers and Sons* (1862).

Saltanova. Bely again distorts the spelling of this word. In the same picture by Makovsky, E. P. Letkova (later Sultanova) posed as the jealous sister. Letkova-Sultanova became a writer of short stories.

Boborykin, Pyotr Dmitrievich. Russian writer. (1836—1921). He produced over 100 novels, novellas and plays in his lifetime, and was considered by many the "Dean of Russian Letters." One of his best known works is *The Fortified City* (Китай город, 1882). Kitai gorod was built in Moscow between 1534—1538 as a second line of defense for the central city and the Kremlin fortress. The word "кита" in Old Russian meant "fortress" and of course, in modern Russian "Китай" is the name for "China." By the nineteenth century this area was "the crowded and irregularly built centre of business." (Karl Baedeker, *Handbook for Travellers to Russia*, New York: Arno Press, 1970, rpt. of 1914 ed., p. 276).

clown. Another instance of how purely verbal associations produce a thought train. Bely uses the word "паяц" for "clown" related to the Italian "pagliacci" which brings to mind the Italian opera and the associations with the Russian theatre which follow. *I Pagliacci* was composed in 1892 by Ruggiero Leoncavallo (1858—1919).

Lentovsky, Mikhail Valentinovich. Russian actor and director. (1843—1906). Famous actor and entrepreneur who staged several vaudevilles and plays.

Ognyov, Roman Yakovlevich. From the Russian "огонь" (fire). In actuality this is Arkady Yakovlevich Chernov. A Russian opera singer. (1858—1904). After several years in Italy he returned to St. Petersburg where his baritone voice became popular from 1888—1898 in the role of Mephistopheles in *Faust* (opera by Charles Guonod written in 1859). He was also the second husband of E. I. Gamalei. It is doubly ironic that Chernov, from the Russian "черный" (black), plays Mephistopheles the evil spirit whose name means "he who does not love life." One other association connected with *Faust* is the fact that Rudolf Steiner, the founder of Anthroposophy and Bely's spiritual mentor, began his career as a Goethe scholar. Even today the complete *Faust* is performed in the summer at Dornach, Switzerland, the headquarters of the worldwide anthroposophical movement.

Mariinsky Theater This is now the Kirov Theater in Leningrad. The Mariinsky Theater opened in 1860 in St. Petersburg as the Imperial Opera and Ballet Theater.

Kondratyev, Gennady Petrovich. Opera singer. (1834-1905). He studied and performed in Italy until his return to St. Petersburg. From 1871 on he was director of the opera in St. Petersburg.

Poliksena Borisovna Bleshchensky. From the Russian "блести" (to sparkle). Actually E. I. Gamalei, one of the closest friends of Bely's mother, who moved to St. Petersburg after her divorce to later become the wife of Chernov.

Napravnik, Edvard Frantsovich. Conductor. (1839-1916). Born in Bohemia, he came to Russia in 1861, where he worked as a composer and conductor of the opera in St. Petersburg.

Moika. A river in Petersburg.

Nevsky. The most famous of the Petersburg Prospects, enshrined forever in Gogol's story "Nevsky Prospect." "The Nevski Prospekt is 115 ft. wide and 2 3/4 M[eters] long, being the longest street in St. Petersburg... it is the busiest street in St. Petersburg... flanked on both sides by business houses." (Baedeker, p. 103).

Yablochkov, Pavel Nikolaevich. Russian inventor. (1847—1894). Inventor of the first widely used system of electric street lighting in Russia, first installed in Petersburg in 1878. One can also make the association with the word "яблоко" (apple) as Bely does in his novel *Petersburg* (trans. by Robert Maguire and John Malmstad, Indiana Univ., 1978, p. 311).

Princess Dagmar. The daughter of King Christian IX of Denmark, she married the future Aleksandr III on October 28, 1866 and was renamed Maria Fyodorovna. In Danish literature Princess Dagmar is the first wife of Danish King, Waldemar the Conqueror. She is portrayed as an example of a pure Christian wife and queen.

"how crabby she can be..." Literally this should be translated as: "to show [one] where the crabs spend the winter." Normally used in the sense of "I'll show you" or the more colloquial English "I'll show you where the sun don't shine." Since these "crabs" reappear, it was important to preserve a form of the word.

Mueller. Author of the well known body-building book called *My System* (Моя система).

Venus. The daughter of Zeus by Dione and the goddess of love and beauty. Another interpretation based on her Greek name Aphrodite (foam-born) is that she rose from the foam of the sea and is the goddess of gardens and flowers. (cf. Charles Gayley, *The Classic Myths*, New York: Ginn and Co., 1893, pp. 31, 32).

Faberge, Peter Carl. The famed jeweler in St. Petersburg and the official court jeweler who had branches in Moscow, London and Paris. He is best remembered for his magnificent Easter eggs prepared for the royal family.

sealskin cap. This is another homonymnic use for the Russian word "котик."

"beauty spots like flies." Russian "мушка" can mean either "little fly" or an "artificial beauty spot on the face." Here both denotations of the homonym are given.

"door was dissolving." The word "раствориться" can mean either "to open" or "to dissolve." While the door is obviously opening, the image of Papa has already been connected with the word in the sense of "dissolve" and the "solution" (раствор).

Mamochka

Pieter. This is the Dutch spelling of the nickname used for the city of St. Petersburg. (Maguire and Malmstad, p. 296).

Kosyakov house. The word "косяк" (door jamb or slope) is related to the root "кос" (crooked or slanting). Actually this was the Rachmanov house built in 1878 and according to Bely the first three-storied house in that area. ("Arbat," p. 165).

Zachatyevsky Lane. From the Church Slavonic and Russian word "зачатье" (conception).

Kovalevsky, Maksim Maksimovich. Russian jurist. (1815—1916). Professor of State Law and the History of Law at Moscow University between 1877—1887. In 1887 he is removed from his post for his liberal political views. He goes abroad, but returns to a post as Professor at St. Petersburg University from 1905 until his death. One of the areas of his research was the theory and forms of matriarchy.

Pompul. This is Ivan Ivanovich Yanzhul. Russian economist. (1845—1914). Professor of Economics and Professor of Financial Law at Moscow University. He was also Factory Inspector for Moscow and later a Member of the St. Petersburg Academy. He was for several years the next-door neighbor.

Dean M. Letaev. Moscow University was founded in 1755 and underwent re-organization in 1863, at which time it was divided into fifty-three departments among four divisions (факультеты): Philology, Physics and Mathematics, Jurisprudence, and Medicine. The University was presided over by an elected rector approved by the Czar and by four deans approved by the Minister of Education. Professor Bugaev was Dean of the Division of Physics and Mathematics from 1887 to 1891.

"It's right under your nose." A literal translation would read: "Beat yourself on the nose" in the sense of "Mark my words well."

Mikhails

not November, but—December. There seems to be some intentional confusion with the dates at this point. St. Mikhail's day could be celebrated on either November 8 or 22, or December 18. However, St. Nikolai's day falls on December 6 or 24. The fictional name for the father is Mikhail, but his real name is Nikolai Bugaev who celebrated his nameday on December 6. By moving the action into December Bely can continue his mixture of fact and fiction.

Tolstopyatov. From the Russian word "толстопятый" (stoutheeled).

"A beadle isn't a beagle." The Russian reads: "Педель не пудель." (A beadle isn't a poodle).

Mass Card. A close cultural equivalent for the "поминанье," which are slips of paper containing the names of those to be remembered in Othodox Church services.

viziga. This is prepared by removing the spinal cord from a sturgeon. It is then cut into pieces and cooked. Used as a stuffing it produced a rich fish fragrance and a melt-in-your-mouth taste.

something burning. "At night during severe frosts on Theater Square and the crosswalks of the central streets big fires were lit for the poor people to warm themselves." (И. А. Слонов, "Из жизни торговой Москвы," in *Ушедшая Москва*, ред. Н. Ц. Асукин, М: 1964, 220, 221).

kulebyaka. "Flaky salmon or cabbage loaf." (*Russian Cooking*, p.12).

Anuchin, Dmitry Nikolaevich. Russian geographer. (1843—1923). Professor of Geography and Ethnography and Head of the newly established department of that title after 1884. He is also the editor of the *Russian Gazette* (Русские ведомости). Bely later wrote his Kandidat thesis for Anuchin. Anuchin is also remembered as one of the main contributors to the first Soviet World Atlas.

Usov, Sergei Alekseevich. Russian zoologist. (1827—1886). Professor of Zoology at Moscow University. Also the godfather of Boris Bugaev. Professor Bugaev authored the eulogy for Professor Usov. Bely notes that his father, deprived of contact with his close friend Usov, became more and more isolated and withdrawn. (*On the Border*, p. 93). Little Borya was indeed surprised by the size of Usov's wart: "Why does Godfather have a strawberry growing on his face?" (ibid., p. 64).

Veselovsky, Aleksei Nikolaevich. Russian literary historian. (1843—1918). He received an honorary doctorate from Moscow University in 1879 where he began to teach in 1881. His better known brother Aleksandr (1838—1906) was also a literary historian and Professor of Literature at the University of St. Petersburg and a member of the Academy of Sciences.

Batyushkov, Konstantin. Russian poet (1787—1855).

theosophy. The Theosophical Society was founded in 1875 by Madame H. P. Blavatsky and continued by Annie Besant. The theosophists attempted to unite the wisdom of much of Eastern thought into a coherent system. Annie Besant in *The Ancient Wisdom* introduces many of the associations which can be found in Bely's novel, including Taoism, the *I ching*, Ahura Mazda, Brahma, reincarnation, Pythagorus, and the monad. Rudolf Steiner was originally associated with the Theosophical movement; later he founded the Anthroposophical movement which attracted Bely as a member.

Severtsov, Aleksei Nikolaevich. Russian biologist. (1866—1936). After finishing Moscow University in 1890, he went on to become a Professor of Biology, first in Kiev from 1902—1911 and then in Moscow from 1911—1930.

Usov, Pasha. The son of Sergei A. Usov mentioned above.

Grot, Nikolai Yakovlevich. Russian philosopher. (1852—1899). Professor at Moscow University from 1866.

multisuckeress. This neologism leads into Mrs. Kislenko, from the Russian "кислый" meaning "sour."

Vindalai Urvantsev. Russian "урваться" (to break away from).

Trumpet of Jericho. The fabled "trumpets" of Jericho at whose sound the walls came tumbling down. (Joshua 6).

Czar cannon. Cast in 1586 by Andrei Chokhov and intended for the defense of the Moscow Kremlin. It weighs 40 tons and has a calibre of 890 mm. While it has never been fired, it is a well-known tourist attraction within the Kremlin walls.

Adam. (Genesis 1:26-5:5).

raising of the dead. In both Matthew 11:5 and Luke 7:22 we read of the miracles being performed by Christ. This later serves as a foundation for the Christian belief in resurrection not only for Christ but for all who believe in him. (Revelations 20:5).

Ahura Mazda

Ahura Mazda. The supreme deity of ancient Persia who forms the basis for Zoroastrianism.

Dadarchenkos. This is Nikolai Ilych Storozhenko. (1836—1906). A Professor of World Literature at Moscow University. He is known as a specialist on English literature and on Shakespeare. In 1894 he becomes the Head of the "Society of Lovers of Russian Letters or Literatures." Bely recalls visits with other children to the Storozhenko home in *On the Border*, p. 117 ff.

Persic. While the usage of "persic" in the meaning of "peach" is considered obsolete in English, the word duplicates the sound play in Russian of "Перс" and "персик." In several instances in the translation I have relied on the original (even when obsolete) usage.

sunbeams. The Russian word "зайчик" can mean either "little hare" or a "reflection of the sun's rays." It is the one homonym for which I have not found one satisfactory equivalent. Both concepts appear regularly in the novel.

The Cathedral of the Redeemer (Храм Христа Спасителя). "The most richly decorated church in Moscow, built in 1839—1883 from the plans of *Thon* in commemoration of the events of 1812—1814, is conspicuously situated in a large square on the left bank of the Moskva. . . . Four massive piers support the *Main Dome*, which is adorned with a large picture of the Lord of the Sabaoth, by Markov. Below are representatives of the Old and New Testament." (Baedeker, pp.304-305). The Church of the Redeemer was demolished in 1934 to make way for the Palace of Soviets, which was to be the largest building in the world. Construction on the building was hampered by water seepage and halted in 1941. During the war the steel skeleton of the building was dismantled to provide metal for the war effort. Eventually in 1960 the sight became the home of the Moscow outdoor swimming pool. (Kathleen Berton, *Moscow: An Architectural History*, New York: St. Martin's Press, 1978, pp. 223-225).

Koshelyov, Nikolai Andreevich. Russian painter. (1840-?). In addition to his original works in the cupola, Koshelyov helped to paint the Saboath according the sketch of Professor Markov.

tigers. "The Tiger still exists in the Lenkoran Territory, around the shores of the Caspian, in Turkestan and on the Chinese bank of the Amur." (Baedeker, p. xxx).

Sarts. Name of the indigenous inhabitants who had settled in what is now Uzbekistan and Turkestan.

Alaska. Alaska was purchased from the Russians by the Americans in 1867. Russia's military concerns in the Balkans and the realization that she could not adequately defend Alaska were considerations in the sale. The actual purchase price was $7,200,000.

Lamsdorfs. The Lamsdorf family had close ties to the ruling circles of Russia. Nikolai Lamsdorf was an aide-de-camp to Emperor Aleksandr II. His father had been a tutor to the Russian Emperor Pavel. Count Vladimir Nikolaevich Lamsdorf (1845-1907) devoted his life to the Foreign Service from his twenty-first birthday. By 1875 he had achieved the rank of First Secretary. From 1901 until his retirement in 1906 he served as the Russian Foreign Minister; and as such he was involved with the crushing defeat of the Russians in the Russo-Japanese War of 1905. It is possible that Bely's recollection at this point contains an anachronism.

Bismarck, Otto Eduard Leopold von. German statesman. (1815—1898). Among his other more well known activities, Bismarck was ambassador to St. Petersburg for four years beginning in 1858. In addition to forging a German alliance with Austro-Hungary in 1879 which provided for mutual assistance in case of a Russian attack, Bismarck also designed the Three Emperors' Alliance of 1881, in which Russia joined with the other two on a policy of benevolent neutrality in the Balkans. The "three hairs" is apparently a reference to the famous caricatures printed in the Berlin satirical journal *Kladderadatsch* where Bismarck is depicted with a mustache and some hair on the sides of his head, but bald on the top of his head except for three distinct hairs which resemble horns.

Kalnoky (Kalnocky) von Koeroespatak, Count Gustav. Austro-Hungarian diplomat. (1832—1898). After serving as Ambassador to St. Petersburg, Kalnoky became the Foreign Minister from 1881—1895.

black Granny. Much of the logic of this paragraph is based on the words: "бабушка" (granny) and "бабочка" (butterfly).

become tired. "стать" (to become) and "устать" (to tire).

beri-beri-beri. This chant which proceeds through the sound combinations "r-b," "er" and "ar" is based in part on Bely's own work on glossolalia. Heavily influenced by Rudolf Steiner's theories of eurythmy, Bely created his own *Glossalolija* [sic] in 1922. He himself describes this process as "an improvisation on several sound themes; since these themes develop in me phantasies of sound-images, thus I lay them out; but I know: beyond the image subjectivity of my improvisations is concealed their outside-the-image, nonsubjective root." (p. 9). This fascination with words was a lifelong obsession with Bely who believed that the word was the key to all existence. "The incarnation of the unions of all letters is — man — he exists, as an entity of the multiplicity of sounds; we are created by the word; and with our word we create, in naming them, all things;..." (p. 101). One interesting attempt to decipher the sound system of the novel according to Bely's *Glossalolija* was made by А. Векслер, "'Эпопея' А. Белого," *Современная литература: сборник статей*, Л: 1925, 48-75).

Zoroaster. Persian prophet. (660 B.C.—583 B.C.) The founder of the religion of Ancient Persia known as Zoroastrianism. He is a descendant of the Spitama (White) family, a curious coincidence with Andrei Bely. "'Zarouster' [sic] is the star of the star of the morning, where 'зор' [see, light] is the nucleus: it is the sun's 'взор' [look]." (*Glossalolija*, p. 61).

Kuznetsky Most. A street known for its better shops in the downtown area.

snappers. These party favors were stuffed with surprises and one had to pop one end in order to open the snapper. Bely associates the "pants" for dolls with the popping sound and the word which can also mean "to fart."

'Rousant'...'Russian' or 'russet'... The key to the sound-sense alternation is found in *Glossalolija*, p. 54: "'rus' — 'rucant'; this is — luminous (in Sanskrit); 'rucant' is russet; 'rus' is Rus; she is a luminance by sound; and 'rusios' is flaming: 'rouge'."

Papa Hit the Nail on the Head

"Papa Hit the Nail on the Head." The actual Russian translation should be to "reach the nail" meaning "This is the last straw." To have translated the sentence thus would be to ignore the literal interpretation which the young boy applies to the sequence of events: whenever his father gets angry he vents that anger by hammering at the wash stand in the study which had been a gift from his wife.

agrement. Bely uses the word "аграмант" instead of the correct French "agrement" meaning "ornament."

salmon. Bely invents the Russian word "сомовой" which is derived from the French "saumon" meaning not only the fish, but also the pinkish color associated with it.

windywintry. "ветрищенские." This is probably an echo of the more famous "Крещенские морозы" (Epiphany frosts).

Yanzhul. This is apparently an oversight on Bely's part. He has been using the name Pompul to substitute for Ivan Ivanovich Yanzhul. Here he uses the actual instead of the fictional name.

Vasilievsky. A reference to Vasilievsky Island in St. Petersburg where the University and residential districts are located.

Lepyokhin. In *The Silver Dove* Mrs. Yeropegin is referred to by her husband as "лепеха" (a flat cake) translated by George Reavey as "dumpling."

Pafnuty Lvovich. This is Chebyshev already mentioned.

"the terrifying Lawgiver, the Sinai one." It is on Mount Sinai that the Lord gives the tablets containing the commandments to Moses. "The glory of the LORD settled on Mount Sinai." (Exodus 24:16).

Samurai. Warrior of feudal Japan.

Hokusai. Japanese painter. (1760—1849). While Japanese do not consider him first-rate, he has achieved considerable popularity in the West and many Europeans feel that he is "the greatest of all the Japanese painters of the Popular School." (*E. B.*, XIII, p. 577).

The Scythian

keekee. Russian has the verb "кикать," meaning to screech out "kee-kee."

Phooeyness

our Church elder, Svetoslavsky. From the Russian words "свет" (light) and "слава" (glory). Bely recalls the actual Church elder, Bogoslovsky, "бог" (god) and "слово" (word) in "Arbat," p. 164.

Berendei. "Each year at the Palm Sunday fair there appeared new toys, for which the merchants thought up the names of persons, who for some reason in recent times had distinguished themselves in a positive, or mostly in a negative sense,..." (И. А. Белоусов, "Ушедшая Москва" in *Ушедшая Москва*, 353). A literary antecedent for Berendei can be found in V. A. Zhukovsky's "Tale of Czar Berendei" written in 1831 and printed in 1833. The more immediate and more likely reference is to the opera *Snow Maiden* (Снегурочка, 1882) by Nikolai Andreevich Rimsky-Korsakov (1844—1908) based on the play by Aleksandr N. Ostrovsky written in 1873. Ostrovsky's play is filled with the residents of the village of Berendeev, who are called Berendeis.

Aphrosim. "'Aphrosim!' — I simply mixed up: 'aphrosyne' in Greek is after all 'thoughtlessness'; and Afrosinya worked as a kitchen maid." (*Kotik Letaev*, 1922 ed., p. 56). An additional association is with the Greek word "aphros," meaning "foam" or "froth."

Pfeffer. German for "pepper."

Pils. German from "Pilsener" or "Pilsner," a special type of beer which requires three pourings from the tap over a five minute span to create a magnificent head of foam. Bely might have also had in mind "Pilz," the German word for "mushroom."

Gorozhankin, Ivan Nikolaevich. Russian botanist. (1848—1904). Professor of Botany at Moscow University and Director of the Botanical Gardens.

Anton's fire. The Russian expression for "gangrene." This is obviously brought to mind by the associations of Anton, the yardman, and the antonovka apples, which the father frequently gives as presents to Kotik.

Sophus Lie, the Swedish mathematician. He is Norwegian, not Swedish.

Smirnov, Sergei Vasilevich. Actually Mikhail Vasilevich Popov, a classmate of Bely's father. ("Arbat," pp. 163, 164). Russian "смирный" (quiet or submissive).

Belkin. M. L. Belkin was a well-known furrier on Kuznetsky Most. The Russian word "белка" (squirrel). Belkin is also the fictitious narrator of Pushkin's "Tales of Belkin" (1830).

Fig. In addition to the reference to fig leaves in the Garden of Eden, there is mention of the Fig tree in the *Upanishads*. The word "fig" is also related to an obscene gesture in Russia. The Russian phrase "to look in a book, and see a fig" means "to understand nothing."

Livland or Livonia. A territory which comprised parts of modern southern Estonia and northern Latvia, including the city of Riga. It became a part of the Russian Empire in 1721 according to the provisions of the Treaty of Neustadt. The inhabitants were primarily Latvians, Estonians and some Germans.

Baer, Karl Ernest. (1792—1876). Member of the Russian Academy of Sciences. One of the founders and pioneers in the science of embryology. He is also associated with Baer's Law of All Development. As a Professor of Anatomy at Koenigsberg from 1819, Baer discovered in 1826 the egg of mammals and expounded his law: "every animal which springs from the coition of male and female is developed from an ovum." The work referred to is probably *Über Entwicklungsgeschicte der Thiere* Königsberg: 1828, 2 vol. entitled in Russian *История развития животных*.

Spring

Kislovka Street. Russian "кислый" (sour). Now Semashko Street.

Popov. While all of the shops and shopkeepers did actually exist, some of the names call forth certain associations. Popov, the wine merchant, comes from Russian "поп" a colloquial and non-complimentary designation for a priest. Thus "Popov" means "son of a priest." There is, of course, a Popov brand vodka in the United States.

Burov. Canes and umbrellas. Russian "бурый" (brown) and "бурный" (stormy).

Neidhard. German "Neidhart" means "envious."

Starikov. Russian "старик" (old man).

Kogtev. Russian "когти" (claws).

Tolstoy, Lev Nikolaevich. Russian writer (1828-1910). The young Boris Bugaev saw Tolstoi on several occasions as a visitor to the Bugaev home. (*On the Border*, pp. 112, 113).

"It's the Germans letting loose the mist!" Having regularly used the word "mist" to translate the Russian "туман," I came across this word play which does not exist in the Russian, but does relate the English "mist" with the German word "Mist," which can also mean "a mist" but more often refers to "dung" or "manure."

Schumann, Robert Alexander. German composer. (1810—1856).

Fellow Traveler

Diogenes. Greek philospher. (412 B.C.—323 B.C.). "He inured himself to the vicissitude of weather by living in a tub belonging to the temple of Cybele." (*E.B*, VIII, 282).

Aesopian. Greek fabulist. (620 B.C.—560 B.C.)

offspring-fumes, like the schismatic priest, Pustosvyat. Russian "чадо" already seen in the sense of "kitchen fumes" can also mean in Church literature "offspring." This homonym brings to mind the next image of Nikita Pustosvyat, a heretic beheaded on Red Square in 1682. One of the heretical stands of these Old Believers was their insistence on making the sign of the cross with two instead of three fingers. The name Pustosvyat can be broken down into "пусто" (blank) and "свят" (sacred).

"Second." This is actually our "ring" or fourth finger, called by the Russians "the nameless one." Russians begin counting with their fingers by depressing first the pinky, then the ring finger and so on.

a savage radish. "свирепая редька." Bely could be thinking of the folktale entitled "Turnip" (Репка) where Grandpa having planted a turnip calls on Grandma who calls on someone else, etc. to pull the turnip out of the ground. The little story is especially marked by alliteration, rhyme and other poetical sound effects. See А. Н. Афансьев, *Народные русские сказки* (М: 1957, I, 131).

Julius,II. Giuliana della Rovere who becomes Pope and reigns from 1503—1513 with the help of Cesare Borgia.

Moro. Ludovico Sforza, il Moro (the Moor). (1451—1508). This famous patron of Leonardo da Vinci received the crown of Milan in 1494 but was driven out in 1499. He was handed over to the French and died in prison.

Este. The House of Este was one of the oldest of the former reigning houses of Italy.

Leonardo da Vinci. Italian painter. (1452—1519).

Raphael, Sanzio. Italian painter. (1483—1520).

Lorenzo di Credi. Italian painter. (1459—1537). He was a Florentine painter who worked as an assistant to Leonardo da Vinci.

Valla, Giorgio. Italian humanist. (c. 1430—1499). A cousin of Lorenzo, who translates Aristotle's *Poetics* in 1498. Bely has obviously made a mistake in his choice of the name Valle. Pietro della Valle, a world traveller, (1586—1652) who visits India and Persia.

Poggio. Gian Francesco Poggio Braccioline. Italian scholar. (1380—1459). Scholar of the Renaissance who devotes his life to recovering the classics. The author of *A History of Florence.*

Borgia, Cesare. (1476—1507). Son of Pope Alexander VI and brother of the well-known Lucretia Borgia (1480—1519).

Attic salt. An expression going back to the Romans meaning "refined, delicate, poignant wit" by reference to the standards of Attica and its capital, Athens. (*OED,* p. 18). The connection between Ancient Greece and the fifteenth century is one for which Bely is clearly indebted to Rudolf Steiner. Steiner describes the three major periods of human culture as 1) Greek civilization, 2) the time of Christ, 3) Raphael, Michelangelo and Leonardo da Vinci. See *The Bhagavad Gita and the Epistles of Paul,* trans. Lisa D. Monges, Doris M. Bugby (New York: Anthroposophical Press, 1971, pp. 4,5).

billygoat hops. "козловак." Berberova (*First Encounter,* p. 112) explains: "A strange dance of the period performed in public by a single dancer, uninhibited and wild, was called a *kozlovak.*" From Russian "козел" (billy goat).

Beethoven, Ludwig van. German composer. (1770—1827).

Socrates. Greek educator. (c. 470 B.C.—399 B.C.). One can find many parellels between Professor Letaev and Socrates in their eccentricity, modes of life and even in their physical appearances. "Outwardly his [Socrates'] presence was mean and his countenance grotesque. Short of stature, thicknecked and somewhat corpulent with prominent eyes, with nose upturned and nostrils outspread, with large mouth and coarse lips..." (*E.B.,* XXV, 332). Condemned to death in 399 B.C., he is forced to drink hemlock.

Monadology. From the Greek term "monas" (unit or one), which for Pythagorus is the basis of his number system. "A monadology is a metaphysical system that interprets the world as a harmonious unity encompassing a plurality of such self-determining simple entitites." The monad is in modern terms: "a simple, irreducible, and sometimes indestructible entity" and "the minimal unity into which the cosmos and all composite things in it can be resolved. (*The Encyclopedia of Philosophy,* ed. Paul Edwards, New York: Macmillan, 1967, V, 362). Leibniz writes *La Monadologie* (1714) as a sketch of his philosophical system. Nikolai Bugaev also publishes a brochure entitled "The Bases of Evolutionary Monadology" (Основы эволюционной монадологии, 1893), which originally appeared in the journal, *Questions of Philosophy and Psychology.*

Andrei the Filler. Russian "Андрей Налив." This is the feast of St. Andrew of Crete (660—740) celebrated on July 4. Archbishop of Crete from 692, he is known as an orator and one of the main hymnologists of the Oriental Church. According to folk beliefs it was at this time that the winter crops were ripe. Two such folk sayings are "Winter's a'fillin, and the buckwheat is a'comin" and "By Andrei's day the winter crops have come to their fill, and Father oats is halfway grown." (Александр Е. Бурцев, *Полное собрание этнографических трудов*, СПб: 1910, 1911, IX, 214-215). There is also a sort of apple called "белый налив."

Kasyanov. Vladimir Ivanovich Taneev. (1840—1921). Taneev was well known for his monthly dinners at the Hermitage restaurant.

Heavenly Empire. Sometimes called the Celestial Empire, this was the name for the Chinese Empire.

bigbrowacorn. "лоборог." Related to the Russian "носорог" (rhinocerous) and "единорог" (unicorn). The unicorn is the symbol on the coat of arms of the Ableukhov family in the novel *Petersburg*.

penates. Roman deities whose duty it was to attend to the welfare and prosperity of the family. From the Latin "penus," which was the innermost part of the sanctuay.

Leyden jar. A device for the storage of an electric charge. "The earliest form of Leyden jar consisted of a glass vial or thin Florence flask, partly full of water, having a metallic nail inserted through the cork which touched the water." The name comes from the University of Leyden (Leiden) where some of the earliest experiments were made in 1746. (E. B., XVI, 528).

Elohims! Actually the form "elohim" is already the Hebrew plural of the word for "god." It is often used in the singular sense of the one God.

Delyanov, Ivan Davidovich. (1818-1897). Minister of Education from 1882. It should be remembered that all deanships were approved by the Minister of Education, or more literally the Minister of Enlightenment (Просвещение).

Ezekiels. Ezekiel was the third and last of the "Greater" Old Testament Prophets. Sometimes called the "Father of Judaism," Ezekiel is credited with the doctrines of resurrection and personal immortality which come from his prophecies.

Traviata. *La Traviata* (The Fallen Woman), opera by Giuseppe Verdi, 1853.

Andersen, Hans Christian. Danish poet and fabulist. (1805-1875). Best known for his *Fairy Tales* (1835) including one called the "Fellow Traveller." Bely recalls having had all of Andersen read to him in the fall and winter of 1866. (*On the Border*, p. 205).

Abraham. As ancestor to the Israelites, Abraham is according to legend the first to worship the True God. Abraham seals a covenant with God, the sign of which is circumcision. (Genesis 17). He is also well known for his total submission to the will of God, including his near execution of his own son, Isaac. (Genesis 22).

Sodom. "Now the men of Sodom were wicked great sinners against the Lord." (Genesis 13:13).

calves. "тельцы." During Moses' absence on the mountain awaiting the commandments, the Jews built an idol of gold in the shape of a calf. (Exodus 32:1-7).

Kraft. German "force."

Lot. The son of Abram's brother, Haran, who lives in Sodom. Lot and his family are the only ones to escape the destruction of the city, but Lot's curious wife who looks back is turned into a pillar of salt. (Genesis 19:26).

Xanthippe. The wife of Socrates, usually associated with a nagging, quarrelsome woman.

Caesar Augustus. The adopted son of Julius Caeser born in 63 B.C. who became the first Roman Emperor in 27 B.C. and ruled until his death in 14 A.D. He is mentioned in Luke 2:1 for ordering the census which brings Joseph and Mary to Bethlehem, where Christ is born.

Pontius Pilate. The Roman Procurator of Judea who condemned Jesus to be crucified. Appointed by Tiberius in 26 A.D. he is reported to have killed himself in 39 A. D. on orders of Caligula.

red downpours. A reference to the destruction of Sodom by "brimstone and fire." (Genesis 19:24).

Dead, bitter Sea. Often called the Salt Sea in Genesis, it is a salt lake at the mouth of the Jordan River. "The water is bitter and distasteful to the mouth,..." (*The Interpreter's Dictionary of the Bible*, George Buttrick, New York: 1962, I, 789).

Om

Om. Most solemn of the mystic syllables of the Hindu religion. A key to internal wisdom. In the *Upanisads* we read: "That which is denoted by the word OM is verily this imperishable Brahman." (*Manduka*, I Khadra, 1).

"Paradise is — a sparkler." In Zoroastrianism heaven is a "place of 'Eternal Light'." (A. V. Williams Jackson, *Zoroastrian Studies*, Columbia: 1928, XII, 147).

the World Tree. Almost all of the imagery which follows is borrowed from Hindu writings, principally the *Upanisads* "The entrance to the True is covered by a shining disk [the sun]." (*Isa vasya Upanisad*, 15). "Grounded in the Highest...is the beginningless Asvattha tree (the universe),[fig tree which is also the abode of God]." (*VI Valli*, 1). Zoroastrianism contains a similar "tree of life," "the sacred white haoma tree, from which is extracted the draft of ambrosia which bestows immortality at the Resurrection." (*Zoroastrian Studies*, XII, 51, 52). The concept of God as light, "The Illuminance," is a familiar one in the *Upanisads* as it is in the concept of "Light of Light" in the Christian tradition. In *Notes of an Eccentric* (II, 149, 152), Bely mentions a translation by Vera Johnson of the *Upanisads*, and goes on to write: "The Upanisads filled the spirit, like a cup, with warmth."

Raphael. One of the three archangels mentioned in the Book of Tobias in the *Old Testament*. The other two are Michael and Gabriel. Raphael is the patron of travellers.

Seven Rivers. A region in northern Turkestan. The Seven Rivers are the Ili, Karatal, Aksu, Bien, Lepsa, Baskan, and Sarkand.

Zarathustra. Another name for Zoroaster. "'Zarathustra' is outstretched by its rays onto everything from the spiritual life-fever of the soul." (*Глоссалолия*, 60).

Euphrates and Tigris. Two rivers located primarily in modern day Iraq. According to Genesis, the Euphrates was one of the four rivers bordering the garden of Eden.

Labrador. The coast of Labrador is located in the Canadian province of Newfoundland.

Brahma. Creator and first God of the Hindu triad. Normally he is depicted as red in color and with four bearded faces.

Mahabharata. One of the longest epics of all time, it has some 88,000 verses. Supposedly written by Vyasa, it was already in existence by the fourth century B.C. It is one of the two great epic poems of the Hindus. The other is the *Ramayana*.

Om-mir... This progression of sounds results in interesting collections of nonsense syllables and words. Each line in the lefthand column arrives at a key word which corresponds to a word in the righthand column. Om—mir [world]—mira—am—amo [I love (Latin)] = I love. Ammo—amo [I love]—mam—mama = mater [mother]. Ram—rama [Hindu deity]—brahm—brahma = god.

Dykirion. A candelabrum of "two-candles" found on the altar in an Orthodox Church.

Babylonian captivity. The people of Israel were taken captive by the city and kingdom of Babylon from 597 B.C. to 537 B.C. According to the *Old Testament* this was God's punishment for their sin of idolatry and disobedience. (Ezra 2:1 and Jeremiah 25:8-11).

Nativity Ruprecht. The German version of Santa Claus. Originally in the seventeenth century the servant Ruprecht follows the Christ child with gifts for the good children on Christmas eve. One century later he is the companion for St. Nikolaus who brings gifts to German children on St. Nikolaus day, December 6.

in fine linen. The form in Russian "виссоны" is the word used in Russian Biblical literature: "clothed in fine linen, and purple, and scarlet." (Revelations 18:16).

Enoch. An Old Testament patriarch, the son of Jored and the father of Methuselah. In contrast to his father and son whose deaths are duly noted, "Enoch walked with God; and he was not, for God took him." (Genesis 5:24).

Methusaleh. An Old Testament, antediluvian patriarch, who lives 969 years. (Genesis 5:21-27).

Melchizedek. He offers Abraham bread and wine as he is returning from his defeat of the four kings. Often known as the "Priest of the Most High God." (Genesis 14:18).

reliquaries The word "рака," a receptacle for relics of the saints, gives rise to the association with "рак" (crab) used in the expression "know, where the crabs spend the winter" meaning "to really know one's stuff." By replacing the word for "winter" with "quarry" I have introduced a substitute for the word play.

Abram. "No longer shall your name be Abram [exalted father], but your name shall be Abraham; [father of a multitude]." (Genesis 17:5).

Isaac. The son of Abraham whom he is willing to sacrifice, until the son is saved by God's angel. (Genesis 22).

Red Anise

Red Anise. A red and green apple sometimes called a "striped anise" and having a slight fragrance of aniseed.

Marusya-dawn. This may be associated with the lines: "a maiden,. . . a czaritza, all shining, like the dawn" (девица, . . . царица, вся сияя, как заря) of Pushkin's "Tale of the Golden Cockerel" (Сказка о золотом петушке, 1834). The tale is adapted from the "Legend of the Arab Astrologer" in Washington Irving's *The Alahambra*. Having received the golden cockerel which warns of impending attack, the czar promises the giver anything he desires. After several attempts by the czar's sons to repel the invaders fail, the czar himself goes to the front. There he meets this dazzling beauty, with whom he returns to his kingdom. Upon his return the advisor asks for the beauty as payment for the cockerel. The czar refuses, kills the sorcerer, and is in turn clawed to death on the forehead by the the cockerel. The sound "kiri ku ku" appears in the poem. Rimsky-Korsakov wrote his famous opera *The Golden Cockerel*, first performed in 1909, on the basis of the poem.

Dadon. The famous Czar Dadon also appears in "The Golden Cockerel."

Prechistenka. Now Kropotkin Street. The Russian "пречистая" refers to the purity of the Virgin Mary celebrated on the holiday of the Assumption.

Stozhenka. Actually Ostozhenka Street, now Metrostroevsky Street. The confusion and mistake comes from the confusion of two words: "остожье" "a piece of land large enough to yield a 'стог' or 'стожок' a 'stack' of hay."

Ganetsky, Ivan Stepanovich. Russian military man. (1810—1887). He reached the rank of Adjutant-General, participated in the Turkish wars and was the one-time commandant of the fortress at St. Petersburg.

Mariinsky Institute Probably the Aleksandr and Marie's Girls' School on Prechistenka Street. Actually several (29) such schools were established in the 1860s.

Madam Chertova. From Russian "черт" (devil). Also another reference to the old woman in the "Queen of Spades."

Levshinsky. There is a Maly Levshinsky Street in Moscow.

Ivan, its finger in a thimble. "The huge bell-tower of Ivan-Veliki (Great)...completed by Boris Godunov in 1600...rises in five stories to a height of 320 ft. . . The tower is surmounted by a gilded dome, 33 ft. in diameter, crowned by a gilded cross." (Baedeker, p. 281).

paschas. "Easter cheese pyramid with candied fruits and nuts." (*Russian Cooking*, p. 90).

"He is risen, truly." The traditional Easter greeting in Russia is "Christ is risen" to which one replies "Truly, He is risen."

Madam Hornung. German "Horn" is "horn." "It was considered customary to renew one's clothes for Easter." (Белоусов, "Ушедшая Москва," 326).

"Behold, the man!" The famous phrase of Pontius Pilate as he presented Jesus to the crowd: "ecce homo." (John 19:5).

Herod's warrior. Herod the Great. (73 B.C.—4 B.C.) King of Palestine from 37 B.C. until his death. Hearing of the birth of the Messiah, Herod sends his soldiers to kill all male children under the age of two in the region of Bethlehem. (Matthew 2:16-18).

Devichy Field. "*The Field of Maidens,* in which, during the time of the Mongolian supremacy, were assembled the maidens who had to be delivered to the Khan along with the yearly tribute." (Baedeker, p. 306).

clinics. Originally called the New University Clinic, this is now the City Clinical Hospital #1 on Pirogovkaya Bolshaya Street, the former Bolshaya Czaritsinskaya.

Giftbearing Hosts. In the "Cherubimic Hymn" of the Orthodox Service there is the passage "that we may receive the King of all, who comes invisibly upborne by the Angelic Hosts." The Church Slavonic form "дороносим" "means literally 'borne on lances' and alludes to the ancient military custom of soldiers raising their general on their shields above the points of their lances and carrying him thus surrounded by troops, so that from a distance, it looked as though he were borne on the points of lances." (D. Sokolof, *A Manual of the Orthodox Church*, Jordanville, N. Y.: Holy Trinity Monastery, 1968, p. 68).

Caiaphas. After his arrest in the Garden of Gethsemane and before being taken to Pilate, Christ is led to Caiaphas. "Caiaphas, who was high priest that year. It was Caiaphas who had given counsel to the Jews that it was expedient that one man should die for the people." (John 18:13,14).

Let this cup pass from me. (Matthew 26:39).

Judea. One of the three main divisions of Palestine along with Galilee and Samaria. The south-western part of Palestine.

Galilee. Northern district of Palestine. Most of Christ's life and ministry took place here.

Sea of Tiberias. A large lake in northern Palestine also called the Sea of Galilee.

"My peace — I give you." (John 14:27).

gift-bearing ciborium. In the Orthodox Church this is a case used to carry the Holy Gifts outside of the Church in order to administer communion to those unable to attend services. In the Roman Catholic Church this case is called a "pyx" and a ciborium is the receptacle for consecrated hosts in the tabernacle.

By Andrei the Filler — you will be filled full with knowledge. This is another echo of the teachings of Steiner who believed that only after a period of probation, enlightenment and initiation, one "is then ripe to hear the real names of things which are the keys to higher knowledge." (*Knowledge of the Higher Worlds,* trans. G. Metaxa, London: Putnam, 1923, p. 63).

Kasyanov. The Bugaev family spent a summer in Demyanov, where Taneev had an estate. (*The Beginning of the Century* [Начало века], 1933, p. 67).

pinapplerie. Bely's fascination with the pineapple may be associated with the Disk of the Sun. The image appears in one of his poems, "On the Hills" (На горах, 1903), which was a favorite of Rudolf Steiner. There is also a poem entitled "Pineapple" (Ананас, 1903—1931). Before the introduction by Dole of canned pineapples from Hawaii, they were an exotic fruit, a sign of wealth and luxury in Russia.

Daniel. It was not Daniel but his three friends, Shadrach, Meskach and Abednega, who were thrown into the fiery oven. (Daniel 3). Daniel was placed in the lion's den. (Daniel 6).

at dawn — it is Nazareth. A play on words in Russian: "на заре — Назарея." Nazareth was the home of Jesus, Mary and Joseph.

Elijah. "A chariot of fire and horses of fire separated the two and Elijah went up by a whirlwind to heaven." Only his mantle was left behind. (2 Kings 2:11).

BOOKS IN ENGLISH FROM HERMITAGE

BELYJ, Andrej. *THE CHRISTENED CHINAMAN* 12.00
A novel. Transl. by Thomas R. Beyer (200 pp.)
BUNIN, Ivan. *IN A FAR DISTANT LAND* 8.50
Coll. of stories. Transl. by Robert Bowie (170 pp.)
DAVYDOFF, Alexander. *RUSSIAN SKETCHES* 15.00
Memoirs. Transl. by Olga Dax. (305 pp., ill.)
DEBRECZENY, Paul. *TEMPTATIONS OF THE PAST* 6.50
A novel (110 pp.)
GRIBOEDOV, Alexander. *THE WOES OF WIT* 10.00
A comedy. Transl. by Alan Shaw (130 pp.)
MONAHAN, Barbara. *A DICTIONARY OF RUSSIAN
GESTURE* (190 pp., illustr.) 10.50
MOSCOVIT, Andrej. *OUR CHOICE AND HISTORY* 12.50
Philos. essay. Transl. by Isabel Heaman (280 pp.)
RATUSHINSKAIA, Irina. *POEMS* 8.50
In Russian, English, and French (134 pp.)
RATUSHINSKAIA, Irina. *TALE OF THREE HEADS* 7.50
Coll. of stories. Transl. by Diane Ignashev
STILMAN, Leon. *GOGOL* 15.00
A biographical study (240 pp.)
STUDEMEISTER, Marguerite. *BOOKPLATES AND
THEIR OWNERS IN IMPERIAL RUSSIA* 26.00
An illustr. survey (220 pp.)
VISSON, Vladimir. *FAIR WARNING* 12.50
Memoirs (250 pp., illustr.)
YAKOBSON, Helen. *CONVERSATIONAL RUSSIAN* 8.50
An intermediate course (210 pp., illustr.)

A catalog of books in Russian is available upon request.

20% disc. with the order of 3 books or more. $2.00 postage and handling.
Send orders to Hermitage, P.O.Box 410, Tenafly, N.J. 07670, U.S.A.